Byline Baltimore

Byline Baltimore

William "Bill" Hughes

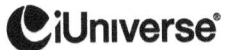

BYLINE BALTIMORE

iUniverse books may be ordered through booksellers or by contacting:

iUniverse
1663 Liberty Drive
Bloomington, IN 47403
www.iuniverse.com
1-800-Authors (1-800-288-4677)

ISBN: 978-1-5320-6276-6 (sc)
ISBN: 978-1-5320-6277-3 (e)

Library of Congress Control Number: 2018913940

Print information available on the last page.

iUniverse rev. date: 11/27/2018

Contents

Politics

Baltimore

Reviews

Travel

Dedication

This book is dedicated, with deep affection, to the blessed memory of my political mentors, all of whom were Baltimore City-based:

Michael "Iron Mike" McHale, City Council Member
Judge John A. McGuire, District Court of Maryland
Julian "Fats" Carrick, Political Boss
Mary Avara, Chair, Maryland State Film Censor Board
Harry J. "Soft Shoes" McGuirk, State Senator

Ackowledgement

My special thanks go out to Tim Maier, editor, publisher and owner of the online publication *Baltimore Post-Examiner*. Without him graciously giving me the opportunity to write/blog for his website over the last few years, this book would not have been possible. All the commentaries/stories, and many of the photos in this book came directly from the pages of Maier's *Baltimore Post-Examiner*, and/or on occasion, its sister publication, *Los Angeles Post-Examiner*.

Epigraph

"Welcome, O Life! I go to encounter for the millionth time the reality of experience and to forge in the smithy of my soul the uncreated conscience of my race."

- James Joyce, *A Portrait of the Artist as a Young Man*

1. Trump's Inauguration Marred by Boycotts, Protests and a Fake Entrance January 21, 2017

I knew that President-elect Donald Trump was going to have his smiley face on at his inauguration as soon as I stepped into Baltimore's Penn's Station early on Friday morning, January 20, 2017. It was packed with Trump true believers carrying all kinds of signs and wearing red baseball caps that barked: "Make American Great Again." There were only a few anti-Trump activists in sight.

Washington D.C. and federal officials were expecting close to 1,000,000 visitors for the weekend. I don't think they even came close to making that number. The MARC line prepared for a huge turnout for the event, too, the 45th in our country's history. It had ordered out more trains than usual for the occasion.

Well, the 8:30 am MARC train out of Penn Station had eight cars. I asked the conductor how many empty seats he had. He said it was only filled to "about one-third of its capacity."

Earlier in the week, a Gallup Poll came out. It found that 55 percent of the Americans polled had "a negative view" of Trump even before he took the oath of office. It was an historic polling low. Most recent presidents had favorable ratings going into the office.

The last inauguration I attended was for the warmonger George W. Bush, Jr. aka "Dubya," back in 2001. That was a very cold day with pockets of Bush-bashers on hand. This time, however, the temperature hovered around the 50 degrees mark for most of the day, with light showers interspersed. And - underscore this - there was "no problem" getting up close to view the inauguration parade at the Bush event.

About 68 members of the U.S. Congress had promised to boycott the ceremony. Maryland's Anthony Brown (4th D.) and Jamie Raskin (8th D.) are in that group. Rep. Elijah Cummings (7th D.), however, said he would attend.

After my train arrived at Penn Station in D.C., about 9:30 am, with its splendid view of the U.S. Capitol, I walked out to Columbus Circle. A spirited anti-Trump demonstration was already in progress. There, I witnessed plenty of anti-Trump posters, signs and banners. Speakers were also blasting away via a loud audio system.

I was told by one of the activists that on Pennsylvania Avenue, at 7th Street, the ANSWER Coalition, a national social justice advocacy group, had erected a 28-foot stage. There, they would be hosting speakers representing a wide array of grassroots issues to share their views.The area is known as the "Navy Memorial Plaza."

I starting walking towards the ANSWER rally by heading out in a westerly direction on "D" Street. No cars were allowed on it. Every side street was blocked with either barriers, huge buses and/or dump trucks. There were cops and security types all over the place.

As I continued my journey, along with others, I was confronted by "Jesus" types hawking Biblical messages of doom. (Maybe, they know something that I don't. Scary though!)

On my left, as I passed along, were entrances to the National Mall and to the Inauguration grounds: They were marked Orange, Blue and Red. However, you needed an "official" ticket to get into the Mall and also to check out the parade on Pennsylvania Avenue. A fellow on the train from Ohio had told me: "I got a ticket from my congressman." Well, good for him.

I passed some social justice activists on the way. They had a banner up. When one of their speakers, Margaret Flowers, was addressing the crowd, a dork-headed Trump supporter got in her face. Fortunately, Flowers' colleague, Kevin Zeese was nearby and gave the interloper a piece of his mind. The irate Trump zealot soon backed off.

At 7th Street, there was a line for the public who didn't have a ticket, waiting to gain entrance. It went back at least three blocks and was about 30 people wide. I waited for over 45 minutes and the line barely moved inches. I drank one decaf coffee waiting. The Secret

Service was in charge of security at this gate/entry point. I decided this was a "fake entrance!"

I gave up and went back to hang out at Penn Station with the anti-Trump protesters.

Oh, by the way, last night, near northwest D.C. in Maryland, according to "USA Today," a large group of LGBT activists hosted a "Queer Dance Party" outside the rented home of VP Mike Pence. The VP is a born-again Evangelical, although he was raised as a Roman Catholic. It all, mercifully, ended peacefully.

I was told that Trump was sworn in about noon, in front of the Capitol, by Chief Justice John Roberts of the SCTOUS. So, as Shakespeare would write, in the play Macbeth, "the deed is done."

Finally, the only thing I know for sure is this: The next four years will give new meaning to the word - surrealism.

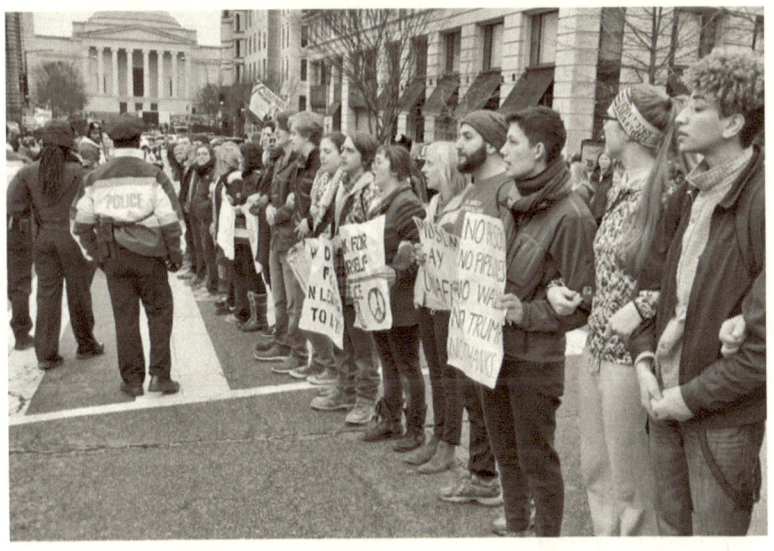

Protesting the Donald Trump Inauguration

2. Spirited Rally Protesting Trump's Executive Orders January 29, 2017

On a chilly, Saturday afternoon, January 28, 2017, a crowd of over 300 gathered, at the Edward J. Garmatz's Federal Courthouse, in Baltimore, to protest President Donald J. Trump's recent torrent of Executive Orders. The building is located at 101 W. Lombard Street in the downtown area, not far from the Inner Harbor.

Speaker after speaker roundly denounced President Trump for his executive actions concerning a wide array of human rights and economic issues, such as: withdrawing federal funding for sanctuary cities, banning Muslim immigrants, building a Border Wall with Mexico, crippling Obamacare and restarting the Dakota Access and Keystone pipelines. He has also threatened to launch a federal probe of supposed voter fraud in last year's presidential election because he thought he should have gotten more votes.

Trump had initially proposed a "20 percent tax on Mexican imports," to help pay the costs for building the mega-wall. Later in the week, he backed off and said that was just "one of many" possibilities.

Meanwhile, as if to set the stage for much worst to come, six journalists were arrested at Trump's inauguration on January 20th and charged with "felony rioting." They can face sentences up to ten years in the slammer.

Activist Steven Ceci said it was important for people to take a stand against "hatred, the anti-immigrant policies of Trump, and to block the pipelines." He also praised students from U.B. and MICA for helping to organized the event. Ceci said it was a "joint effort." He called for a "people's movement" to rise up and take on Trump and his gang.

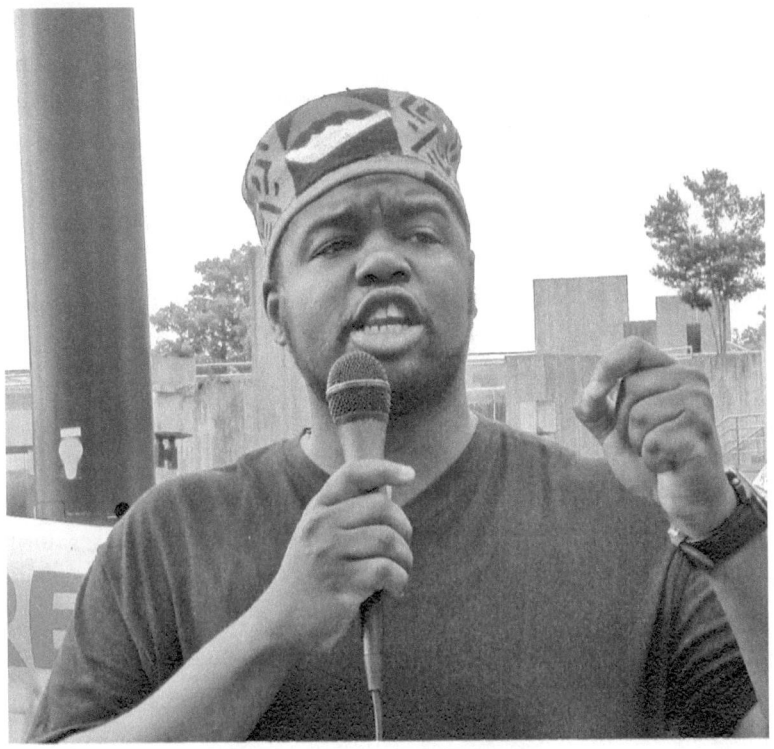

Activist Elder C.D. Witherspoon

3. Protesting Catholic Church Cover-up of Sexual Abuse Cases March 26, 2018

On a brisk, Palm Sunday morning, March 25, 2018, about twenty activists, carrying signs and posters, gathered at the Villa Assumpta on North Charles St. at Bellona Avenue in Baltimore County, MD. The Villa Assumpta is a retirement home, a convent for nuns run by the School Sisters of Notre Dame. (SSND).

Back in the 1970s, Sister Eileen Weisman was the principal at the Catholic Community Middle School (CCMS), formerly Our Lady of Good Counsel School in Locust Point. It was a SSND school. One of the lay teachers under her supervision from 1972 to 1979, was the later convicted - sexual predator - John Merzbacher.

The protesters claim Merzbacher's tenure was "a reign of terror" for many of his students - male and female alike. They insist Sister Weisman knew, or should have known, about his serial sex abuses and other outrageous conduct, including repeatedly threatened students with a loaded hand gun - and did nothing.

The coverup, they claim, continues to this day! Sister Weisman and the SSND, along with Archdiocese of Baltimore (AOB), have denied any wrongdoings on their part in this sordid matter. The AOB said it didn't learn of the demented Merzbacher's abuses until 1988.

Merzbacher was finally convicted of raping of one of the students in 1995, at a criminal trial in Baltimore City. He received four life sentences for child rape. Charges involving other victims, about 12 in number, were dropped. Merzbacher, now age 76, is currently serving his sentence at the Eastern Correctional Institution in Westover, Maryland. His conviction was affirmed on appeal. https://courts.state.md.us/data/opinions/coa/1997/99a96.pdf

Media accounts of the rape trial indicated that Merzbacher held a "loaded gun" to the head of his victim, Elizabeth Ann Murphy, then 11 years of age. Since then, a civil suit was filed by numerous other victims, including Linda Malat Tiburzi.

Ms. Tiburzi said Merzbacher sexually abused her and threatened her with a gun, when she was a student at CCMS from 1973-76. That suit, which included 14 plaintiffs, was dismissed because it ran afoul of the three-year statute of limitations.

In her civil lawsuit, Tiburzi claimed that on one occasion when Merzbacher was abusing her, she had been pinned to the ground and her blouse was wide opened, when Sister Weisman suddenly unlocked the door and walked in. The nun made a comment about his keeping the door locked. Tiburzi continued, but Sister Weisman "did nothing. There was no investigation, there were no questions."

At the protest, Marsha Wise, a former student at CCMS, told me that Sister Weisman "facilitated" Merzbacher's wrongdoing. There was no way she couldn't have known. Her office was on the second floor and when she came in and out of the building using the front door, she had to pass Merzbacher's classroom, which was also on the first floor.

Two other fellow students at the rally, Bill Stankiewicz and Kathie Lewandowski Richardson, had similar terror stories to tell me. They all underscored how the trauma of those early years at CCMS, "the living in fear" still stays with them.

One of the students related to me an account of how Merzbacher, at the time an uncontrollable wild man, had supposedly shot a gun off in one of the classrooms to intimated everyone. She related also how one student who complained about Merzbacher and Sister Weisman's suspected conduct was arbitrarily shipped off to a mental institution for a year's confinement!

Some of the survivors want Sister Weisman to come clean, others want her to be indicted as an accessory to Merzbacher's evil doings. As one of the students put it: "She deserves to do time in jail." They all agree on one thing: "We need closure on this issue."

Another teacher at the the CCMS, during that same time period, was Gary Homberg. He said that Sister Weisman was told about Merzbacher's sexual misconduct, including his bringing a gun to class. Homberg's plea went nowhere. He was told by church officials, including the then-parish priest, Father Herbert Derwart, now deceased, to "shut up" about his complaint.

Homberg repeated his claim of misconduct about the case on a recent WJZ-TV expose, featuring Denise Koch, one of the station's anchors. He said, "church officials just looked the other way. They would have to be deaf, dumb and blind not to know what was going on." See: http://www.bishop-accountability.org /news2018/03_04/2018_03_05_Denise_Baltimore_Did_Catholic.htm

After leaving, the CCMS, Sister Weisman became the principal at the "The School of the Cathedral" of the AOB, on North Charles St. When the dispute involving her knowledge of Merzbacher's wrongdoings heated up with his criminal trial, she reportedly was soon afterwards transferred to Rome. Now, she's back in Baltimore, "living in a convent on school property," according to a source.

The protest rally was sponsored by the "CCMS Alumni & Friends Against Abuse." Its tag lines for the event were #ccmsvictimsunite and #sheknew.

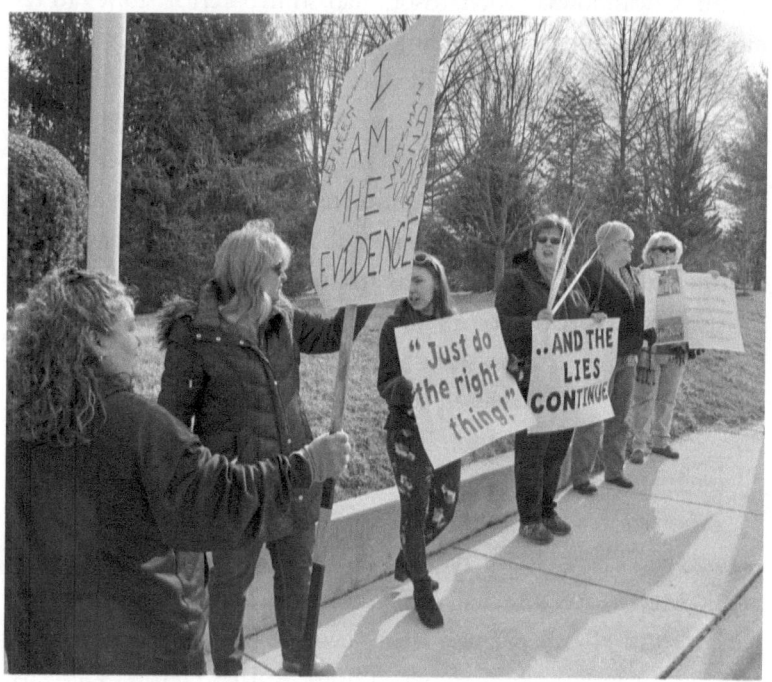

Protesting Roman Catholic Church Cover-Up

4. Michael Phelps Testifies on Capitol Hill February 28, 2017

On Tuesday morning, February 28, 2017, Michael Phelps testified before a House Subcommittee on Oversights and Investigation, in Room 2123 of the Rayburn Office Building. He was one of five witnesses. The Subcommittee's chairman is Rep. Tim Murphy (R-PA).

This subcommittee is part of the Committee on Energy and Commerce, whose chairman is Rep. Greg Walden (R-OR).

The focus of the inquiry dealt with ways to "improve and strengthen" the anti-doping process dealing with international sports, particularly the Olympic Games.

After the completion of the Rio Olympics, in 2016, Phelps retired from swimming competition. He had competed in five games and ended his career as the most decorated Olympian in history. He won a total of 28 gold medals. Phelps was born in Baltimore City and raised in the Rodgers Forge area of Baltimore County.

In his testimony, Phelps expressed his deep concerns about the inadequacy of the current anti-doping testing system. He underscored that in some cases, "no testing at all was done" and that he had suspected that "some athletes were cheating."

Phelps mentioned how one of his teachers had told him very early on that "you will never amount to anything." He underscored that, despite that kind of negativity, he had worked hard all of his life to be the best in his sport.

His full testimony, along with the other four witnesses can be viewed at: https://energycommerce.house.gov/hearings-and-votes/hearings/ways-improve-and-strengthen-international-anti-doping-system

There is a huge amount of credible evidence on the record that Russian officials had "orchestrated a doping program at the Olympics." See: https://www.nytimes.com/2016/12/09/sports/russia-doping-mclaren-report.html?_r=0

Phelps urged the sub-committee and the groups supposedly policing the Olympics "to do what is necessary to ensure the system is fair and reliable, so we can all believe in it."

The written testimony that Phelps submitted to the sub-committee can be found at: http://docs.house.gov/meetings/ IF/IF02/20170228/105613/HHRG-115-IF02-Wstate-PhelpsM-20170228.pdf

After the hearing adjourned, Phelps and the other four witnesses, including Chairmen Murphy and Walden, participated in a press conference.

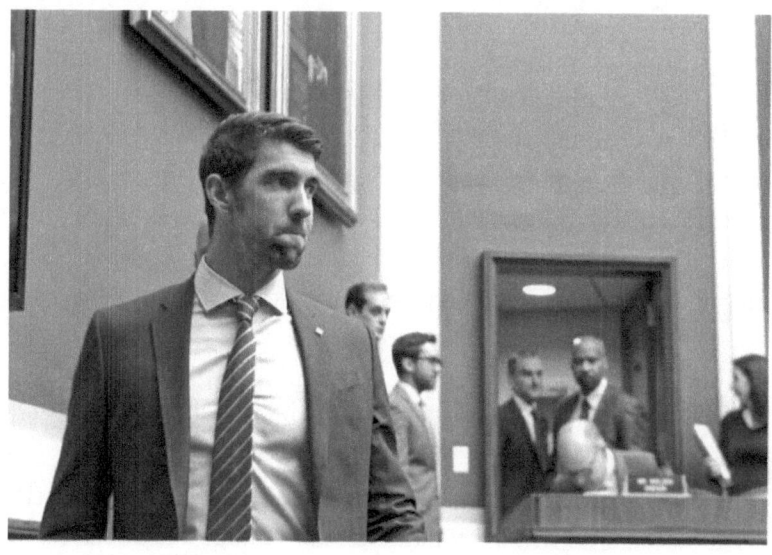

Michael Phelps Testifies at Congressional Hearing

5. Are Steve Bannon's "America First" Days as a White House Insider Numbered? April 9, 2017

Intrigue inside President Donald Trump's White House burst out into the open this week. Steve Bannon, one of the president's most loyal strategists during his upset winning campaign for office, and an advocate of an "America First" policy, was unceremoniously demoted.

Bannon was kicked off the powerful National Security Council and given a lesser position in WH affairs. He is known as a "flaming populist."

Meanwhile, Trump also decided, without Congressional authorization, to use military force against the Syrian regime headed by Bashar al-Assad. About 59 Tomahawk cruise missile were launched. This kind of military action puts America right in the middle of Syria's dirty Civil War.

The lethal strikes also apparently write "finis" to Trump's supposed "America First" policy. Think instead - Global Cop!

(At press time, elements from both the Left and Right have labeled the Syrian chemical attack a "False Flag Op." Former Rep. Ron Paul (R-Texas) said it was most likely carried out by U.S. backed "Al Qaeda-filled rebels." Scott Adams, a Liberal, and creator of "Dilbert," thinks it was a "false flag Op," since Assad had nothing to gain from such an horrific action.)

Naturally, Trump's White House is playing Bannon's ouster down, labeling it as "insignificant." Hardly anyone on the Planet Earth believes that line however.

Coming out on top in this shocker of a reorganization are, among others, two White House aides. One is the president's son-in-law, Jared Kushner, age 36, whose influence continues to grow daily by leaps and bounds.

Kushner is married to Trump's daughter, Ivanka. (She also works in the WH). Kushner's initial portfolio as a senior advisor called on him to focus on China. Now, his father-in-law has enlarged it to include the Middle East. His post is titled: "Office of American Innovation." (That sounds important as Hell to me.)

Another key White House advisor, Gary Cohn, doesn't give a good hoot about Bannon, or his right wing politics, either. His specialty is economics. Its economics, however, from a Globalist/Banker's point of view.

Cohn is linked to one of the Wall Street Banks most powerful entities - Goldman Sachs. He once held the post of president of that prestigious company. Cohn and Kushner are close buddies. Together, they make up a formidable White House-based, one-two punch.

Kushner, compared to Bannon, has really deep pockets. In 2007, he purchased the building, k/a "666 Fifth Avenue," in Manhattan for $1.8 billion! Kushner also owns the "New York Observer," an online newspaper.

"Politico" is reporting the embarrassing demotion of Bannon as a big victory for the "West Wing Democrats" over the "Nationalists." It is also a huge defeat for the "Deplorables," who faithfully supported Trump's candidacy. Kushner and Cohn, in this fight, are obviously the "West Wing Democrats."

There has also been speculation in the MSM that because Bannon was getting a lot of airtime, such as his mug on the cover of "Time" magazine, Trump's fragile ego just couldn't handle it. If that were true, then it wouldn't have taken much effort for the ambitious duo of Kushner and Cohn to play off of that kind of situation.

Some will remember how the then-First Lady, Nancy Reagan, took an intense dislike to her hubby's publicity hound of a Secretary of State, Alexander Haig. It wasn't long after that, the chain-smoking Haig was out of office. (His face also made it on to a "Time" magazine's cover.)

"Salon's" pundit, Heather Digby Parton, has a interesting take on Bannon' sudden fall from grace. First, she blasted him as "an apocalyptic fruitcake" and his worldview as "daft." (Oh, Heather, you are such a meanie!)

Parton noted that the late journalist, Wayne Barrett, who did a bio on Trump, thought that Bannon was the kind of dude, that a President Trump would use up "quickly" and then, with no regrets, just "step over."

Parton sees Kushner and his wife Ivanka as the emerging "power couple" in the White House, who probably ordered the "hit" on Bannon. She gives them the cute moniker of "Javanka."

This kind of "Family First" thought was first espoused by author Timothy O'Brien, who also did a bio on "The Donald." He said it was a "kiss of death," for anybody other than a "family member to get more attention" than Donald Trump. I think Parton' spin is right on the money.

Final warning to Steve Bannon: If you know what's good for you, ride clear of "Javanka!"

Update – Bannon did get the heave-ho as a White House fixture, and insider, on August 18, 2017. His Populist Movement's ideas for Europe, according to published reports, are also falling flat.

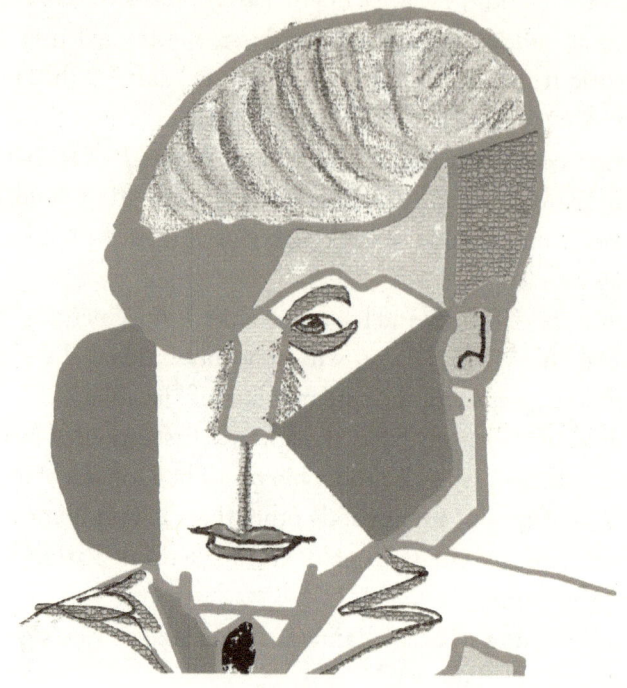

"I, The Donald!"

6. CODEPINK Rallies at U.S. Justice Department May 11, 2017

At noon on Wednesday, May 10, 2017, a vibrant rally was held by CODEPINK and its allies, on the steps of the U.S. Justice Department, in Washington, D.C. Its purpose was to protest the fact that three of its members were recently found guilty of disorderly conduct by a court in the District and each of them faces a possible sentence of 12 months in jail and a fine up to $2,000.

The three activists are: Desiree Fariooz, Tighe Barry and Lenny Bianchi. Their supposed "disorderly conduct" took place at the confirmation hearing on Capitol Hill, on January 10, 2017, of the then-U.S. Sen. Jeff Sessions. He was appointed by President Donald Trump to be the head of the Justice Department. (His confirmation was approved by the Senate.)

Two of the defendants were arrested before the hearing even began. The third defendant, Ms. Fairooz, was locked-up because she was caught laughing out-loud when Sen. Richard Shelby (R-Al), (with a straight face), had referred to Sessions as someone who had a documented record "of treating all Americans equally under the law."

Keep in mind, that U.S. Sen. Elizabeth Warren (D-Mass) was barred from reading, at Sesssions' hearing, a letter from the widow of MLK, Jr., (Coretta Scott King), which had sharply criticizing Sessions on his Civil Rights record.

CODEPINK is a national organization working for Peace and Justice on a wide array of issues. It is known for conducting demonstrations, but always in a peaceful and nonviolent manner.

The fear, as expressed by some activists, is that the Justice Department under the Trump-Pence regime may go out of its way to "crackdown on dissent, especially in the form of nonviolent protests." In the past, they added, charges would not have been brought in this type of situation. Trump is well-known to be very thin-skinned about any criticism directed his way.

One of the defendants, Tighe Barry, appeared at the rally, as Attorney General Sessions in a clown outfit. His antics mocking his arrest brought a lot of laughter from the demonstrators.

The sentencing hearing for the three defendants is set for June 21, 2017, before the Hon. Robert E. Morin, Chief Judge of the Superior Court of D.C.

Speaking at the rally was Medea Benjamin, co-founder of CODEPINK. She expressed her concerns about the status of the three cases and how justice wasn't served by the jury's verdicts. Her remarks can be found on Vimeo, at: https://vimeo.com/216911488

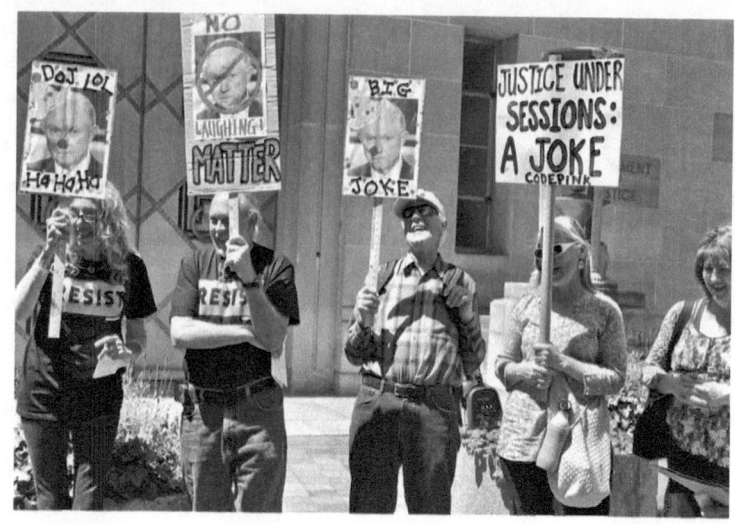

CODEPINK Activists Protest US Justice Department

7. Native Americans Rally Over Pipeline (DAPL). March 11, 2017

On Friday morning, March 10, 2017, a huge rally and march was held in Washington, D.C. by Native American tribes from around the country. They were supplemented by their allies from the Peace & Justice community.

Despite periods of rain and some light snow, thousands gathered at 10 am in front of the main office of the Army Corps of Engineers. Then, they marched about two miles to the White House.

The focus of their protest action was to stop the Dakota Access Pipe Line #NODAPL from being built. However, the Trump/Pence Gang has given it a green light. For background on this controversial issue, check out: http://www.bbc.com/news/world-us-canada-37863955

After their first stop at the Corps of Engineers, they stopped at one of President Donald Trump's luxury hotels. It's called the "Trump International Washington, D.C." The luxury lodgings are located about 1,000 yards from the National Mall.

After that symbolic stop, the spirited social justice activists, some in Native Costumes, moved on to Lafayette Park, directly in front of the White House. There, they set up a speakers' stand.

David Archambault, the chair of the Standing Rock Sioux tribe, was the lead speaker at the event. He said the tribes were marching today "against injustice." Archambault added that Native Nations cannot continue to be pushed around for the benefit of what he labeled "corporate interests and government whim."

While the speakers were talking, supporters of their cause continued to protest peacefully just outside the White House fence.

At press time, it was estimated, absent judicial intervention, that the company operating the disputed pipeline, expects to have "oil flowing by the end of this month."

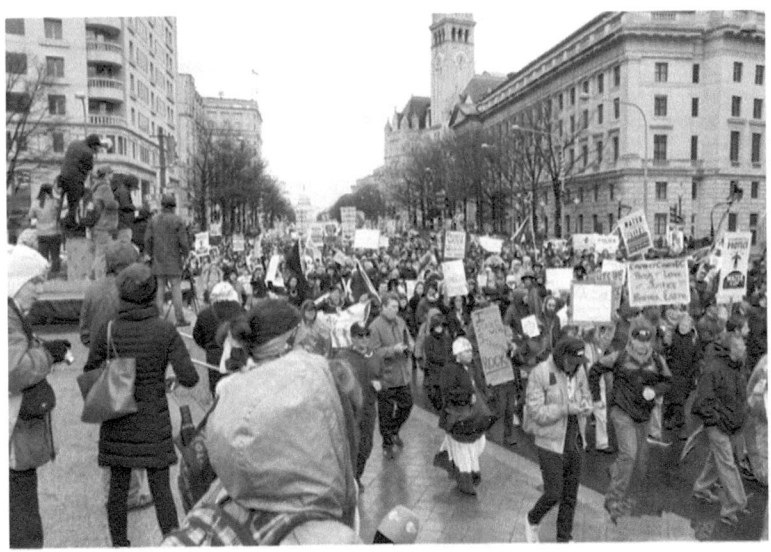

Native Americans Protest Pipeline in Washington, DC

8. Who Killed Sister Cathy?
April 24, 2017

"The evil in man is of gigantic proportions." - Carl Jung

Did the Archdiocese of Baltimore (AOB) lie about Father Joseph Maskell's crimes? This is one of the key questions that came up in Netflix's "The Keepers" docu-series, ("Justice for Sister Cathy"), a program launched on May 19th of this year.

More on the background of Sister Cathy's murder in just a moment. But first, let's look at this key issue.

The AOB claimed it didn't know that Father Maskell (now deceased) was a sexual pervert, who we now know was viciously preying on school children, male and female alike. The AOB claimed that it wasn't until the early 90s, that it knew of his criminal activity.

The credible evidence in this series, however, strongly challenges the AOB's version of history. In the late 60s, the mother of a one of Maskell's victims told church officials about Maskall sexual abusing her altar boy son, Charles Franz.

Franz said that at first, Maskell treated him as a "golden boy" - then the abuse began. Franz eventually became a successful dentist, but he also battled with alcoholism and low self-esteem for nine years as a result of his abuse. His courageous contribution to truth-finding, along with his late mother's, (bless her memory), makes him a true "golden boy" in my eyes.

How did the AOB's respond to the charges brought by Mrs. Franz? In 1967, it moved Maskell from St. Clement RC parish in Landsdowne (where young Franz was as an altar boy), to Archbishop Keough, an all-girls, Catholic high school, in Baltimore City, run by the School Sisters of Notre Dame (SSND). This change gave Father Maskell a whole new crop of victims.

Franz commented: "If the Catholic Church had dealt with this properly in 1967, there would be no murder. We wouldn't be here."

This case reminded me of what happened in the Archdiocese of Boston a few years back. In Boston, the church's wrongdoings were later exposed by the "Boston Globe" in their "Spotlight" series.

We now know that the "Spotlight" disclosures weren't the end of the Catholic Church's troubles. It was only the beginning!

Ryan White is the producer of "The Keepers." His work deserves an award. The questions that come up after watching "The Keepers" are endless.

Investigative reporter, Tom Nugent's role, is pivotal in this drama. He has been working on the case of Sister Cathy since the early 90s. In episode one, you see him moving around his attic checking out boxes of old files, with articles and notes on the case. This setting is a perfect place to start telling this saga. One of his sources, "Deep Throat," was a police official familiar with the case.

This is a case nearly fifty years old. Some key players were priests, policemen and neighbors, but many memories have faded and some of the main characters have died. Nugent is in all seven episodes. His narration and questioning is a road map through the tangled web/murder mystery on the killing of Sister Cathy. Check out Nugent's article, in 2013, on Sister Cathy, at: https://whokilledsistercathy.wordpress.com

The prime keepers of the memory of what happened to Sister Cathy are two of her former students at Keough - Abbie Schaub and Gemma Hoskins. They remind me of those amateur detectives on the British TV shows who go sleuthing around looking to solving mysteries.

Sister Catherine Ann Cesnik, (Sister Cathy), age 26, who was a faculty member at Keough, was prepared to blow the whistle on Father Maskell's wrongdoing. Before she could act, however she was murdered by party or parties unknown on November 7, 1969. She was last seen leaving her apartment to do some shopping. Her badly-battered body was found on January 3, 1970, by two hunters in a landfill, off Monumental Avenue, in Baltimore County.

Sister Cathy shared her apartment with another nun, Sister Russell Philips, now deceased. Sister Russell has always refused to talk about the case. Why? I have to wonder: Was she also in fear of Father Maskell? Could she have set Sister Cathy up?

Father Maskell was a suspect in Sister Cathy's killing, but never charged. He fled to Ireland and later died in 2001, in Baltimore County. Recently, his body was exhumed, but no DNA could be found that matched the crime scene. Some insiders theorize that Maskell probably had one of his cronies kill Sister Cathy.

Around the same time, that Sister Cathy was murdered, Joyce Malecki's body was found. She was only 20 years of age. She lived close to Sister Cathy. There are similarities in these two unsolved cases that have intrigued investigators. Her throat was slashed and her hands tied behind her back. She was a parishioner at St. Clement at the same time Father Maskall was a pastor there. Could the killer or killers of Malecki be the same ones who were in on the murder of Sister Cathy?

The FBI investigated Malecki's murder. Her body was found on federal property. The agency has a file on her case, that supposedly contains forensic evidence. If true, it needs to share that file with both the Baltimore City and County police and do it - now!

An attempt to have Father Maskell indicted as a sexual predator in Baltimore City, back in the 90s, was unsuccessful. The Assistant D.A., Sharon A.H. May, said the case wasn't strong enough to bring to trial.

Two of the heroes of this saga are Jean Hargadon Wehner and Theresa Lancaster. They were the plaintiffs in a civil case against Maskell and the AOB in the early 90s.

The case, however, was tossed out by the trial judge because it ran afoul of the statute of limitations. The duo have continued to fearlessly speak out for justice in this matter. Four other students from Keough have also joined them in going public about their stories of abuse.

Mrs. Wehner told the police that Father Maskell took her to the place where Sister Cathy's body was dumped soon after she went missing. Her memory on this issue is very credible. She added that Maskell, at the site, threatened her by saying that she could end up dead like Sister Cathy if she got out of line.

The AOB has paid out, without admitting fault, $472,000 to the victims of Father Maskell.

Thanks to "The Keepers" series, the unsolved murders of Sister Cathy and Joyce Malecki are getting more attention than ever from the police, the media and those intrepid daughters of Keough who have refused to let this matter go. Let's hope it leads to justice for all of the victims of this deplorable saga.

9. Protesting MedStars's Discriminatory Policies May 11, 2018

A spirited protest action was held at MedStar's Union Memorial Hospital on Thursday morning, May 10, 2018. The hospital is located at 3333 N. Calvert Street, at 33rd Street & University Parkway, in Baltimore.

About forty activists showed up for the rally/press conference, which was sourced by the Maryland branch of "Health Care is a Human Right" (HCHR)" campaign. MedStar was the target of the protest action.

The protesters charged that the institution had recently arbitrarily dropped Dr. Shawn Dhillon, a primary care doctor at Union Memorial for 20 years." This action was supposedly done without cause by cutting him from "MedStar's insurance plans." This also had the effect of terminating half of the patients in his practice. It was reported MedStar "pressured him to leave."

The protesters further alleged that roughly "400 Medicaid patients in Dr. Dhillon's care were gotten rid of by assigning them to an inner-city clinic unaffiliated with Union Memorial." MedStar's conduct in this situation, the activists charged was similar to the discriminatory action at Franklin Square Medical Center where allegedly "critical services were closed without warning."

One of Dr. Dhillon's patients, the Rev. Annie Chambers, spoke at the rally. She claimed: "Our basic rights as patients are being violated and access to our doctor is being taken away...We are not going to be silent about this."

Another patient, Ian Schlackman, said: "Patients are being used as pawns in MedStar's strategy of putting profits ahead of the needs of patients and the health services needed for communities." Donna Simone Plamondon of Hampden is another of Dr. Dhillon's patients. She couldn't make it to the rally, but wrote: He's been my primary care physician for over 15 years. MedStar said the office was closing on Sept. 1st, 2018, and that he was retiring. It prevented us from contacting him in anyway. I'm pissed!"

Maryland Healthcare Is a Human Right Campaign was the sponsor of today's action. Margaret Flowers, MD, one of its co-founders, ripped MedStar for using "the community as a profit center to make their executives and investors wealthy. Health care is a human right, not a commodity," she added.

MedStar denies all of the activists' claims. It said its priority "is to provide quality care to all patients, and, as such, has properly informed patients of other providers in their network." MedStar further said the dispute regarding Dr. Dhillon and the hospital was really a matter between that physician and the "insurance division of MedStar."

While the rally was proceeding, the Dr. Dhillon took a few minutes off from seeing patients inside the hospital to made an appearance. He thanked everyone for their support. He warned that on the ongoing important issue of health care "peoples' voices aren't being heard." Dr. Dhillon regretted the fact that because of MedStar's arbitrary actions, he would soon be leaving the hospital after twenty years of faithful service.

See Dr. Dhillon's full remarks on You Tube at https://youtu.be/yNHOo9MqEtc

To follow up on this issue, go to http://www.stopmedstar discrimination.org

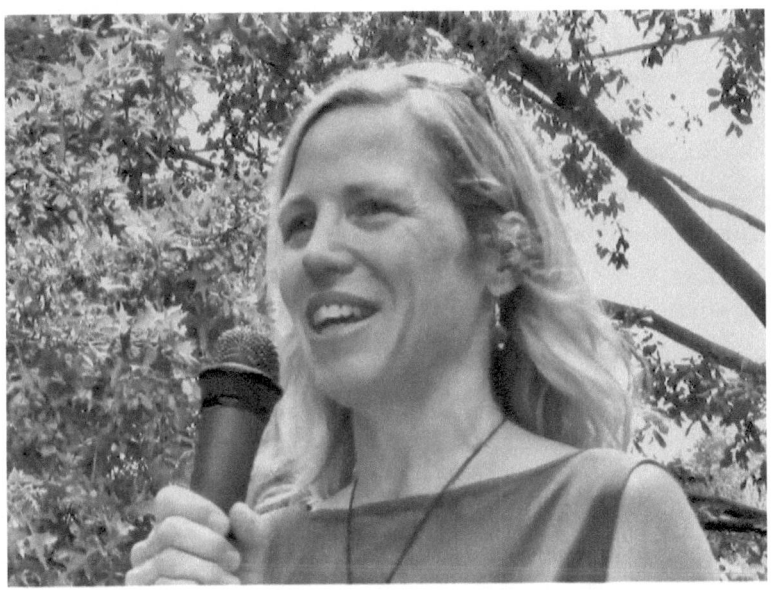

Activist Dr. Margaret Flowers

10. Bishop Eugene Sutton Champions "Dreamers" September 17, 2017

A lively rally was held on the afternoon of September 13, 2017, in Bishop's Park, Baltimore, Maryland. A crowd of about one hundred and fifty were present. The park is located at the corner of University Parkway and North Charles Street.

The purpose of the event was to support the cause of the "Dreamers." They are the 800,000 young undocumented immigrants in the U.S. who are now at risk of deportation. The program is known as "The Deferred Action for Childhood Arrivals," (DACA).

Recently, President Donald Trump decided to end the DACA program. Then, instead, he passed the buck onto the U.S. Congress, which has a Republican majority.

The rally was sponsored by the Episcopal Cathedral of the Incarnation. One of the speakers was Bishop Eugene Taylor Sutton of the Diocese of Maryland.

The Bishop, an African-American, traced his family's history back to the days prior to the founding of the American Republic. He said his "forebears were brought to this country in 1619, to Jamestown, VA. The first peoples enslaved in America. We had no choice about coming here, they wanted our labor. We were treated as slaves. We were property."

The Bishop was standing in front of a pedestal that had recently held a large monument - a tribute to the lost cause of the Confederacy. It was taken down a few weeks ago on the orders of Baltimore's Mayor, Catherine Pugh.

The Bishop added that the Confederates fought for an idea of America that was contrary to the "vision of God." These so-called Christian people used their tradition and their scriptures "to subjugate another people."

The Bishop said he would like to see a new monument in the park that "is for everyone." He said America seems to be saying to the "Dreamers" we want "your labor but we don't want you."

"Just as my forebears had to say 'no' for many of hundreds of years, we are standing with our brothers and sisters here, (the Dreamers), today and saying, "No. That is not going to happen."

The Bishop said, "it's time for a new America. An America that look more like the people of God…What makes a difference is that you are a child of God."

The fact that this rally had to be called, the Bishop continued, is "shameful" for America. "'Send them back' is never a defensible notion for people of faith. Send them back? Where did you come from?"

The Bishop went on the underscore that the Christian faith stands on "the side of the outsider, the aliens." He quoted Jesus and both the Old and New Testaments to make his moral and spiritual point.

The Bishop said that we are still fighting against the kind of negative thinking, and belief system, of 150 years ago, that gave us the "Confederate monument" that once stood in Bishop's Park.

In concluding his remarks, the Bishop asked the crowd to shout out what democracy looks like. They responded, loudly, and in unison: "This is what democracy looks like!"

After the rally, Bishop Sutton marched with the audience over to the Cathedral of the Incarnation, only one block away, where a "teach-in" on the issues was to be conducted.

There are 11,143 "dreamers" in Maryland. A recent study supported the argument that they are making an "important economic contribution to the state." See: http://www.mdeconomy.org/dreamers-make-important-contributions-to-maryland/

To learn more about the DACA program, go to: http://www.cnn.com/2017/09/04/politics/daca-dreamers-immigration-program/index.html

At press time, the White House denied a deal had been made with the Democratic leadership to protect DACA with new legislation. Stay tuned on this issue.

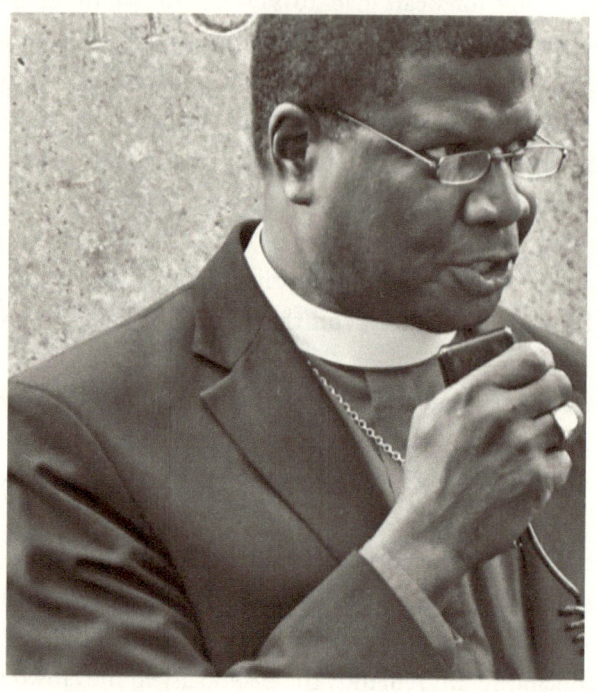

Bishop Eugene Sutton Champions "Dreamers"

11. Grand Jury Action Needed in Unsolved Murders, Sexual Abuse of Keough Students & Its Cover-up June 5, 2017

"To the dead we owe only the Truth." - Voltaire

Notice to the Archdiocese of Baltimore (AOB): Three high ranking Penn State College officials were sentenced to jail, on June

2, 2017, for not reporting the child abuse allegations against scumbag Jerry Sandusky.

This is a final warning to those who enable child predators to perpetrate their crimes. No more cover-ups!

Now, to that end, let's re-open a window to the past:

Joyce Malecki, age 20, was working in an office of a liquor distributor. On November 11, 1969, she went shopping in the Glen Burnie area and was abducted. Her body was found two days later in a creek located on the U.S. Army's Fort Meade military base.

That salient fact makes her murder a Federal case! It gives jurisdiction to the U.S. Attorney's Office in Baltimore. The FBI is the investigatory arm of that office.

Unfortunately, little has been done by the Feds in this matter. In the case of Malecki, her hands were tied behind her back, her throat was slashed and she was strangled. Her murder remains unsolved.

Malecki was a resident of Landsdowne, in Baltimore County. She attended St. Clement RC Church, the same church where the degenerate Father Joseph Maskell, now deceased, was an assistant pastor (1966-68.) The record shows that Malecki attended a religious retreat during that period with Maskell in charge of the (gasp) "spiritual" program.

The AOB knew Maskell had sexually abused an altar boy at St. Clement. In the late 60s, the boy's mother had reported it directly to them. Its shameful reaction: Move the predator to Archbishop Keough H.S., where he would continue his unholy reign of terror over the innocents.

Enter Sister Cathy Cesnik, age 26. She was an English teacher at Keough during a time period when Maskell was the so-called "guidance counselor" and chaplain at the school.

The Netflix's docu-series, "The Keepers," revealed that she was prepared "to blow the whistle" on Maskell and his crime accomplice, Fr. Neil Magnus (also deceased). Close to thirty students came forward since then declaring that both Maskell and Magnus, and parties unknown, repeatedly raped, sodomized and sexually abused them at the school and at other sites.

Before the beloved Sister Cathy could take action, however, she was murdered. Her body was found on January 3, 1970, in a garbage dump in Landsdowne, not far from St. Clement. She had been choked and suffered a fatal head wound. Her case also remains unsolved.

How large was this evil ring of sick pedophiles and sexual predators? Some believe that besides members of the Roman Catholic clergy, cops, politicians, and a shadowy character, "Brother Bob," were also involved.

On WBAL-TV, on the night of June 2, 2017, popular attorney and civil litigator, Joanne Suder, was interviewed. She said, in talking about "The Keepers" series, that there may have been "over 100 victims" of this sexual predator clique at Keough during the period of time in question.

A list of crimes associated with the "sexual exploitation of children" is catalogued in the federal code.

Sister Cathy was a potential witness against Fathers Maskell and Magnus. If the wrongdoers in her murder used a phone, or U.S. mail, for example, to plot her killing, the Feds may have justification to take over her case, too.

In an article dated June, 2015, investigative reporter Tom Nugent, "Inside Baltimore," suggested a possible "link" between the Keough rapists, particularly Fr. Maskell, and the notorious John Merzbacker. He's doing hard time in a state slammer for convictions on four rape charges at a Catholic Middle School in Locust Point.

If Merzbacker does know more than he's been saying, that could be helpful in solving some of these cases, maybe the authorities can figure out a way to get him - legally - of course - to talk. Just a suggestion.

What about that principal at Merzbacker's Catholic Middle School - Sister Eileen Weisman? She was an intimate of his. Was she also acquainted with Maskell or Magnus? Was she part of the cover-up? Sister Weisman has repeatedly denied any wrongdoing. Like Keough, the School Sisters of Notre Dame operated a school in Locust Point.

There are also unsolved murders, cold cases, of other young victims in the same time period and vicinity as Sister Cathy and Melecki. Are these cases related? In that category are Pamela Lynn Conyers, age 16, in 1970, in Anne Arundel County; and Elizabeth "Gay" Montanye, age 16, whose body was found in South Baltimore, in 1972.

During the inquiry into Maskell's wrongdoing, back in the early 90s, some of the State's evidence was destroyed by a suspicious "basement flooding" at the Court House. These were the boxes of files and documents that Maskell had ordered buried in the Holy Cross Cemetery, which were later recovered, via a search warrant, by city detectives.

Supposedly, nude photos of children were found in this cache. Had Maskell sent or received them through the mail? If so, a federal crime may have also been committed by him. The "flooding" ended that line of inquiry.

When I was working in the Court House, in the 60s and 70s, evidence for a trial was kept either in police custody and/or in the office of the assistant D.A. If it had to be stored, it was placed in a file cabinet in the assistant's office under lock and key!

Question: If the critical evidence was "flooded," why weren't any serious efforts made to restore it?

Bottom line: The victims, their families, and the public want answers to their questions, and they want all the above cases solved. The FBI should take the lead and coordinate with the City and Baltimore County police. It should be a team investigative effort for the sake of the public good.

Federal, Baltimore City and Baltimore County Grand Juries need to be empaneled - now - and begin calling witnesses!

Justice can't wait any longer.

Update: On September 21, 2018, the "Baltimore Sun" reported that the Attorney General of Maryland, the Hon. Brian Frosh, had opened a state-wide probe of child sex abuse by Roman Catholic clergy and cover-ups by church leaders.

12. DAPL Pipeline Protest
Featuring Activist Kate Wyer
February 16, 2017

Social Justice and environmental activists, in solidarity with Native Americans, staged an emergency protest action on late Wednesday afternoon, February 15, 2017, in down town Baltimore, Maryland. The purpose of the their action was to draw public attention to the fact that grasping corporate interests, (members of the 1% Gang), aided and abetted by the administration of President Donald Trump, have been granted a green light to build a pipeline, k/a the "Standing Rock & DAPL Pipeline." The focus of the protest action was the office of the Army Corps of Engineers (Corps).

Backstory: After the election of President Trump, the Corps caved in and, despite serious environmental objections, approved the permit process for the $3.7 billion project. Check out: http://ktla.com/2017/01/31/army-corps-of-engineers-ordered-to-approve-final-step-to-finish-dakota-access-pipeline/

The proposed pipeline, Dakota Access, will travel along 50 counties and four states, 1,172 miles, reaching from North Dakota to the state of Illinois. It runs through the Standing Rock Sioux reservation. This land is sacred to Native Americans. There is also a genuine fear the pipeline could contaminate the waters of Lake Oahe and the nearby Missouri River. #NoDAPL

A coalition of groups, hosted by "Solidarity Maryland," came together today to sponsor the emergency protest action. There were activists lined up in front of the office of the Army Corps. An estimated 25 protestors participated in the rally. To learn more, go to: https://www.facebook.com/events/1308417289215950/

Here's the latest news from Standing Rock, at: http://www.counterpunch.org/2017/02/15/standing-rock-come-help-come-prepared-an-interview-with-dawn-neptune-adams/

I talked at the rally with one of the activists, Ms. Kate Wyer. She shared her views on the need to protest not only the DAPL, but the Keystone Pipeline as well. Check out her remarks at: https://vimeo.com/204269299

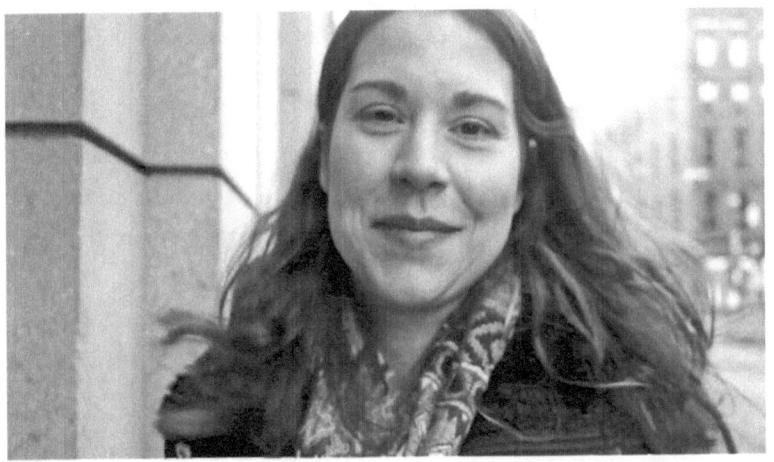

Activist Kate Wyer

13. Del. Shane Robinson: "We Need to Move Towards Clean Energy"

On Thursday afternoon, August 24, 2017, a press conference promoting clean energy in Maryland was held on Federal Hill, in Baltimore, just north of the Inner Harbor. The event was sponsored by the "Food & Water Watch" organization.

One of the speakers was Delegate Shane Robinson, 39th District. He was introduced by Ms. Rianna Eckel, the Maryland organizer for the Food & Water Watch.

Del. Robinson said: "We can't wait another five years to act. We need to move Maryland to 100 % clean energy immediately." A new bill, sponsored by the Delegate, has been introduced in the General Assembly to that end. It will call for "100 % renewable energy by 2035."

Del. Robinson continued: "Maryland took a major step to protect its residents from the negative impacts of fossil fuels banning fracking last year, but that simply won't be enough in the long run. We know that sea level rises will devastate cities like Baltimore, Annapolis and towns across the Eastern Shore."

As a lead sponsor of the bill Del. Robinson is also seeking to remove incentives for problematic energy options currently considered "renewable" in Maryland, such as trash incineration and burning methane from factory farm, according to a memo from the Food & Water Watch organization.

The Food & Water Watch memo continued: "United Nations Framework Convention on Climate Change (UNFCCC) agrees that preventing the planet from warming 1.5C above pre-industrial levels would significantly reduce the risks and impacts of climate change."

Other speakers at the event were: Fred Tutman, Patuxent Riverkeeper; Mike Hersh, Progressive Democrats of America; and Del. Eric Luedtke, District 14.

Mr. Hersh said in his comments: "When we launched the effort to protect our water, air, land and people, and climate from the threat of fracking - right here in this very spot - many told us we couldn't possibly prevail. But we did prevail, and now Maryland is leading the way…"

It's only fair to point out that Maryland's Governor Larry Hogan, an independent Republican, did endorse the statewide fracking-ban in our state. He signed the bill into law on April 5, 2017, in a State House ceremony.

Mr. Tutman in his remarks said: "Marylanders have had to put up enough with coal dust, waste products and toxins released by fossil fuels simply because they're cheap or available. The time is now for Marylanders to break ties with energy options known to be toxic to our future. The measures provided in this legislation will help us ratchet down the persistent reliance on dirty fossil and set a course for using greener options that are more sustainable."

I leave the final word on this issue to Ms. Eckel. She said: "With enough political will, a swift, just transition to 100 % renewable energy is possible but we must act now."

Del. Robinson's full remarks can be found, at: https://vimeo.com/230967862

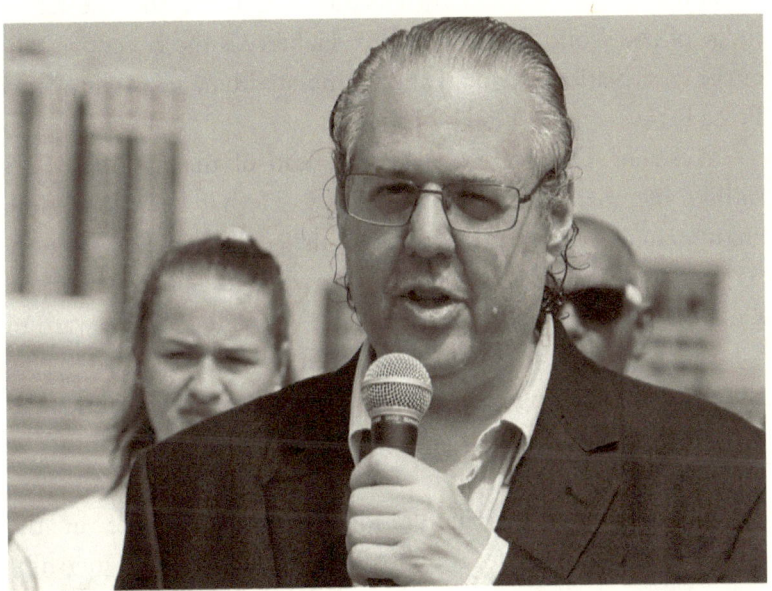

Mike Hersh

14. Richard L. Trumka Gets World Peace Prize
June 20, 2018

On Tuesday afternoon, June 19, 2018, Richard L. Trumka, President of the AFL-CIO, was presented with the inaugural "World Peace Prize for Labor Leadership." The event took place at the headquarters of the AFL-CIO, in Washington, D.C., in the George Meany Conference Room.

The award was presented before a capacity audience by Fr. Sean Mc Manus and Ms. Barbara Flaherty. He is the President of the Washington, D.C.- based Irish National Caucus, and the Chief Judge of the World Peace Prize. Ms. Flaherty is the Executive V.P. of the Irish National Caucus and Corporate Manager of the World Peace Prize.

President Trumka has been the head of the national, 12.5 million-member AFL-CIO since 2009. He has been long time champion of social and economic justice. When he was only 33-years old, Trumka was elected the youngest president of the United Mine Workers of America (UMWA). He looks forward to "an economy of shared prosperity for all working families." This is part of the working class aspirations that President Trumka had carried with him from his earliest days laboring in the "mines of southwest Pennsylvania."

To learn more about President Trumka's career in the Labor Movement, go to: https://aflcio.org/about/leadership/richard-l-trumka

To view President Trumka's acceptance remarks, check out https://vimeo.com/275953504

Father Mc Manus said: "President Trumka was selected for this inaugural Award for the year 2018, because of his life-long dedication to social justice and fair employment. The latter are the very foundation of peace, because peace is the fruit of justice. Those who work for justice are therefore, the real peace workers."

He continued, "It's easy to talk about 'peace' if one leaves out justice…Working for justice is not a part-time endeavor. Rather it is, instead, the work of a life time…Peace Prizes can too often be associated with politicians or so called 'Great Statesmen,' who may have just spent a short time actually working on a peace agreement.

"So, we felt that Peace Prizes also 'belong to people' who spend their lives, day in and day out, working for justice…The way for the ordinary person to get a chance at basic justice is to get a decent job, with a just wage, without any discrimination for any reason.

"Fair employment is… the nexus between justice and peace… Those who spend their lives working for decent jobs with just wages, are indeed the true and steadfast 'peace builders.' And if any American group personifies this, it is surely 'the Labor Movement and, in particular, the AFL-CIO…' And that is why the 2018 initial recipient of the 'World Peace Prize for Labor Leadership' is the honorable Richard L. Trumka, President of the AFL-CIO.

"No one more deserve this award than President Trumka. He has shown a lifetime of dedicated service to the cause of Labor. He is a most impressive leader, a very fine man, and a fearless defender of the rights of working men and women," concluded Father McManus.

Background on the World Peace Award - According to the program from the event, "it was founded in 1989, by the Rev. Dr. Han Min Su. He is from Seoul, Korea and is a Presbyterian Minister. The World Peace Prize is not only International, but also Inter-faith. The Board of Judges symbolically represent the nine major religions of the word." To learn more about Rev. Dr. Su and this organization, go to: http://www.wppac.net

Entertainment for the ceremony was provided by Derek Warfield & the "Young Wolfe Tones." One of the ballads they sang was in memory of the legendary labor hero, Joe Hill, entitled: "I Dreamt

I saw Joe Hill Last Night." It was written by Alfred Hayes. To learn more about Hill's history, check out: https://aflcio.org/about/history/labor-history-people/joe-hill

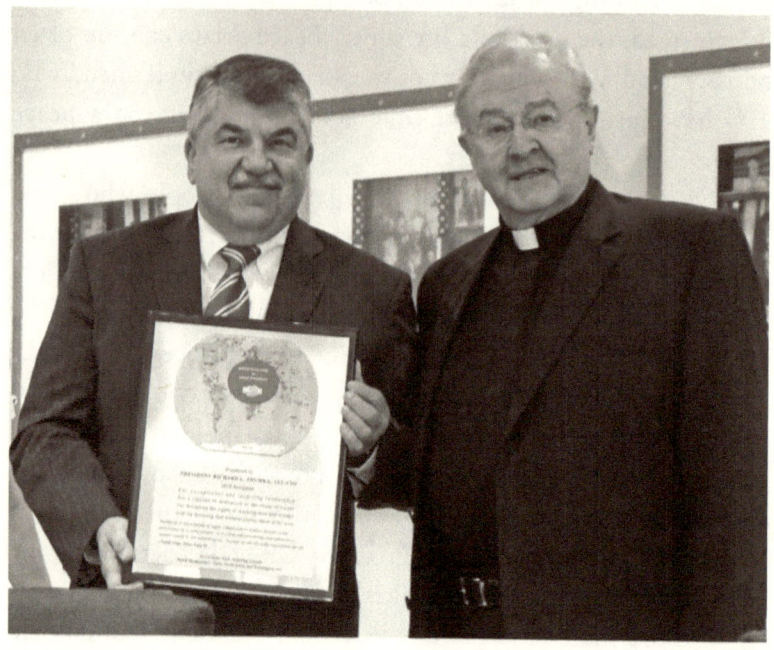

Richard L. Trumka with Father Sean McManus

15. "The Fiddler of Dooney" - Reading by Ray McGovern June 2, 2017

When is the last time someone read the poem, "The Fiddler of Dooney" in front of the White House? Try Tuesday afternoon, May 30, 2017.

First, some background:

At around 2 pm on that date, social justice activists, in the hundreds, gathered in front of the White House. They had just marched from the Lincoln Memorial, under the leadership of the "Veterans for Peace," a national organization.

They had rallied earlier in front of the Lincoln Memorial. A coalition of ten other antiwar, peace and justice organizations had participated in that spirited demonstration.

At the White House, the activists had one simple message for President Donald Trump. It was: "Stop the Endless Wars!"

One of the speakers in front of the White House was Ray McGovern, political activist, ex-U.S. Army veteran and a former CIA analyst. Check out his bio, at: https://www.charterforcompassion. org/truth-religious-leaders/truth-ray-mcgovern

McGovern fondly recalled his early days of peace-making activism and his relationship with two legends in that area of concern - both now deceased - Phil Berrigan and his brother Fr. Dan Berrigan, S.J.

Phil Berigan, some may recall, spent many of his years of activism, including the "Catonsville Nine" action, in Baltimore and environs. To learn more about the fabled Berrigan brothers, go to: http://peace.maripo.com/m_jonah.htm

(Phil's daughter, Frida, recently wrote a popular book about what it was like growing up with parents - Liz McAlister is her mother - who were full time "peacemakers." See: https://www.wbai. org/programupdates.php?programupdate=472)

McGovern, a native of the Bronx and a U. of Fordham graduate, then read from a popular Irish poem, "The Fiddler of Dooney." It was authored by Yeats in 1899.

Here are the words from "The Fiddler of Dooney:"

"When I play on my fiddle in Dooney,
Folk dance like a wave of the sea;
My cousin is a priest in Kilvarnet,
My brother in Mocharabuiee.

    I passed my brother and cousin:
They read in their books of prayer;
I read in my book of songs

I bought at the Sligo fair.
      When we come at the end of time
To Peter sitting in state,
He will smile on three old spirits,
But call me first through the gate;
      For the good are always the merry,
Save by an evil chance,
And the merry love the fiddle,
And the merry love to dance:
      And when the folk there spy me,
They will all come up to me,
With 'Here is the fiddler of Dooney!'
And dance like a wave of the sea."

After his reading, McGovern wished all his colleagues "joy" in the spirit of the Fiddler of Dooney.

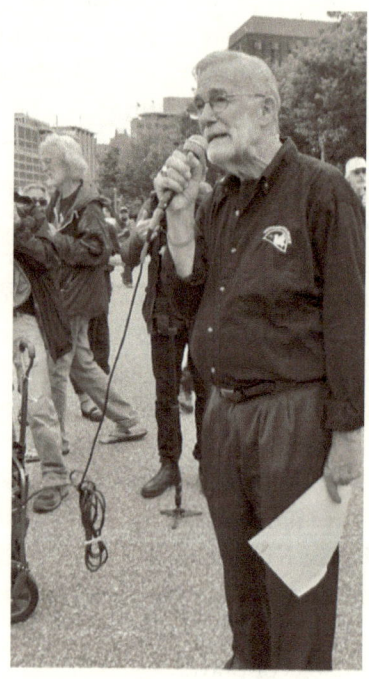

Activist Ray McGovern

16. Women's in Solidarity Vigil In Baltimore Features a Rousing Speech by Marilyn Mosby January 21, 2017

On Saturday afternoon, January 21, 2017, social justice activists held a vigil in Baltimore. It was in solidarity with the Women's March on Washington, also being held today. Over 500,000, at press time, were expected to attend the D.C. rally.

Under cloudy skies, social justice activists, about 2,000-plus strong, gathered on North Charles at 33rd Street around noon. A monument to Johns Hopkins, the founder of Johns Hopkins University, stands on the campus of the school and fronts on North Charles Street. It was there, that the large one-hour vigil began.

Thanks to the excellent cooperation of the Baltimore City Police Department, all vehicle traffic on Charles Street were blocked from University Parkway to 32nd Street. Also, 33rd Street was closed from St Paul to Charles Street.

In light of the inauguration of Donald Trump as President, the women of Baltimore, in solidarity with their sisters across the country, convened this action in the hopes of raising awareness about the issue of "social justice in the incoming administration." They underscored on their F/B page, the need for "social, racial and gender justice" to be preserved and protected over the next four years. To learn more, go to: https://www.facebook.com/events/1931161697106012/

There was a lot of loud chanting at the spirited demonstration, songs were belted out, like my fave, "This Land is Your Land," and there were colorful homemade signs and posters of every description. Plenty of children in the crowd, too, and I think, that most of them enjoyed every single minute of it. (I have the photos to prove it.)

One of the speakers at the event was the State's Attorney for Baltimore City, Marilyn Mosby. See focused on the topic of "Warrior Women." See her remarks at: https://vimeo.com/200504495

Another speaker was social justice activist, Ralph Moore. His comments covered the famous ballad: "We Shall Overcome." To review his reflections, go to: https://vimeo.com/200507654

I also interviewed longtime Women's Movement activist, Loretta Waltemeyer. Check out her comments on the Movement, at: https://vimeo.com/200505525

By any standard, the Women's Vigil in Baltimore was a rousing success. It ended around 1:30 pm.

More photos can be viewed on my Facebook page, at: https://www.facebook.com/media/set/?set=a.10211772065120486.1073742221.1334685315&type=1&l=c509b30313

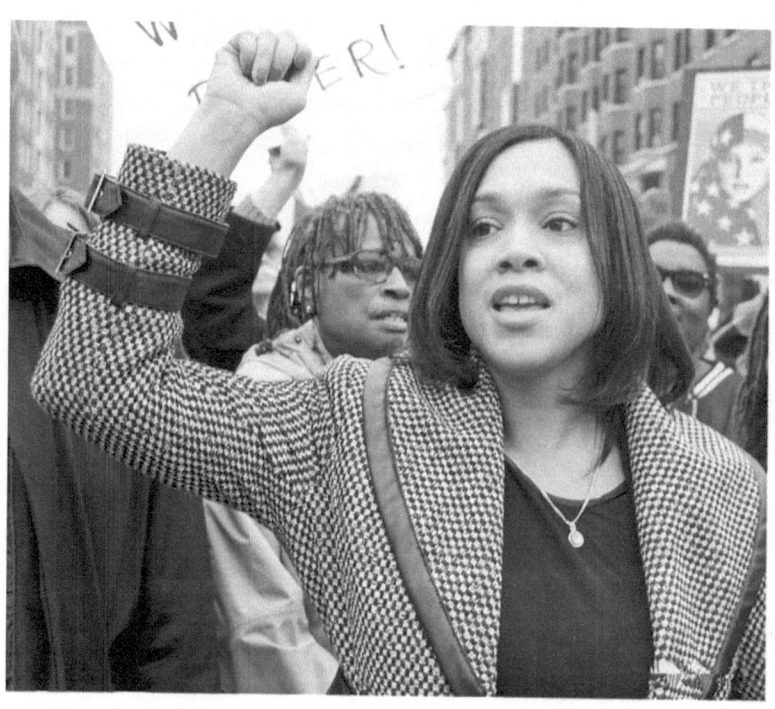

State's Attorney Marilyn Mosby

17. Martin O'Malley Demands Justice for Native Americans: Blasts "Neanderthal" Trump March 10, 2017

On Friday morning, March 10, 2017, a huge rally and march was held in Washington, D.C. by Native American tribes from around the country, supplemented by their allies from the Peace & Justice community.

Despite periods of rain and some light snow, they gathered at 10 am in front of the main office of the Army Corps of Engineers. Then, they marched about two miles to the White House.

The focus of their protest action was to stop the Dakota Access Pipe Line #NODAPL from being built. For background on this issue, check out: http://www.bbc.com/news/world-us-canada-37863955

At Lafayette Park in front of the White House, the protesters set up a speakers' stand. Meanwhile, in front of the White House, supporters of their cause peacefully continued to protest.

At the southern end of Lafayette Park, I had a chance to do an interview with the popular former Maryland Governor, Martin O'Malley.

He said he stood in "solidarity" with the cause of justice for Native Americans. O'Malley while pointing to the White House, added that President Donald Trump, "has a backward-looking, Neanderthal vision of our relationship to the earth."

O'Malley, a Democrat, was twice governor of Maryland, (2007-15); and twice Mayor of Baltimore City (1991-1999). In 2016, he ran for president on the Democratic ticket and finished third. He emerged, however, from that national contest with a significant amount of positive, new recognition.

O'Malley shares his views on this controversy, at: https://vimeo.com/207861744

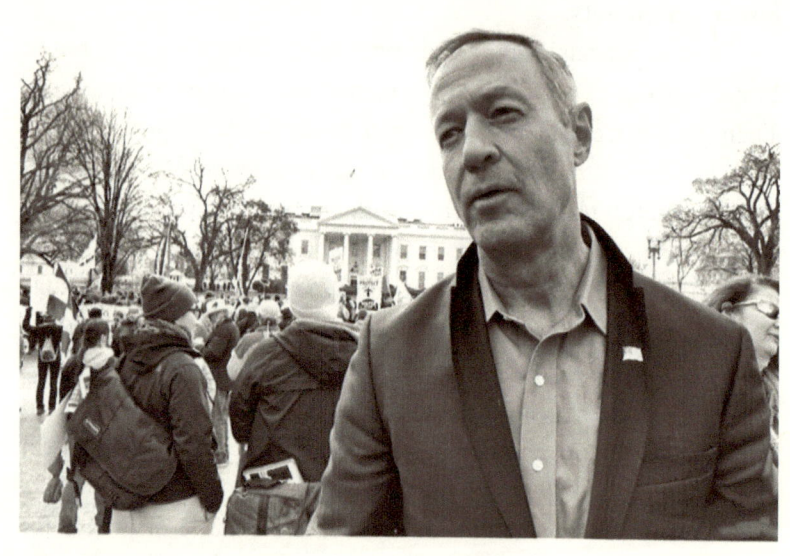

Hon. Martin O'Malley

POLITICS

18. The Campaign from Hell: Blame Barbara Walters! March 1, 2016

By any definition, the 2016 national campaign for the office of the President of the United States is the absolute pits. Nothing in past memory comes close to it. The personal mudslinging by the major candidates, particularly on the Republican side, have reached new lows breaking all prior taboos. It is all like your watching some off-the-wall reality TV show.

On that point, think Donald Tump's TV show, "The Apprentice." It later morphed into the "Celebrity Apprentice." More about that foolishness and his role in it later.

But first this key question: Who is mostly to blame for this unholy presidential election year farce and the trivializing of an otherwise important political event? Try Barbara Walters!

Stay on board, now, and hear me out. The dumbing down of America's media and the way it has polluted politics didn't happen overnight. It has a history and Walters has had a major role in it.

In the opinion of some media critics, Walters was never a journalist, but alway "an entertainer." In fact, it was in her blood. Her late father was well connected in New York City and Las Vegas to show business personalities. He once owned the Latin Quarter nightclub in Manhattan, a penthouse on Central Park West, along with a fancy pad in Miami Beach. Growing up, Walters was surrounded by luxury and celebrities. Her only connection to the reality of the working class were the servants in her family's homes.

When the ever-so-gabby Walters entered the network news circuit, in 1976, Professor Jeffrey M. McCall underscored, she had "no journalistic credentials." This is a fact that bothered "the grizzly news veterans of the day." She left the NBC's "Today" show to co-anchor ABC Evening News. It became clear quickly to observers that her talky facade with its focus on shallow and soapy personalities, didn't translated into a "serious news anchor desk."

At that time, the ABC Evening News network was stuck in last place in the ratings. When Walters, mercifully, bailed out two years later from that job, McCall reminds us, "ABC was still dead last."

Veteran newsman, the late Harry Reasoner, was the co-host with Walters. He hated every single minute of it. Reasoner had founded CBS's "Sixty Minutes." Walters was paid $1 million-a-year for the ABC gig, five times what Reasoner was making. Go figure.

This process, like so many Walters influenced, blurred deeply the distinction between entertainers and journalists. McCall added, "Entertainers made huge money, not journalists. Entertainers were celebrities, journalists were supposed to be - journalists."

Walters then drifted over to ABC's "20/20" doing "soft interviews and hosting specials," McCall continued. ABC News furthered empowered her fascination with the cult of the celebrity by letting her loose on a show entitled," Most Fascinating People."

On the latter program, the now "superstar" Walters raved about such "carnival attractions" as Honey Boo Boo, the (gasp) Kardashians and Miley Cyrus. It's clear that none of this was the "stuff of journalism." In further creating what McCall labeled, "the world of infotainment," Walters also interviewed a number of presidents and politicos. The majority of those segments, true to her lightweight record, heavily emphasized personalities over any real news.

When she wasn't busy interviewing famous people, Walters was "partying and vacationing with and occasionally dating them," wrote media critic, Alex Pareene. Her former romantic relationships, included the late Sen. Edward Brooke and the Wall Street Bankster, Alan Greenspan. Walters also enjoyed and bragged about her "buddy" connections with the likes of the shadowy Henry Kissinger; New York Yankee's owner, George Steinbrenner; Sen. Joe McCarthy's lawyer Roy Cohn; and of course, "The Donald" Trump.

Pareene highlights one of Walters' "Big Scoops," an interview in 2011, with the Syrian dictator Bashar al-Assad. When she was vacationing in Syria in 2008, she met Assad and his wife, Asma. Walters called them "very charming and intelligent." After the interview, "while Assad's military was killing demonstrators across the country, Walters wrote letters recommending one of Assad's aide who had set up the interview for a plum American media internship. With her help, the aide was accepted at Columbia."

Walters' record, Pareene wrote, "includes her tendency to interview her close, personal friends...and her habit of using her position to protect and cover for some of the worst abusers of power in the world." He added this hard punch to the gut, Walters' attraction to the "most soulless exemplars of American power is probably why she's been so phenomenally successful." Ouch!

Now, let's look at Walters' glorified chatfest, "The View." She confessed that it wasn't "Meet the Press." The mini laugh-in show has been on ABC for close to 18 years. Walters was a co-owner, and co-host, for most of that time. Over the years, just about every leading political figure, such as President Barack Obama, would make an appearance. Serious political issues were mostly ignored and/or trivialized. Mindless gossip was its mainstay. Take one of the regulars on the show, windbag Whoopi Goldberg. She was one of the most persistent defenders of (double gasp) Bill Cosby!

All of the above is just a small sampling of how celebrity-obsessed Walters has negatively influenced the reporting of news and how it has, like a plague, impacted on the world of politics.

Enter Donald Trump: Billionaire, casino mogul, real estate magnate and TV personality! The transition of Trump into a serious Republican candidate for president was made possible, I submit, by the dismal track record of his Manhattan confidant - Ms. Infotainment, herself - Barbara Walters!

As a candidate, Trump has simply changed TV "sets." He's doing that same ignorant, foul mouthed, bossy, intimating Trump persona, not on the scripted "Celebrity Apprentice" entertainment show, but now in the national political arena. Absent a near-miracle, Trump will be the standard-bearer of the Republic Party for the office of President in the general election in November, 2016.

In conclusion, America, you can thank mostly Barbara Walters, who zealously merged news with entertainment and politics, for this unholy mess.

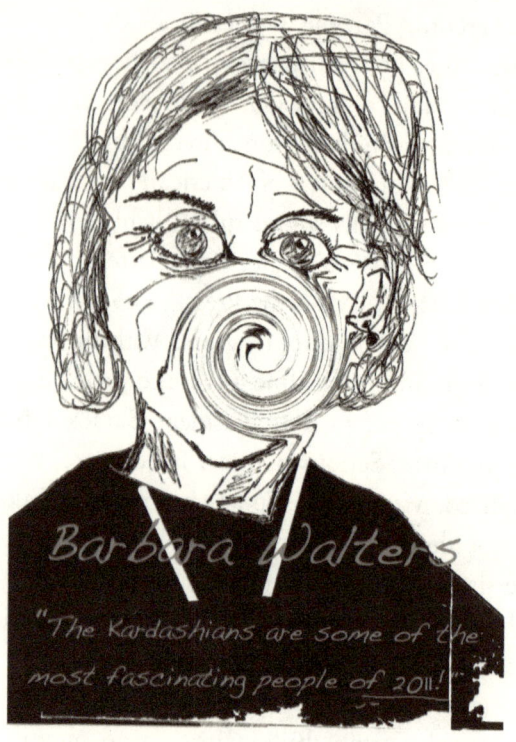

Barbara Walters

19. Comedian Roseanne & President Trump: The Odd Couple
April 1, 2018

Roseanne Barr, a TV comedian, now 65 years-old, is riding high. Her family sitcom, which originally ran on ABC for nine years - 1988 through 1997 - is featured again on the TV sets of Americans.

In fact, the two-episode debut, "Roseanne," about a working-class family, scored huge ratings on its renewal on March 27th, attracting more than 18 million viewers. Featured in the reboot are its two original stars, the wisecracking Roseanne, of course, and her partner-in-comedy, the lovable and talented John Goodman.

In the current program, Roseanne is a grandmother who voted for U.S. President Donald Trump. This aspect reflects reality since she has bragged about "voting for Trump" in the 2016 election.

Isn't this cute? President Trump personally called Roseanne to congratulate her on her program's high ratings debut. He also made sure the world knew about it. Sounds like fake news to me!

Question: Is Roseanne's support of Trump genuine or was it contrived to maximize publicity for her new TV show? In 2012, Roseanne ran for president on a Green Party ticket. That's right, the very liberal, lefty-leaning Green Party of Jill Stein.

Shifting from Green Party politics to sucking up to Trump, the enabler of the grasping 1% Gang, is the mother of all leaps. I think this big switch-up was a calculated, shabby move on Roseanne's part. (A new report by Suisse Credit Bank shows the 1 % Gang owns more of the world's assets than the bottom 99 percent combined.)

Roseanne, who is now worth $80 million, lives in Hilo on the Big Island in Hawaii in a huge mansion on a 46-acre farm. That wasn't always the case. Roseanne was raised under modest circumstances in Salt Lake City, Utah, the oldest of four children. Her parents were Jewish immigrants.

Roseanne began her show business career as a stand-up comic in 1980. One extremely low point for her came in 1990, on July 25th, at a nationally-aired major league baseball game, between the San Diego Padres and the Cincinnati Reds. She chose to deliberately trash our national anthem, the "Star-Spangled Banner." She belted it out in an insulting off-key manner. To add insult to injury, Roseanne finished it off with a gross obscenity by "grabbing her crotch and then spitting on the ground." Check out: https://www.youtube.com/watch?v=ZuD5IPHa5h8

The fans roundly booed Roseanne's crude performance and the national TV audience didn't like it either. Generally, the response was one of utter disgust. San Diego is a military town. The stunt was a mega-disaster and almost sank Roseanne's career. Somebody commented: "She's lucky she got out of there alive."

If anything, Roseanne is resilient. She has bounced back from the national anthem fiasco, but deep scars remains. She now has her own star on the "Hollywood Walk of Fame." Some will respond by saying: "So what! Rin Tin Tin, a dog, also has a star there?"

Roseanne definitely has a serious political itch. It was revealed again in a tongue-in-cheek performance way back on Mother's Day, May 8, 2010, in Washington, D.C., when she took the opportunity to announce her candidacy for president. See the video at: https://vimeo.com/11585318

The setting was a peace rally at John Marshall Park, near the National Mall. It was sponsored by CODE PINK, a peace and justice organization and clearly on the Left side of the political spectrum. I'm sure CODE PINK organizers had no idea what Roseanne was going to say.

Medea Benjamin, CODE PINK's co-founder, introduced her to the small, but lively, crowd gathered there. She stepped up to the microphone and pulled out her written remarks. Pure Roseanne anarchy followed.

For the most part, Roseanne's comments were, as expected, funny. She had the crowd laughing with her. She said she would "outlaw b… s…!" She also got plenty of laughs when she underscored that, besides running for president, she was also going to toss her hat into the race for prime minister of Israel!

In a heartbeat, Roseanne's dark side came out yet again. She proposed bringing back the - the guillotine! She labeled it "blessed and holy." Lethal was the punishment that she wanted to inflict on the wrong doers in our society. That bloody notion brought out groans from the audience. (During France's "Reign of Terror" about 16,500 victims were executed via the guillotine.)

Roseanne's voting for Trump in 2016, and embracing CODE PINK in 2010, is yet another contradiction in terms. Maybe her politics simply depends on which way the wind is blowing? She bizarrely tweeted on March 31st, that "Trump has freed so many children held in bondage to pimps." See "Fox News."

To prove she has a serious side, however, Roseanne will be one of the 21 speakers at the all-day "Jerusalem Post Annual Conference," set for New York City on Sunday, April 29, 2018.

I don't intend to tell the folks sponsoring the NYC event what to do, but out of a sense of caution, they might want to pre-screen Roseanne's speech before she gives it. Having somebody standing by to cut off the sound, might turn out to be a prudent measure, too! If the past is prologue, you can't be too careful with our wisecracking, belief-shifting comic - Roseanne!

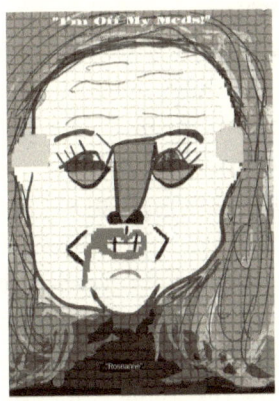

"Roseanne"

20. The "Deplorables" Give Hillary Clinton a Kick November 12, 2016

On presidential election day, November 8th, I was traveling in the northern part of Portugal and staying in the city of Porto. At bedtime, the news readers on the TV had projected a huge lead for the Democratic nominee, Hillary Clinton. They were supposedly using exit polling. (The U.S. is five hours behind the time in Portugal.) It looked like a Clinton win was a done deal. Wrong!

The next morning, a stunning reality had set in. The election from Hell was over! Donald Trump, the Republican Party nominee, had won the day in a bitterly fought political battle filled daily with the most unsavory kind of vitriol. What the heck happened?

Cutting to the chase: The so-called "deplorables" have spoken, that's what happened! One of the major gaffes, Clinton had committed during her failed campaign for the highest office in the land was referring to Trump supporters as the "deplorables."

Into that basket, she recklessly tossed the "racists, sexists, homophobic, xenophobic, Islamophobic - you name it." Clinton's gratuitously branding millions of Americans with a hateful tag was one of her dumbest mistakes. It may have cost her the election.

The fact that many voters also didn't trust Clinton added to this mix, as did her inflammatory anti-Russian, anti-Putin rhetoric. She came off as an agent of the Oligarchs.

Simply put, the demonizing of Trump backfired badly. I believe also that the polls were off so much because his backers (a neo-"silent majority" if you like) simply didn't want to go on record as being in his camp.

I think Clinton's "deplorables" crack also represented an out-of-touch "elitist" view of a huge segment of the voting population in our America. It was mirrored in the heavily-biased reporting and commentary sections of the know-it-all Establishment-controlled press, such as the "New York Times" and the "Washington Post."

These ivory tower media dudes looked down on the Trump brigade as mostly unwashed red necks, losers from the Rust Belt and gun nuts. This gave journalism yet another black eye.

Keep in mind that both of these newspapers were also wrong on the Iraq War. They were asleep at the wheel as the Bush-Cheney Gang deceptively dragged the country into the lethal, immoral and illegal Iraq War. The current chaos in the Middle East can be traced to that reckless decision by Dubya to invade Iraq over Saddam Hussein's supposed possession of "Weapons of Mass Destruction."

Closer to home. Who are the deplorables? Post-election analysis shows them as an emerging Populist Movement comprising many blue collar workers and huge segments of the Middle Class. You can call them "The Forgotten Americans," if you so choose.

What do they want? They want a bigger slice of the pie. They are sick and tired of: the shenanigans of the 1% Gang; their stooges in the media; the endless wars; the unfair trade deals; and, the outsourcing of jobs that have devastated our manufacturing base.

Trump ran as an outsider in his own party. Now, he's its leader. He also has a Republican-controlled House and Senate at his beckoning.

Both major parties were clearly out of touch with the vast majority of Americans. If you thought House Speaker Paul Ryan was a reactionary in this last session of the Congress, just wait for 2017.

I recall a few months ago a labor leader saying: "There's a lot of anger out in the country." Little did he know just how right he was. And, if this angry populist uprising doesn't get that bigger "slice of the pie," they are seeking from Trump, there's going to be hell to pay.

Many in the Liberal/Left column wanted to see Vermont's Bernie Sanders in the White House. When he stumbled, they were forced reluctantly into the Clinton camp. Not that many were happy with that association. Chances are, if Clinton had won the election, the U.S. would have been at war with Iran within six months. Her Mideast track record reeks of blood-stained, impetuous warmongering.

Now for the really bad news. Trump is a card carrying member of the 1% Gang! If you didn't know that, you soon will.

Beginning with a new appointee to the Supreme Court, Trump's policies over the next four years, on issues as varied as: the economy; the environment; Health Care; consumer protection; military spending; foreign affairs; immigration; border control; Labor Unions: and, the privatizing of public assets, will define our nation for decades to come.

There is little, if anything, to be optimistic about, except at press time, this: Trump indicated he was looking to make a rapproachement with Russia, re: Assad's Syria. Good news, indeed, if he, in fact, follows through on it.

All of this, however, can be taken as a challenge for the Liberal/Left and their allies in the Labor Movement. Suggestion: Stop whining about the results of the 2016 election.

Instead - the Liberal/Left should get out in front of the Populist Movement which brought Trump to power. Grow it, re-direct and re-organize it, to include their progressive concerns and agenda for our America.

Bottom line: Buckle-up your seat belts America! You are in for a bumpy ride.

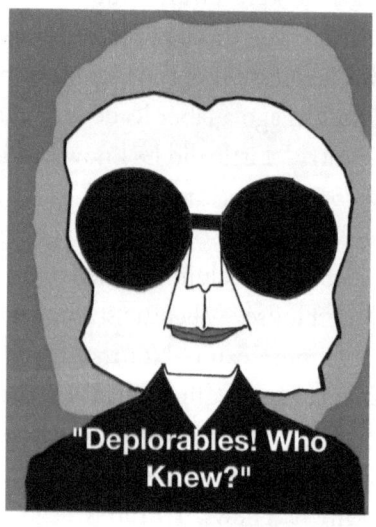

"Deplorables! Who Knew?"

21. A Modern Day Mystery: What Is Deep State? April 16, 2018

From the sensational murders of John F. Kennedy, Martin Luther King, Jr., and Bobby Kennedy to the bloody lethal 9/11 attack, you can eventually count on an entity known as "Deep State" to get mention as a possible culprit. What is this mysterious "Deep State?" How does it operate? Who is behind it? Well... it depends.

An instructive article in the "Moyers & Co.," 02.21.14, by pundit Mike Lofgren, addressed the question under the heading: "Anatomy of the Deep State?" He wrote: there is "another goverment concealed behind the one that is visible...a hybrid of public and private institutions ruling the country according to a consistent pattern...The state within a state is hiding mostly in plain sight... In terms of its scope...the American hybrid state, the Deep State, is in a class by itself and relentlessly well entrenched."

Lofgren continued: "Far from being invincible, its failures such as those in Iraq, Afghanistan and Libya, are routine enough...that it allows them to escape the consequence of their frequent ineptitude." Ouch!

The words "Deep State" came into fashion again recently when President Donald Trump claimed that an entrenched Establishment "was out to get him!" His ongoing bitter feud with the FBI, its former director, the (6-foot, 8) James Comey, and his then-deputy, Andrew McCabe, underscored that heated conflict.

The President has described Comey as a "slippery... untruthful slime ball." Comey fired back and claimed the president has acted like an "ego-driven Mob boss" and that his administration is a "forest fire." Just the other day, Comey added that Trump "is a serial liar...treats women like meat and is a stain on all who work for him."

There is also a book out by Jerome R. Corsi that says there is a "secret plan" to destroy President Trump's regime. It's called: "Killing the Deep State: The Fight to Save Donald Trump's Presidency."

At press time, even Trump's supporters on the Right were turning against him because of his shocking decision to join the Coaliton's strike against Syria. Tucker Carlson, Laura Ingraham and Michael Savage were furious with him. Savage tweeted: "We're lost. War machine bombs Syria. Warmongers hijacking our nation."

Ann Coulter went even further. She said the chemical attack may have been "faked" and called Syria "a country 7k miles away and of zero stragetic interest." (Elileen AJ Connelly, "NY Post," 04.14.18). This is the same sentiment expressed by many Americans, mostly on the Left, about the Syrian conflict and also about the Bush-Cheney Gang's starting the Iraq War.

The phrase "Deep State" is generally meant to suggest that there is an "architecture of government that operates outside the democratic system," according to Hunter Schwartz, CNN, 03.11.17. A few pundits have described Deep State as the military establishment and the spy agencies and their "top secret workings."

No doubt, its meaning has shifted over the years. Some, historically, have referred to Deep State as a kind of "Shadow Goverment." This bring me to a new book on the subject: "JFK-911: 50 years of Deep State." It is written by a Frenchman, Laurent Guyenot.

The author claimed his book "exposes the hidden powers at work" in this country, going back to the start of the Cold War, the murder of JFK and up till 9/11, along with a host of other subjects. In some ways, he does succeed. In others, Guyenot falls way short of the mark. But, nevertheless, he does make you take a second look at some of these confounding controversies.

Keep in mind, all alternate theories, that is, non-Establishment views, on the JFK case, and the other ones mentioned by the author, such as 9/11, are usually dismissed out of hand as "conspiracy theories."

For the historical record, however, here are just ten so-called "conspiracy theories" that turned out to be true. http://theantimedia.com/10-conspiracy-theories-that-turned-out-to-be-true/

One of the ten was a hairbrained scheme, via the Joint Chiefs of Staff. It called for (gasp) a mass shooting of innocent civilians in the U.S. to be blamed on Fidel Castro's regime. Fortunately, JFK declined to appove it. It was known as: "Operations Northwoods."

As for the illegal and immoral Iraq War, the Bush-Cheny Gang, Guyenot underscored, relied on the carnard that the demented Saddam Hussein had weapons of mass destruction (WMD). This was a classic example of "fake news." Sadly, this deceitful message was championed by both the "NY Times" and the "Washington Post" as though it were the Holy Gospel Truth.

The Bush-Cheney Gang's main source for that disgusting lie was an Iraqi "con artist," Ahmed Chalabi. He had previously been sentenced to 22 years in prison in Jordan for bank fraud, according to Guyenot.

Paul Wolfowitz, whom "Time Magazine" tagged "the godfather of the Iraq War," pushed the hawkish "Preemptive Strike Doctrine in 2001," Guyenot continued. This is the same party line Trump relied on to attack Syria. Wolfowitz was then a Deputy Defense Secretary.

Powerful sources outside the government had also repeatedly argued for a link between 9/11 and Saddam. When that didn't pass the smell test, the Bush-Cheney Gang went with the WMD lie. As we now know, mayhem, death and destruction followed in its wake.

Finally, Guyenot doesn't have all the answers to JFK's murder and/or the mystery of 9/11, but he sure does raise a lot of compelling questions about them. Since the past is prologue, if the American people don't wake up soon and demand transparency re: "Deep State," then we won't have much of a country left to worry about.

22. David Simon Blasts President Donald Trump's Muslim Ban February 14, 2017

On Monday evening, February 13, 2017, a rally was held at the Beth Am Synagogue in Baltimore's Reservoir Hill neighborhood. David Simon hosted the event, which was also a fundraiser, to protest President Donald Trump's immigration orders.

One of Trump's first executive orders barred entry into the U.S. from seven Muslim-majority countries. It was successfully challenged in federal court. Now, the Trump administration, at press time, is requesting the full appellant court of the 9th Judicial Circuit to hear the case.

Another one of the Executive Orders from Trump would defund "sanctuary cities." (Baltimore, however, under Mayor Catherine Pugh, has declined to take on that role.)

Simon is a former reporter for the "Baltimore Sun." He later went on to create the HBO show, "The Wire." His production company, according to its press release, will "donate up to $100,000 in matching funds" to further this cause. Simon has repeatedly made know his strong opposition to Trump's executive orders.

Meanwhile, US Immigration and Customs enforcement agents (ICE) have arrested hundreds in a nationwide sweep, since Trump's orders were made public. The agency said its conduct is only "routine" and focused on "undocumented immigrants who have criminal records or pending deportation orders." Critics sharply disagree with ICE's conduct.

On TV over last weekend, Stephen Miller, a key Trump advisor addressed this ongoing dispute. He said that it all comes down to an "ideological disagreement between those who believe we (the United State) should have borders and those who believe there should be no borders and no controls."

Speaking at the rally, before a near capacity audience of about 650, besides Simon were twelve other notables. Three of them are very well known to the local community. They include Beau Willimon, the creator of the Netflix series, "House of Cards"; Internet- activist, DeRay McKesson, who also ran for mayor on the Democratic ticket in 2016 and finished in sixth place; and author Taylor Branch. He won a Pulitzer Prize for his "King Era Trilogy."

Rabbi Daniel Cotton Burg of Beth Am Synagogue gave the welcoming remarks. Musical entertainment was provided by American rock, country & folk singer/songwriter, Steve Earle.

In his remarks, Simon praised the community for quickly raising close to $50,000, most of it online. He said he got "mad" when he was watching the recent scenes of distress at our nation's airports as a result of Trump's executive orders. He brought up the fact that "ten of his relatives" could not escape from Europe during that horrific Nazi era.

The idea of "America First" was derided by Simon. He said that today, unlike in the past, that he's confident that we as a people "can do more."

23. Debunking the Icons, Like that Creepy Bill Cosby February 9, 2017

An "Icon" has been defined in the New Oxford American dictionary as an "object of uncritical devotion"... and also as "a person or thing regarded as a representative symbol of something."

For me, George Herman "Babe" Ruth and Muhammad Ali are by far my top sports' icons, with Baltimore Colts great, John Unitas a close third. In American history, it would be General George Washington, followed by President Abraham Lincoln, with General

George Patton bringing up the rear. In the realm of professional movie actors: I like the Australian Russell Crowe and the British actress, Emily Blunt, with the actor, Jamie Foxx, a close third.

From time to time, however, some of the icons of the great mass of the people are tarnished and fall quickly from grace for a variety of reasons. Mostly it's because of egregious conduct of their own making. We've seen a lot of that lately.

In show business, we've had Roman Polanski, convicted child molester; Bill Cosby, multiple sexual assault charges; and Paul Reubens, aka "Pee Wee" Herman, obscene behavior in a porno movie theater. All three, so to speak, fell on their own sword.

In the political arena, the late Spiro T. Agnew, ex-V.P. of the United States; the late Walter "Wally" Orlinsky, former President of the Baltimore City Council; and Sheila Dixon, former Mayor of Baltimore, are three examples of icons who crashed at the top of their game. In their cases, greed was a factor in ending their careers. I'm sure the reader can thing of many more examples.

With respect to iconic institutions, the Roman Catholic Church in the United States may have taken the hardest hit of all. The massive scandal involving its pedophile priests abusing children came close to bringing it to its knees. Although, it's true to a much lesser extent, Protestant clergy and Jewish Rabbis, haven't been immune from this type of wrongdoing.

There are, however, thousands of cases documenting pedophile Catholic priests sexually abusing children in this country, and others. How long will it take for the Church, as an institution, to recover - spiritually, financially and otherwise - from this shocking, revolting and debilitating scandal? Your guess is as good as any.

Much will depend on its coming fully clean, fairly compensating victims, expelling the priestly wrongdoers and requiring the Bishops who cover-up the scandals to, finally, face the music.

Take what happened in the archdiocese of Boston as Exhibit "A". It was discovered by the "Boston Globe" newspaper that there had been a pattern of abuse of children by parish priests in Boston going back to the mid-1990s, that had been ignored by the Bishops. (See, https://www.bostonglobe.com/news/special-reports/2002/01/06/church-allowed-abuse-priest-for-years/cSHfGkTIrAT25qKGvBuDNM/story.html

An award-winning movie, "Spotlight," was made about the priest pedophile scandal in Boston. Based on the top-notch investigative reporting done by reporters at the "Boston Globe,"
it won two Oscars in 2015, including best picture.

Cardinal Bernard Law, who was in charge of the archdiocese, when this firestorm erupted, resigned in December, 2002. He denied that he had covered up the serial priestly wrongdoing. http://www.bostonglobe.com/news/special-reports/2002/12/14/church-seeks-healing/WJS0tI6gQP8zQAHjAHVhmL/story.html

Many don't believe him. They say that Cardinal Law needs to own up to his role in this scandal. Windy Bill O'Reilly, a Rightwing Catholic, said he thinks that Law "belongs in prison," and that the then-Pope John Paul II, "utterly failed to deal with the crisis." http://www.irishcentral.com/news/bill-oreilly-says-cardinal-should-be-in-jail-for-pedophile-cover-up-90422259-237691481

Like O'Reilly, there are more hardliners on this issue from both the Right and Left side of the spectrum. Many of them won't be satisfied until Cardinal Law confesses completely to his role in this matter and does public penance in each and every parish in the archdiocese of Boston. Nothing less will suffice for them.

I have personally known two young men who were abused by priests in South Baltimore. One of them became an alcoholic, the other, tragically, committed suicide. Of course, there were many more victims of these predatory clerics.

Huff Post blogger, and author, Annie Stein, on December 12, 2015, let loose her strong views on this subject at: http://www.huffingtonpost.com/annie-stein/beasts-of-our-nation_b_8683578.html Her commentary was appropriately entitled: "Beasts of our

Nation." She added this compelling line, which she directed at the Vatican, who may still be hiding clerical criminals, "For the love of Christ punish the bastards!"

Shifting gears to a local spiritual leader in Baltimore - Bishop Heather Cook, in the Episcopal Church, pleaded guilty to a hit and run automobile charge while driving drunk on Roland Avenue. The accident took the life of a cyclist, Tom Palermo. Cook was forced to resign as result of the notorious case and was sentenced on October 27, 2015, to seven years in a state prison. Cook had been the first female bishop in the history of the Episcopal diocese of Maryland.

Jumping to the bigger scene. Even the supposedly impregnable National Security Establishment has suffered a stab in the back to its iconic image as the protector of state secrets.

A former Navy intelligence officer for the government, Jonathan Pollard, who is Jewish, pleaded guilty in 1987, to spying for Israel and giving it "top-secret, classified information." He received a life sentence for his gross violation of the "Espionage Act." He served 30 years in a federal slammer and was paroled on November 20, 2015.

Pollard, an avowed Zionist, cannot leave the U.S. for five years. He has been granted citizenship in Israel and "a public square" in Jerusalem has been named in his honor by his advocates in Israel. His supporters in this country, such as ex-Rep. Anthony Weiner (D-NY), implied Pollard's spying wasn't that harmful to the U.S. Others, however, strongly disagree with that view.

Pundit Philip Giraldi, an ex-CIA counter-terrorism specialist, said that Pollard "did more damage to the United States than any spy in history and it was genuine damage..." See: http://original. antiwar.com/giraldi/2010/09/29/wake-up-america/ Our National Security Establishment has, undoubtedly, learned some bitter, and costly, lessons from the Pollard spying case.

As for the general public (myself included) with its tendency to make icons out of individuals and institutions, let me suggest that it is time for a sea change. This is so, especially in the rocky era of Fake News, Alt-Facts and the Trump/Pence Gang. Let us have MORE, not less, skepticism about our putative heroes.

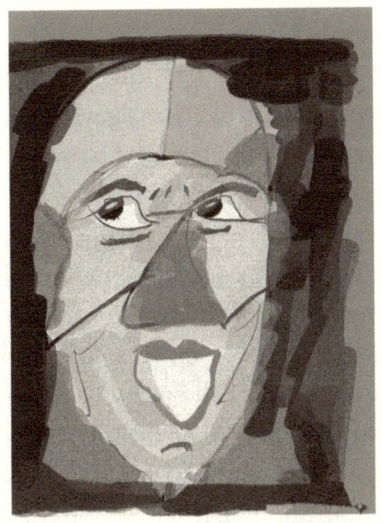

Bill Cosby

24. Democratic Leader Kathleen Matthews Speaks at "Baltimore Women United" Forum
July 11, 2017

On Monday evening, July 10, 2017, Kathleen Matthews was the guest speaker at a forum of the "Baltimore Women United (BWU)." The lively discussion event was held at the Bird in Hand bookshop, in Charles Village in Baltimore City.

Matthews is the Chair of the Maryland State Democratic Party. She was introduced by Ann Loar Brooks, who is on the BWU's "Communication Committee."

Ms. Brooks also moderated the Q&A part of the night's spirited program before a near-capacity audience. Helping to set up the event was Odette Ramos, who is co-chair of the BWU. She is also a member of the Democratic Party's State Central Committee for the 43rd district (Baltimore City).

The state's Democratic Party is still reeling from the fact that Larry Hogan, a Republican, was elected governor in 2014. Although Democrats still dominate the General Assembly, it is Hogan, who currently calls the shots from the State House in Annapolis.

Matthews labeled Hogan "an artful dodger," who must be replaced in 2018. However, a recent Goucher Poll showed Hogan still a very popular governor with a "63 percent job approval rating."

Matthews, age 63, has been moving around the state since she assumed the chairmanship of the party last May. She has visited all 23 counties and Baltimore City for the purpose of rallying the troops, and "energizing the party faithful" to prepare it for the next election and beyond. She is particularly urging "more qualified women to run for public office." Matthews also spotlighted the necessity to "renew the state's party infrastructure."

A strong public speaker, Matthews lives in Chevy Chase, Maryland. She is married and has three children. Her husband is Chris Matthews, the popular host of the nationally syndicated cable TV programs, "Hardball" and the "Chris Matthews Show."

Matthews underscored that a primary goal for the party in Maryland is to create "a grass roots Army to help change America in 2018." A former journalist, writer, news anchor and producer, she worked for ABC's WJAL-TV in Washington, DC for over 25 years. Later, Matthews was a public affairs officer for Marriott International. As a journalist, she won a prestigious "Edward R. Murrow Award."

In the 2016 election, Matthews ran for a congressional seat in Montgomery County's sprawling 8th district, but she lost in a competitive primary race. One of the lessons, she said she learned from that contest was that "politics is tough," and that for the most part, "it is local."

As for the Baltimore Women United, it is a coalition of activist Baltimore women that was formed for among other reasons, "to encourage women to vote in the upcoming primary election," set for June 28, 2018. It is also looking to unite women "together to be a force of engagement, action, solutions and hope in the city."

Another of BWU's aims is to "support qualified women candidates and to increase voters turnout." To learn more details about BWU's progressive, diversity-seeking agenda, go to: https://www.facebook.com/baltimorewomenunited/

During the Q&A session, Matthews promised the party would put up a qualified candidate to take on not only the incumbent Governor Hogan, but also the reactionary Republican Congressman, Rep. Andy Harris (1st District-MD), in the 2018 election. Harris, a favorite of the Tea Party types, has been in office for five terms.

Finally, Matthews owned up to the fact that the Democratic Party needs to learn from the past and to do "more listening" to the rank and file and also to the independent voters. This is, and will be, Matthews promised, "a summer of renewal for us."

Matthews concluding remarks at the program can be found at: https://vimeo.com/225037110

More of my photos can be found on my Facebook page, at: https://www.facebook.com/media/set/?set=a.10213494910270538.1073742254.1334685315&type=1&l=4fc320c121

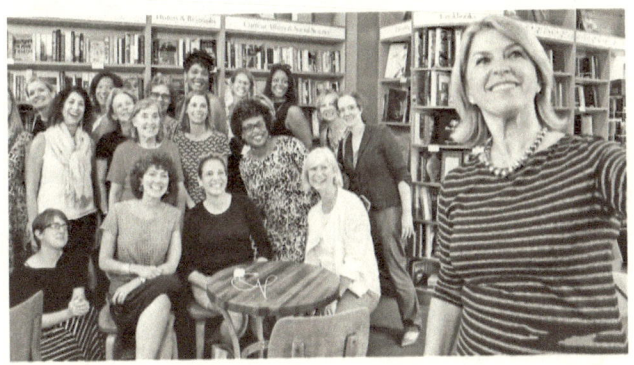

Kathleen Matthews

25. Is Another 2008 Financial Crisis in our Future?
April 20, 2017

On Tuesday, April 11, 2017, President Donald Trump met at the White House with top CEOs from some of America's leading corporations. He boasted: "We are doing a major elimination of the 'horrendous' Dodd-Frank regulations. Keep some obviously, but getting rid of many."

The cozy CEO clique of twenty honchos belong to something called "The Strategy and Policy Forum." Tax reform was also on their agenda. You better believe that any so-called "tax reform" will benefit the 1% Gang more than any member of loser Hillary Clinton's long forgotten and unfairly-maligned "deplorables."

What is Dodd-Frank? It has been described as the most "extensive financial regulatory policy since the 'Great Depression.' It created a host of new protections, rules and oversight authorities." Its laudatory goal was to 'prevent another 2008-style financial crisis," wrote Samuel Taube, in "Investment U," on Jan. 24, 2017.

Ex-Sen. Chris Dodd (D-CT) and ex-Rep Barney Frank (D-MA) were co-authors of the 2010 law that became known as "Dodd-Frank." The measure a few insisted didn't go far enough; others, Wall Street friendly types for sure, whined that it was too top heavy with regulations.

The use of the phrase "financial crisis," is, of course, a gross understatement. The national economy did a "meltdown" of historic proportions in 2008, because of the wrongdoings, and excesses of some of the Wall Street Bankers, hedge fund managers, and other grasping financial insiders; coupled with the disastrous repeal of the Glass-Steagall Act in 1999. Glass-Steagall had separated "commercial and investment banking for seven decades."

The financial crisis of 2008 cost the U.S. economy a staggering $22 trillion. Check out the grim details at: http://www.huffingtonpost.

com/2013/02/14/financial-crisis-cost-gao_n_2687553.html The severe collapse set off a yearlong "banking panic and deep recession."

(Meanwhile, the Iraq and Afghanistan Wars have cost the beleaguered taxpayers $5 trillion and rising to date.)

You can blame then-Democratic President "Bubba Bill" Clinton and then-Sen. Phil Gramm (R-Texas), an arch-conservative, for joining political forces to repeal Glass-Steagall. Why did they choose to do that? Because, they were acting at the "request of the big banks," according to James Rickards in "US News & World Reports" (August 27, 2012). The writer also warned that without something like Glass-Steagall on the federal statute books, "another greater catastrophe is just a matter of time."

Who is listening to Rickards' dire warning in the Trump-Pence Gang? Nobody, it looks like. Another financial expert, Bart Chilton, on "CNBC,"(02.07.17), predicted that it would be "a monumental mistake" for a repeal of Dodd-Frank to be enacted.

Trump's choice for the key post of Treasury Secretary in his administration was Steven Mnuchin. Was that a good idea? I thought Trump was going to "clear the swamp!" Mnuchin has vowed to "strip back Dodd-Frank." He was, for seventeen years, a hedge-fund manager for Goldman Sachs and a partner in the power-packed firm. It is fair to call Mnuchin a "Wall Street insider."

On the Congressional front, the Chair of the House Financial Services Committee, Rep. Jeb Hensarling (R-TX) has been working on proposed legislation to "eliminate Dodd-Frank" and replace it with his brainchild, something labeled, the "Financial Choice Act." He plans to introduce his updated legislation, which covers a wide array of topics, before the end of April, according to Rachel Witkowski, writing in the "Wall Street Journal," on April 11, 2017.

One of Hensarling's proposals would put an end to shareholders' resolutions as we now know it. Advocacy groups, in the realm of social and environmental activities, are upset about the suggested changes. They say it would eliminate shareholders' advocacy for worthy causes.

Under current law, advocacy is opened to anyone who owns $2,000 worth of shares for one year. If Hensarling's proposed changes are passed, one would have to own "$2.5 billion in shares for one year!" It's obvious then that the ordinary citizen, investor and consumer will be left out of this bargaining process.

Finally, how can Trump, in good faith, talk about putting "America's First" and still go along with trashing Dodd-Frank and the rights of Mr. and Mrs. Consumer?

26. Rome, Italy Bans Offensive Monuments: Big Brother Is Pleased! (Satire) August 19, 2017

In a secret meeting of Rome, Italy's City Council, a controversial ordinance was passed by a 12-3 vote to ban all "offensive" monuments in the city.

It's fair to say the "Eternal City" will not be the same after this action is implemented. A city known for its monuments, some centuries old and designed by master artists, intends to get rid of many of them as result of a rising public outcry.

The Council concave was held on the Ides of March, 2017, in the Julius Caesar City Hall, on the Via De La D'Alesandaro, near the ancient Coliseum. Your fearless reporter has obtained copies of the minutes of that meeting.

The City Council's decision will be published on Labor Day. It will take effect 24 hours later absent heavenly intervention.

"It's my sacred duty to make sure my people don't unnecessarily feel bad, "said Mayor Maria Octave, at a press conference on the issue. She intends to sign the bill come hell or high water.

"If people feel bad looking at a monument, then that monument has got to go! It's that simple," the mayor added. "This is one of the legal tests. To start with, all monuments to any Emperor or regime, who either owned and/or endorsed slavery, will be removed. They will no longer be part of our history," she intoned solemnly.

I asked the Mayor if this law also applied to sculptures. She answered, "It does." "Will it cover paintings in our museums, as well," I continued. She cracked sharply that she wouldn't answer any more stupid questions from me and that I should work on getting that smart-ass smirk off my face.

I asked her if she was letting her emotions get the best of her. She responded with a veiled threat: "The waters of the Tiber River are cold tonight!" Then, she said this, staring me straight in the eye: "I don't like bald-headed reporters with mustaches!"

The minutes of the Council revealed a heated session. Councilman Guido Crassus, said, "We will not copy stupid American antics, like in some of their hick towns. Because we don't like a monument, we will be not vandalize it with paint," underscored Crassus. "Instead, we will simply crush it. We will melt the monument down and then reuse the material to erect a memorial to one of our heroes, like - ex-PM, Silivo Berlusconi, for example."

"You are a right wing barbarian," screamed the smallest member of the Council, the feisty Barbarameo Mickulsia, at Crassus. "Where is your sense of history? Your appreciation for how civilizations evolve and how we learn from the past and from our successes and our failures?"

"Throw that windbag Mickulsia out of this hall," roared Crassus' ally, Sergio Cato. "She's a Lefty, who was a fan of the ex-US President Barack Obama." With that cutting remark, the eleven other supporters of the bill rose up as one to loudly boo Mickulisa, a former Senator in the Forum. This brought tears to Mickulsia's eyes, according to one observer.

Another effect of the Council's draconian decision is that the fabled Roman Coliseum itself will surely be destroyed. It holds tons of bad memories for descendants of slaves and gladiators, lovers of abused Barbary lions, fans of the Christian martyrs, and ancestors of former-circus ringmasters and their wives and mistresses, too. Prediction: the Coliseum won't be spared the wrecker's ball! Sadly, it dates from the reign of Emperor Vespasian in AD 72.

I recall feeling lousy myself when I visited the Coliseum a few years back. Why couldn't I have been there when that guy from Jerusalem, Ben Hur, was riding around that track in his chariot whipping his horses and, when he got a chance, his Roman opponent, too? Hur, I understand, looked a lot like the Hollywood actor, Charlton Heston.

To be fair, there were also some pretty awful theatrical productions held at the Coliseum over the years. A few were presented by the demented Emperor Nero. He insisted on not only writing and directing his plays, but (gasp) starring in them, too.

To add some balance here, when the Christians zealots later seized power in Rome, they didn't hesitate to "burn" their enemies to death at the stake - in a public square. One such victim was the priest/philosopher – Giordano Bruno. Should those public squares be flooded now with the waters of the Tiber?

Dissenters to this new law are hoping that the Rome-based chapter of the ACLU will be able to stop it in court. Well, good luck with that "Hail Mary" pass.

Mayor Octave, according to a reliable source, was heard mumbling as she was leaving the press conference, "Did I just pull a Taliban?"

I wondered to myself: If a government can cavalierly ban monuments, what's next - books? - plays? - peace rallies? - war crime memorials? - even, God forbid, Frederico Fellini movies?

In closing, I need to note that the minutes of this historic meeting were signed by the Clerk of the City Council of Rome - one Giorgio Orwellia! He added this telling comment: "Big Brother is pleased!"

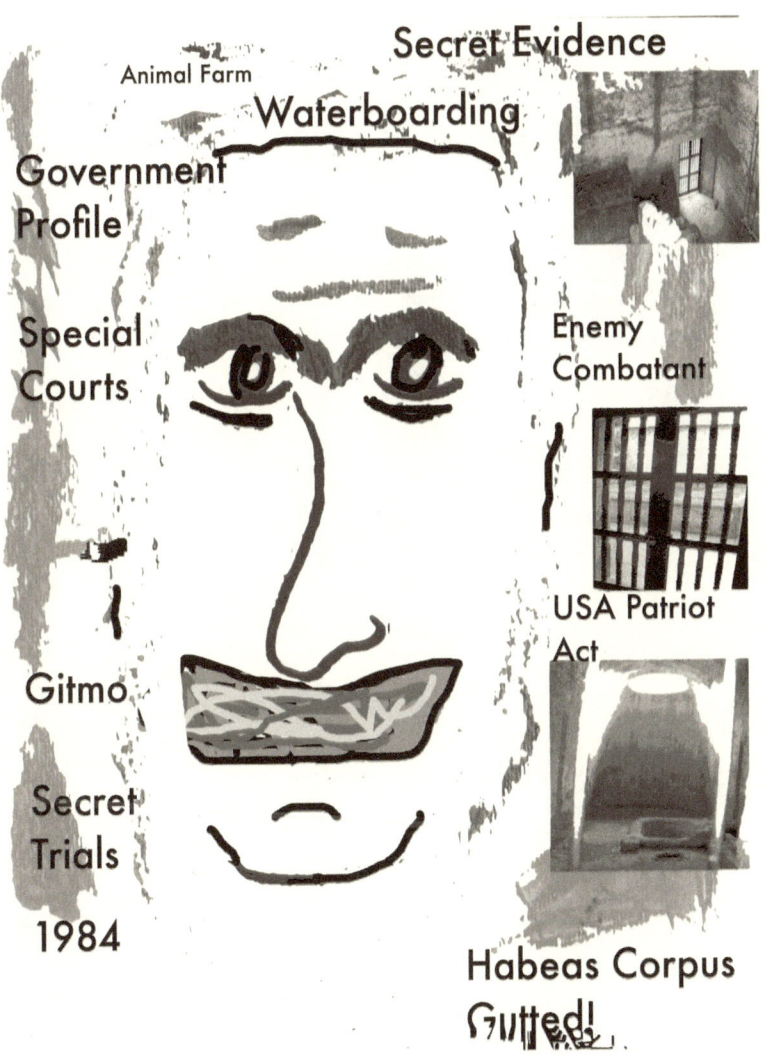

"Big Brother Is Watching"

BALTIMORE

27. A Final Farewell to Judge Tom Ward
March 12, 2016

"And until we meet again, May God hold you in the hollow of his hand." Old Irish Proverb

Corpus Christi R.C. Church, located in the Bolton Hill area, was filled to capacity. In fact, it was standing room only. On Saturday, March 12, 2016, at 11 AM, a funeral Mass was held there for one of Baltimore's finest sons - Judge Tom Ward.

With Father Martin Demke presiding, the Corpus Christi choir added to the ambiance of the occasion with their fine voices. They had a lot of help from the audience, too, which particularly enjoyed singing along with the popular hymn, "On Eagle's Wings."

I knew it was going to be a memorable service when one of my favorite ballads, "How Great Thou Art," was introduced by the Cantor, Anita Hampson, accompanied by pianist, Dan Meyer.

During his 89-years, Judge Ward had a very remarkable career that touched many lives in a positive and deep way. Try newspaper route carrier; union member; B&O Railroad worker (like his father before him); U.S. Army Paratrooper; "Baltimore Sun" reporter; Baltimore City Councilman; Chair of the Liquor Board, Environmentalist; Politico; Irish Preservationist (Irish R/R Workers Museum on Lemmon Street); Founder of the Bolton Hill Democratic Club; Conservationist (Baltimore City & West Virginia); Lawyer; Jurist and devoted Family Man. The truth is: They don't make them like Judge Ward anymore.

When Judge Ward was practicing law as a young, feisty advocate, where do you think his office was located? In some high tower building in the Inner Harbor? Hell, no! It was in Hampden, (Hon), right on "The Avenue," near Elm Street.

Naturally, there were gathered in the church many of Judge Ward's colleagues from the legal arena. Former Chief Judges of the

Maryland Court of Appeals; Robert M. Bell and Joseph F. Murphy were there; along with the former Chief Judge of the Circuit Court of Baltimore; Joseph H.H. Kaplan; and a current City Circuit Court Judge, the Hon. John C. Themelis.

Mayoralty candidates Catherine Pugh and Carl Stokes were also seen in the large assemblage. They are two of the thirteen candidates on the Democratic side seeking that office.

The man responsible for appointing Judge Ward to the chairmanship of the Liquor Board, ex-Baltimore City Mayor and ex-Maryland Governor, Martin O'Malley, (aka "Marty O'Gov"), also made an appearance at the service. Their close friendship goes back, at least, to O'Malley's days as a Baltimore City Councilman.

Two of the Judge's children spoke at the service. Their fond recollections of their father brought both laughter and tears to the audience. The laughter came roaring out when they reminded everyone how their strict father "would not permit a television set in their house!" The tears showed up when they talked about the great love of their father's life, their late mother Joyce (nee McCartney), who died in 2011. They underscored how "desperately lonely" he was after the Lord had called her home.

Attorney Frank Lidinsky, whose late father, Richard A. Lidinsky, Sr., served for decades at the Deputy City Comptroller, wrote a note for the service's program, which struck a responsive cord with me. He said of Judge Ward: "His love of Baltimore City will long be remembered and appreciated. What an honor to the Irish and Catholic community to claim him as their son."

Giving the eulogy was ex-State Senator, Julian "Jack" Lapides. For over fifty-five years, the Senator and Judge Ward were both neighbors and intimate friends. Lapides (a flaming liberal if they ever was one); and Judge Ward (an arch-Conservative), with a capital "C," jointly ran the Bolton Hill Democratic Club. It was, like my old political, now defunct hangout - the Stonewall Democratic Club in South Baltimore - one of the last bastions of freedom in Western

Civilization (or something like that.) It has now, regretfully, gone the way of the DoDo Bird. The club used to meet in the Fifth Regiment Armory.

Somehow, Judge Ward and Senator Lapides survived and overcame their ideological divide. I was so pleased to hear him remind the audience that it was Judge Ward, as a young City Councilman from the 2nd District, and as an bright and energetic attorney, who stopped the East-West Expressway, with plenty of help, too, from the activist communities. (U.S. Senator Barbara A. Mikulski, PLEASE copy this note!) That Monster Highway from Hell would have destroyed and/or seriously impaired the historic neighborhoods of Federal Hill, Little Italy, Fell's Point and Canton.

An honor guard from the Ancient Order of Hibernians, led by a bagpiper, accompanied Judge Ward's casket out of the church and onto the sidewalk, where the hearse was waiting. Former member of the House of Delegates, Brian McHale, was in that group. His friendship with Judge Ward goes back to his late father, Michael "Iron Mike" McHale, days in the City Council.

One of the ballads, the piper played was another old favorite of mine, "The Minstrel Boy." It was so appropriate since Judge Ward was a take-no-prisoners' fighter on every issue that touched his big, lovable and very Irish heart. The Irish patriotic tune was penned by Thomas Moore and was extremely popular with Irish soldiers fighting on the Union side in America's Civil War.

I end this commentary with a short poem, written by one of Judge Ward's many admirers, Ms. Usha Nellore. It's entitled: "In Memory of Dad." Here's it is:

> "I loved the man.
> He was a character!
> I loved the way he tackled a mugger.
> I loved the way he tackled the liquor barons.
> I loved the way he tackled life.

Long life.
Well lived.
Unique and fun filled.
Strong moral fiber.
Stubborn ethical streak.
In this era of cyber,
He was quintessential
old world chic."

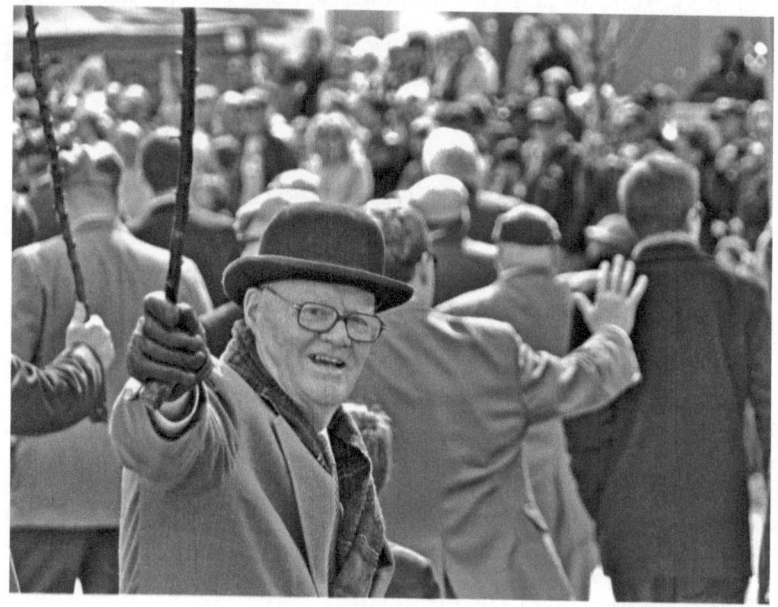

Judge Tom Ward

28. Baltimore Symphony Orchestra Does "Pop Up" at Penn Station September 14, 2016

It was a fun time in the main lobby of Penn Station today. Travelers were welcomed on Wednesday, September 14, 2016, just after noon, by music coming from the string section of the Baltimore Symphony Orchestra (BS0). The surprise visit by the musicians is all part of the BSO's ongoing effort to get the orchestra "out into the community."

This movement has a name. It's called "Pop Up!"

Now, this isn't the first time the BSO has made such efforts to connect directly with the community. Many recall that after the April, 2015 Freddie Gray-related Uprising in the city, a few of its members performed at North & Pennsylvania Avenues, in the heart of West Baltimore.

The BSO did a similar gig, on April 28, 2015, with close to a full orchestra, in front of the Meyerhoff Symphony Hall, under the baton of its talented music director, Marin Alsop. See slideshow/video of that splendid happening at: https://www.facebook.com/bill.hughes.1297/media_set?set=a.10210463220280183.107 3742198.1334685315&type=3&pnref=story

That very special "Peace and Healing" performance couldn't have been better timed. It was also much appreciated by those who were working hard to get our city back up on the right track.

Getting back to today's musical adventure, train travelers were also welcomed to "guest conduct" the string players. A few of them took up the challenge.

Ms. Alsop said all of this is a fun way to introduce the BSO "to new audiences." Well, I think it's fair to say that the impromptu performance was a laudable effort and by the look of the smiling faces at the scene, a good time was had by all.

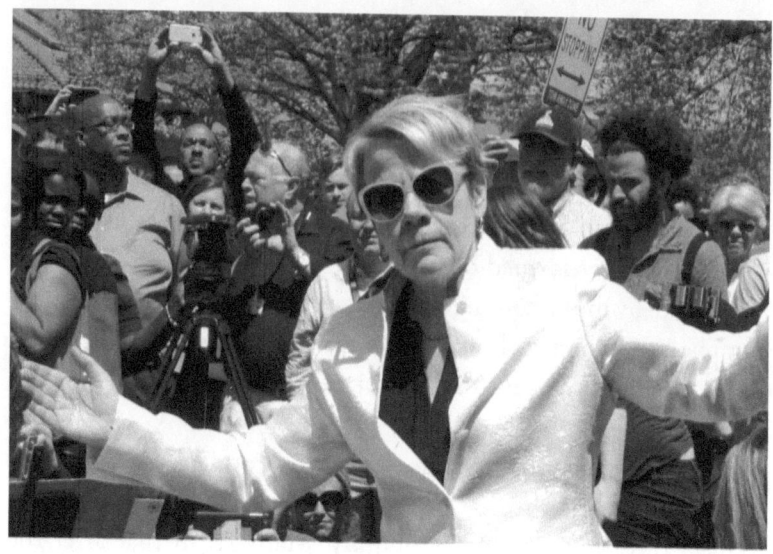

BSO's Conductor, Marin Alsop

29. Al Kaline: Baseball Great from Westport, in South Baltimore
August 19, 2013

Al Kaline is in the Major League Baseball Hall of Fame. He played 22 years, (1953-1974), mostly in the outfield, for the Detroit Tigers of the American League. He set all kinds of records, including hitting 399 career home runs.

Born in 1934, in Westport, a working class South Baltimore neighborhood, his family had to struggle to make it in the world. Kaline's mom scrubbed floors and his dad worked in a broom factory. Although other children in the family went to work at an early age, Kaline's parents chose to allow Al to focus on his baseball aspirations. Bless them for that move.

When you're driving south on Russell Street before you get to the Baltimore-Washington Parkway (BWP), you pass the two stadiums: one for the Orioles and another for the Ravens, both on your left side. The last neighborhood you see before you leave Baltimore City and hit the BWP is Kaline's Westport.

Some of Kaline's cousins labored at the now-defunct Carr-Lowery Glass company, then the largest employer in Westport. A few had participated in semi-pro baseball, others were known around town as pretty good athletes and softball players.

Carr-Lowery was located on the middle branch of the Patapsco River, not too far from where the new "Horseshoe Casino" is currently under construction and where big plans for waterfront development are still, despite some setbacks, in the works.

If you take a spin over the Hanover Street Bridge heading towards Cherry Hill and look hard to the right, you can see where the Carr-Lowery plant was once situated. It closed its doors for good in 2003. It was yet, in a broad sense, another victim of the deliberate de-industrialization of our once, great country. That's a subject, I will leave for another commentary.

The first time I saw Kaline, he wasn't playing baseball! He was playing basketball! It was a sandlot game and it was held at Southern High School. Then, it was located at Warren Avenue and Williams Street in South Baltimore, just opposite fabled Federal Hill Park. Southern High is also where Kaline attended school from 1949 to 1953, and where he first came to the attention of the major league baseball scouts. He didn't go to college.

At the basketball game, I notice this player speeding down the court in front of me, about 6 ft. 1 in. tall, slender, stopping on a dime and getting off a near-perfect jump shot to score. He was pure poetry in action. You couldn't help but pay attention to him. I asked my buddy from Locust Point who was sitting next to me: "Who is 'that' guy?" He answered: "That's Al Kaline!," as if there was much more to the story. And, indeed, there was.

From his baseball playing at Southern H.S. and in the sandlot leagues around town, Kaline was creating a lot of buzz. Was he for real? Would he get signed by a major league club? This was before there was a major league Baltimore Orioles team.

The scene shifts to Latrobe Park's baseball field, off Fort Avenue in South Baltimore and just west of historic Fort McHenry. It's the early '50s. Kaline is playing for United Iron and Metal, a sandlot baseball team - one of the best in Bmore at that time. The competition is the highly regarded Amusement Machine Operators (AMO), a Locust Point-based team coached by George Klemmick.

Mr. Klemmick, now deceased, was a neighbor of mine and a Detective Lt. on the Baltimore City Police Department and one of my favorite people. I was the batboy for the AMO team. The field faced south where it was bordered by the railroad tracks of the B&O Railroad. On the east was a row of trees and a grassy field that stood outside the parameters of the playing area.

The first time up to the plate, Kaline went down hard swinging and missing on three straight pitches! Hey, maybe he wasn't that good after all, I thought to myself. The next time up, however, he changed my mind quickly. Kaline whacked a home run to right field that landed on the far reaches of the railroad tracks. Wow! It took my breath away. He wasn't done yet.

Kaline, a right-handed hitter, slugged home runs to the deepest parts of center and left field on his final two times up at the plate. His team won easily. Bottom line: Al Kaline was the real thing, no ifs, ands or buts.

In 1953, Kaline, then 18-years old, got a $35,000 bonus (over $300,000 in today's dollars) and signed with the Detroit Tigers. The rest as they say is history. In 1980, Kaline, one of Westport's greatest sons, was elected into Baseball's Hall of Fame. The last Baltimorean to be so honored before Kaline was "the Bambino" - George Herman "Babe" Ruth - one of Southwest Baltimore's greatest sons in 1939.

As for those three home runs balls Kaline hit at Latrobe Park that memorable day, I think they're still looking for them!

30. In Honor of Black History Month in Baltimore January 31, 2018

Black History Month is an annual observance in the United States and is held in the month of February. It dates back to at least 1926. It has also been called "African-American History Month."

In 1976, the U.S. government officially adopted the title of "Black History Month." At that time, the then-President the Hon. Gerald Ford urged his fellow Americans "to seize the opportunity to honor the too-often neglected accomplishments of black Americans in every area of endeavor throughout our history."

To learn more about its background, go to: http://www.history.com/topics/black-history/black-history-month

The individuals in my poster - entertainers, artists, educators, religious and labor leaders, peace and justice activists, a football great and politicos alike - are representative of the many, who work tirelessly to make our Baltimore a better place for all.

This poster is my way of paying tribute to them and to the "Black History Month" celebration in the year 2018.

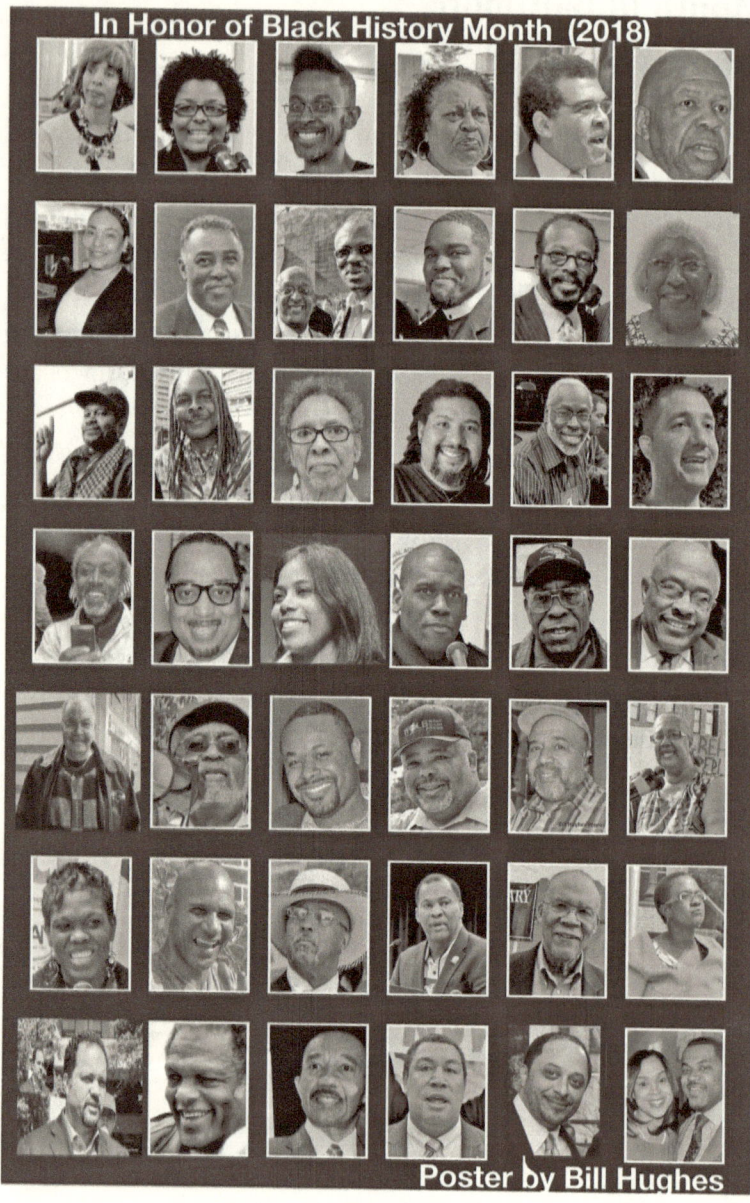

31. Mary Avara: An All-American Gal
April 25, 2016

In the late '50s, I was working on the Baltimore docks as an ILA member in Locust Point, and occasionally, with the late Michael "Iron Mike" McHale (ex-Del. Brian McHale's father). McHale was also a neighbor. He lived on Haubert St., while I resided around the corner on Hull St. A popular City Councilman from South Baltimore, McHale served for three terms from 1951-1963.

One night, McHale took me to a political meeting over in Southwest Baltimore near the Hollins Street Market. I was his designated driver during the campaign season. I was also his precinct captain for the 10th and 11th precincts of the 24th Ward on Fort Ave.

We had to climb up a steep flight of stairs to the meeting hall. When we got to the top, a half-inebriated character came up to McHale, put his ugly mug in front of his, and started bad-mouthing him in a very loud and hostile manner.

Before McHale could respond, this smallish woman, with coal-black hair, rushed out of the shadows. She grabbed the drunk by his coat lapels, shook him as hard as any stevedore could and yelled in his face: "Don't you dare insult Mr. McHale! He's my guest!"

The drunk wisely nodded his compliance and slid back into the crowd. McHale then turned to me - by then my jaw had nearly dropped to the floor - and said, "Billy, I want you to meet Mary Avara!"

I called her "Miss Mary." She had her own "Ladies Democratic Club," on South Carrollton Street in "Pigtown." One of 18 children, Avara (nee Serio), a proud Italian, was widowed at age 36, with four young children to take care of. Her husband, a barber, had died in 1946, in a tragic car crash.

In order to put bread on the table, Avara went to work as bail bondswoman. If you were arrested and needed to make bail, you could turn to Miss Mary for help. She also knew who the best criminal lawyers were in the police district courts. It was simply unheard of for a woman back in that era to be in the bail bonds business. Avara did it, however, and she was darn good at it, too.

Politically, Avara was aligned with McHale and his political boss, Julian "Fats" Carrick aka "The Chicken Man." He was my boss, too. When I knew Mr. Carrick, he was blind. The club's meetings were held in the back of a darkened tavern on Cross Street, in South Baltimore, near Light St. This is long before the area became yuppified.

Sometimes, I would take down the minutes of the meeting. Mr. Carrick would call the group to order. Then, he would pull out his hand gun from his coat pocket and put it on the table. He would, without missing a beat, lead the assembly in saying the Pledge of Allegiance. I recall reading the minutes with a shaky voice.

Getting back to my relationship with Miss Mary. Carrick's club backed J. Millard Tawes, a Democrat, for governor in 1959 election. He was an Eastern Shore politico. Tawes won that election and then served two terms in that post.

As a result of Tawes' victory, I got appointed to a job as a deputy clerk in the Baltimore City Court. This was perfect for me, since I was then going to law school at night at the University of Baltimore.

Who do you think took me to work on that very first day and introduced me to the Clerk of the Court, John Rutherford? It was Miss Mary herself! This is in 1961. She knew everybody in the court house.

Miss Mary also got a very nice political perk from Governor Tawes. It was an appointment as the chairwomen of the "Maryland State Board of Motion Pictures Censors." And, censoring those "trashy, filthy films," as she called them, Miss Mary did with a religious zeal. This upset a lot of the powerful merchants of smut in the biz.

Avara held that post until 1982, when a Supreme Court decision struck it down as unconstitutional. It was the last movie censor board in the country. It was this controversial role that made Avara into an endearing national celebrity. She came off as a feisty grandma fighting the good fight against the pushers of XXX-rated films.

The nightly TV talk show hosts loved Avara. She was a guest many times, while captivating the audience with her folky persona, on the Johnny Carson, Merv Griffin and Dick Cavett programs.

Avara once told the "Baltimore Sun," that she had looked "at more nude bodies, than 80, 100 or 50,000 doctors." If she could, she would have preferred to rate some of the movies she reviewed, as an "R" for rotten, or "G" for garbage. She particularly loathed "Deep Throat."

In the early 70s, a young underground filmmaker in Baltimore, John Waters, regularly clashed with Avara. Although his films were far from the X-rated types, she routinely gave them "the scissors" and considered them as "trash." Their rivalry, however, had the effect of making his movies, like "Pink Flamingos," even more popular and transformed him into a famous name.

By way of full disclosure, back in the 90s, I was in four of Waters' popular flicks, two of them cameo roles: "Pecker" and "A Dirty Shame." Enter another talented filmmaker, Steve Yeager. He did a classic of a documentary, in 1998, on Waters, entitled, "Divine Trash." Somehow, Yeager got Avara to make an appearance in that film.

On or about Avara's 75th birthday, I got a hand-written note from her penned on yellow-colored paper. She said she was keeping busy working as a "cashier" at her son "Cy's" barber school down in Dundalk. On the bottom of her note was printed this phrase from Genesis 21:22, "God is with thee in all thou doest."

Avara died on August 9, 2000, at age 90. Her Requiem Funeral Mass was held at her long time parish, St. Peter the Apostle RC Church. It's located just north of the B&R R/R Museum on Poppleton Street. The church was filled to capacity. This is the same parish, where the baseball immortal, George Herman "Babe" Ruth, was baptized. I'm grateful I got my chance to say good-bye to Miss Mary.

I note for the record, St. Peter's was closed in 2012, by the big shots of the Archdiocese, despite 165 years of continuous service to the community. Trust me when I say this: if Avara were still alive then, there is no way those nervous nellies on North Charles Street would have ever gotten away with shutting down her beloved parish without one hell of a fight.

Finally, as for that All-American gal, Mary Avara, I don't think we will see the likes of her again.

32. Helen Delich Bentley: My Recollections of a Feminist Icon August 8, 2016

Before the word "Feminist" was coined, Helen Delich Bentley had already created the iconic image of one. She did it by fearlessly, and with skill and tenacity, working her butt off.

Bentley died on August 6, 2016, at age 92, in Timonium, Baltimore County. It's fair say, she had a darn good run.

The "Baltimore Sun," Bentley's "newspaper," ran a lengthy tribute to her the very next day, authored by Michael Dresser.

The piece recounted Bentley's fantastic career as a "Sun" reporter and maritime editor; as a producer of the popular TV show, the "Port that Built a City and State"; her ten years as a member of the House of Representatives; her chairmanship of the Federal Maritime Commission; and various other noteworthy public achievements.

These things are all well-known. What I want to relate here are the stories of the first and the last time that I met this amazing woman. Let me set the initial scene:

Back in the mid-1950s, I joined Local 829 of the International Longshoremens Association (ILA). I was 18 years old. It was located in the 1200 block of Hull Street in Locust Point - just opposite where the popular pub/eatery "Hull Street Blues" is today. Our home was in the same block, just a few houses up the street.

My father, the late Richard P. Hughes, Sr., was a boss on the docks for the Aloca Steamship Company, then at Pier 9 N/S Locust Point. He loaned me the $180 to join the local.

You remember the legendary movie, "On the Waterfront?" Well, this was the final era for it. It was in its last hurrah, as the container ships, and modernization, loomed on the horizon. Colorful Marlon Brandon-like dockworkers, with their ubiquitous "stevedore hook" hanging in their back pockets, would soon pass from the setting.

I started working as an extra - picking up a job with a stevedoring gang here and there. I liked hanging out at the union hall with my cronies, playing cards and just shooting the breeze.

Herb Pearce, a neighbor of mine then, was the President of Local 829. He was an imposing figure, who looked and dressed like a movie star. He was also a darn good amateur softball player - a home run slugger at the plate.

The caretaker for our union hall was a hillbilly from West Virginia named - I'm not making this up - John Strange! He also worked as an extra stevedore when they needed one. Strange also liked his drink, so Pearce had to keep an eye on him. He normally slept in a small room in the back of the hall.

Pearce got into some kind of trouble as the president of Local 829. I don't remember the details, but an emergency meeting was called to deal with it. Pearce was potentially facing serious charges and possibly dismissal. The meeting was at night and the hall was packed full - SRO.

There was a lot of yelling and cursing going on. Some idiot set off a firecracker! John Strange was so drunk, he couldn't stand up straight and was badly singing his ass off. The cry went up: "Throw that bum out!" But, then somebody else pitched in: "You can't throw him out, his dues are paid up!" Solution: They locked him in a back room, behind the stage, which meant that all during the meeting from hell you could hear him screaming his bloody head off.

I was standing in the back of the hall, when there was a loud banging on the front door. When it was opened, I could see there was a woman trying to get in. It was Helen Delich! I knew her mug from the TV show. The sergeant-at-arms said firmly, "get f......lost!" Delich persisted pushing, shoving and barking loudly: "This is a public meeting." The predicable response from the union guy: "Go f... y.......!," as they jockeyed back and forth.

Then, I spotted a cop. It was Sergeant Burke from the Southern District. He gently grabbed Delich's arm and told her that the meeting was for "members only." It was only then that the feisty and irate Delich's backed off. Absent Burke's appearance, I think she would have spent the night out there banging away on the front door, then leading to God knows what.

As for the heated meeting, after a lot of vitriol, Pearce, who was a masterful public speaker, stood up and told his side of the story. After a brilliant 15-minute spiel, he had a majority of the members, including myself, standing up cheering for him. By acclamation, all charges were withdrawn.

Pearce is deceased. Local 829 is now part of labor history, having merged with Local 858 into Local 333, on December 3, 1970.

This brings me to the last time, that I saw Helen. It was at a funeral Mass for my brother, Richard, on September 19, 2013. At his death, he was the retired head of the 65,000 membered ILA national Union.

Helen spoke with sincere affection at his funeral, held at Our Lady of Good Counsel RC Church in Locust Point. As the quintessential authority on the maritime industry, her kind words about Richard, and her deep and genuine admiration for his work, meant a lot to not only his family, but to his colleagues on the waterfront. It was, indeed, a beautiful send off for brother Richard.

Helen Delich Bentley - Feminist icon - and a class act if there ever was one.

33. The Demon Suicide Haunts Our Psyches
June 24, 2018

"There is but one serious philosophical problem and that is suicide." - Albert Camus

I recall stepping into a funeral parlor in my old neighborhood, Locust Point, located within walking distance of historic Fort McHenry in Baltimore, Maryland. This was back in the early '80s.

I had repeated this ritual hundreds of times over the years to pay my final respects to family members and friends alike. This time, however, it was to be different. The deceased was a suicide! I'll call him "Joe." He was a retired Baltimore City worker. I burst into tears as I approached his casket. This, too, was a first for me. Joe was a lovable, big bloke! He wouldn't hurt a fly and didn't have a mean bone in his body.

Joe was a player-coach on our sandlot softball team. On Sundays, during the football season, he was also a regular at the Baltimore Colts' games. A bus, which left from a local bar, provided the transportation. (This was when the games were played at Memorial Stadium on 33rd Street.) Joe loved to play pinochle, too.

I had seen Joe two times before he took his own life. Once while he was seated on a bench in the plaza over in Fell's Point. Another time, he was taking a walk around Fort McHenry. On both occasions, he was friendly but unusually quiet and had little to say.

Joe chose a bridge as the place to take his own life. When he jumped off of it, he had weighed his feet down so he wouldn't come back up to the surface.

As the fates would have it, Joe's father, also a city worker, was also a suicide. He shot himself to death. I have to wonder what effect that tragedy had on Joe's impressionable psyche? He was only a teenager when it happened.

(Flashback Note: on December 6, 1928, Clarence Hemingway, the father of the novelist, Ernest Hemingway, shot himself in the head at his home in Oak Park, Illinois. He had been depressed over his health and money problems. On the morning of July 2, 1961, his son, Ernest, by then a heavy drinker suffering from both depression and alcoholism, took his own life, too, with a shotgun blast to the head at his home in Ketchum, Idaho. This pattern of suicides running in families, sadly, is not that unusual.)

Getting back to the topic of Suicide. It has gotten a lot of attention recently as the result of celebrities taking their own lives.

First, there was the fashion designer Kate Spade, of New York City; and then the popular celebrity chef - Anthony Bourdain. The latter, age 61, hung himself in a hotel in Kaysersberg, France, on June 8th. (It's called "Le Chambard," and its rated with five-stars.) Spade took her own life, via a hanging, too, on June 5th, in her luxurious Park Avenue Manhattan-based apartment.

Spade, age 55, was married and left behind a teenage daughter. Her husband, Andy, is now saying that she suffered for years from "depression and anxiety." Spade reportedly left a suicide note for her daughter, telling her "This is not your fault." Kate was known to the public as a vibrant person and a very keen, much-respected businesswoman. Her death on June 5th was a total shock to the public and to many of her business associates.

Spade was separated from her husband Andy at the time of her death. How big a factor that was in her suicide is a matter of speculation. Her husband in a zany kind of reaction wore a "mouse mask" after leaving his apartment one morning after her body was found. He also reacted in a "testy" manner to reporters' questions. Where was the dignity in all of that?

Bourdain had recently acquired a new girlfriend, Asia Argento, an actress, about twenty years younger than himself. She was in Italy when he died. Supposedly, they had just became a "hot item" and he was happier than he had been in years with his new cozy relationship.

However, just before Bourdain's suicide, photos showed up in the international media showing Argento, while walking through the streets of Rome, kissing and embracing a young French reporter - Hugo Clement. Did Bourdain see those photos before his suicide and did they influence his decision to take his own life? We may never know.

Like so many suicides, Bourdain's and Spade's will forever remain a mystery as to why they decided to take their own lives. At press time, the Kate Spade Foundation has pledged $1 million to "suicide prevention groups."

Pundit Anne Kingston, writing for "Maclean's" magazine, (08.17.14), said that we need "to pay more attention to depression and its potential consequences" with respect to the prevention of suicides. She focused her comments on the suicide of the comedian/actor, Robin Williams. Kingston wrote about the array of feelings, "including anger," left behind for the comedian's family and friends to deal with because of his death. Williams died on August 11, 2014, at age 63.

A good book on Williams's life and suicide, he also hung himself, has recently been released. Its called "Robin." The author is David Itzkoff. He covers it all, including the "dark corners" of Williams' life and work. I recommend it.

Then, there are the disturbing numbers of veteran of our wars, 22 a day, who commit suicide in the U.S. It's fair to say the Veterans Administration has been overwhelmed by this ongoing crisis. A new report from the VA found veterans are "two times more likely to die by suicide than non-veterans." https://www.newsy.com/stories/va-veterans-twice-as-likely-to-die-by-suicide-than-non-vets/ More needs to be done - now!

Finally, the "demon suicide," for use of a better term, doesn't rest. It can effect the rich or poor, celebrated or unknown. Your status makes no difference to this voracious predator. It has become a plague of our times. What can it teach us about depression and what's really valuable? Somehow, someway, it must be stopped!

34. Illustrator Barry Blitt at JHU's Center for Visual Arts April 4, 2017

On Monday evening, April 3, 2017, the popular satirical illustrator/cartoonist, Barry Blitt, made an appearance at the Johns Hopkins University's "Center for Visual Arts." It was held on campus in the Mattin Center of the F. Ross Jones Building, at North Charles & 33rd St., in Baltimore, MD.

The event, entitled: "Barry Blitt: In One Eye and Out the Other," was hosted by Craig Hankin, the director of JHU's Center for Visual Arts, before a capacity audience. Besides working as an instructor at the school, Hankin is also an author, musician and a painter. In his salad days, he was the co-founder of Baltimore's "City Paper."

At the moment, "The New Yorker" magazine is Blitt's home base. To put it mildly, he's been on a roll with one outrageous, on target, front cover illustration after another.

One of Blitt's latest funny-as-hell efforts was dated March 6, 2017. It showed Russia's President, Vladimir Putin, as an iconic monocled character, who turns his piercing eye toward a small, fluttering, mouthy-looking butterfly in the upper left hand corner of the cover. Who do you think it is? Why, it's America's pseudo-hero himself, President Donald "Make America Great Again" Trump!

Some history is needed here. The first cover of "The New Yorker," which now goes back 92 years, featured a monocled character k/a "Eustace Tilley," by artist Rea Irvin. Thus, Putin's transformation into "Eustace Vladimirovich Tilley."

When Blitt goes to bed at night, I'm sure he thanks the good Lord for the election of Donald Trump as president. The comedy-loving "Saturday Night Live" show on NBC-TV is in the same boat. Satirists and Republican-bashers alike love Trump and his off-the-wall antics.

Why do they love him? Because, without trying, Trump is a buffoon of a character "Writ large." You don't have to make anything up! Just read the paper everyday, and his crazy tweets. It's all right there.

Blitt is a native of Quebec, Canada, and currently calls Connecticut home. Michael Cavna of "Comic Riffs," (02.24.17), labeled Blitt a "topical artist extraordinaire."

During the program, Blitt narrated a slide show of his work over the years for "The New Yorker," "The New York Times," "Vanity Fair," "Rolling Stone," and other leading publications. He jokingly said that he's not crazy about making public appearances, since he "doesn't have nice pants to wear!"

Blitt, who's built on the short side, a la comedian Jackie Mason, got started doing political illustrations, back in the 80s, during the reign of President Ronald Reagan. This was around the time, he added, when Reagan was "losing his donuts."

One of Blitt's personal fave' sketches of Trump didn't make the final cut. It showed him as a statue, like the one of President Andrew Jackson in the middle of Lafayette Park, with lot of pigeons pooping on him. Oh, too stinky!

Like many of us, Blitt said he was "shocked" when Trump won the presidency. (Yeah, and so was Hillary Clinton!)

Another of Blitt's "New Yorker" illustrations that I personally liked a lot showed a befuddled Dubya, Condi Rice, Dick "Darth Vader" Cheney and Donald "Rumi" Rumsfeld in the White House's Oval Office. The room is filled with water right up to their shoulders. This was during the tragedy of "Hurricane Katrina," which the inept, arrogant Bush-Cheney Gang badly mismanaged - some would argue - they "criminally" mismanaged.

For years, Blitt's has also done illustrations for the "NY Times'" Op Ed pundit, Frank Rich. Blitt is also an author and has won numerous awards for his creative artistry over the years.

Of course, you can't do what Blitt does without stepping on a few toes. His 2008 illustration/cover for the "The New Yorker" is a case in point. It was entitled "The Politics of Fear," and it satirized the false rumors about Barack Obama and his wife, Michelle, as he was running for president.

It showed President Obama, in the WH, dressed in traditional Muslim clothes, and the First Lady, Michelle, in combat boots, with an assault rifle hanging over her shoulder. And, to top it all off, Blitt portrayed an American flag burning in the fire place. Yikes! Even the ex-49ers Q/B Colin Kaepernick (who deigned not to stand for the National Anthem before NFL games) wouldn't go that far.

The illustration was quickly condemned as "tasteless and offensive" by a White House spokesman. It was also roundly criticized by Sen. John McCain (Rep-AZ), among others card-carrying conservatives.

Well, controversy comes with the territory in Blitt's business. It took some time for folks to take his illustration "as a joke." Some, however - and this is understandable when you touch on that ethnic/religious "third rail" - just didn't see it that way. To be honest, they probably never will. Beauty, like comedy, as they say, "is in the eyes of the beholder."

Finally, Blitt is a very entertaining speaker. He also enjoyed the Q&A part of the program and dishing out some pretty good one-liners for the audience to laugh along with him.

You can check out Blitt's personal website at: http://barryblitt. com, where you can also peruse some of the cover illustrations referred to above. To learn more about this event, go to: https://www. facebook.com/events/255136668230667/.

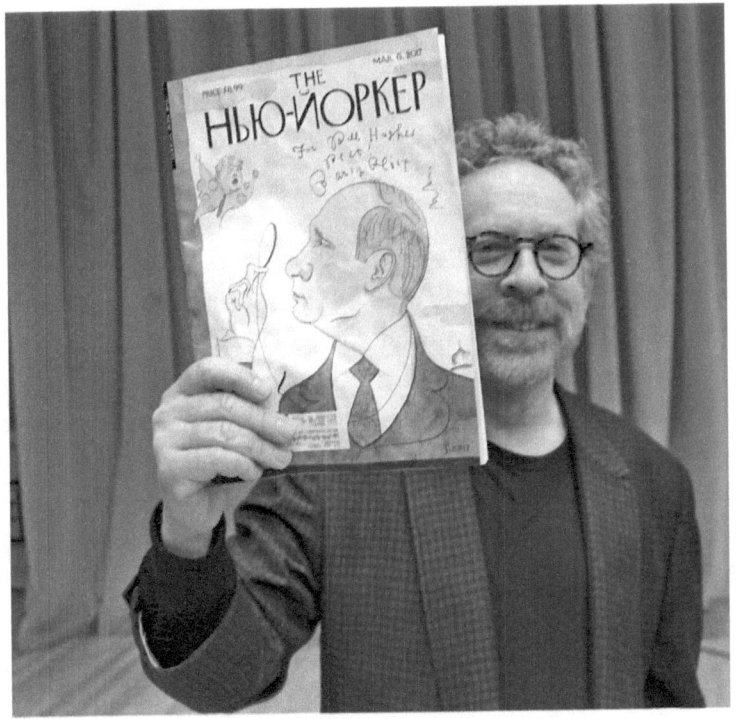

Barry Blitt

35. My Days as a Longshoreman on the Baltimore Docks
July 18, 2017

In the 1940s, a blacksmith shop was located one block from the harbor at the very foot of the 1100 block of Haubert Street in Locust Point. It was next to the then-thriving Procter & Gamble (P&G) plant, in South Baltimore, now occupied by the bustling Under Armour facility. The tracks of the Baltimore & Ohio R/R, plus Nicholson Street, separated the shop from that then- sprawling soap-making plant, which operated 24/7. The shop was also just around the corner from Phil Klemkowski's popular bar on the 1100 block of Hull Street. More on that blacksmith shop in just a moment.

First, let's focus on Klemkowski's emporium. It catered to the merchant seamen more than it did to the local stevedores. There was some resentment about that. When I was about twelve years old, my first freelance job, circa 1949, was shining shoes in the local bars in my neighborhood, such as Klemkowski's. Invariably, the seaman customer would ask me this question: "Do you have any sisters?" My response: "Yea, I do and my dad's a cop!" That would end that conversation! The shoe-shining gig went no where, plus there was a lot of competition, especially from my neighbor, Frankie "The Greek" Pappas. I was raised, first, at 1237 Haubert Street - a two-story house. There was no swimming pool in our neighborhood. We all learned how to swim in the murky waters of the harbor, mostly at the foot of Hull Street. No trunks either. We swam in our undies. Somehow we survived the water pollution from the P&G plant. It may have built up our immune system. Who knows?

At dusk, when the "Moonlight Cruise" boat would pass by Hull Street, with its dancing couples and music, on its journey out of the Inner Harbor, we, (the Locust Point boy-ohs, all six or seven of us), would often "moon" the vessel! The ship's captain was in on the joke. First the passengers would scream; then the screams would turn quickly to laughter. In grade school, my twin brother Jim and I got a weekly job delivering circulars to homes in Locust Point for a local food market owned by two guys, named Ben and Lou. It didn't pay well and often the weather was brutally cold or boiling hot. So one day, we decided to dump the flyers down a sewer and instead take in a movie at the Deluxe Theatre on Fort Avenue at Lowman Street. Putting aside the ethical question, it was a dumb idea! A day or so later, there was a flash flood and all the circulars came spewing-out onto the street! OMG! Since the pay was a joke and the circulars brought in little in the way of new business, nothing happened. In fact, Jim wound up working in the food market. Go figure.

My next job, while in my freshman year of high school, (1951), was delivering the "Baltimore Evening Sun" newspaper to homes in Locust Point for a hefty $2.50 a week! My boss was Louis Gilweiser, a hard-working man, who also enjoyed playing a musical instrument in Baltimore City's orchestra. Yea, the city had a municipal orchestra back then! "The Evening Sun" gig lasted about a year and taught me some solid work-related habits. For example, there was lesson # 1: If I didn't show-up, the newspapers didn't get delivered! There were then about twenty taverns in Locust Point. During and just after World War II right until the early 60s, they all made a pretty good living. Locust Point, then a blue collar bastion, is located on a peninsula which juts out into Baltimore harbor. At its tip was found fabled Fort McHenry. How blue collar was it? There were five International Longshoremen's Association (ILA) union halls located there, all within walking distance of each other. Also, in some of the bars on Locust Point, a portrait of John L. Lewis, the hell-raising boss of the United Mine Workers of America would be found proudly hanging on their walls. Locust Point was Union-strong! The sound of the trains rumbling through the neighborhood and of the ships and tugboats doing their cargo loading/vessel docking businesses were music to the ears of most residents. In that era, the Port was booming with work. There were plenty of dollars also to burn away on automobiles, clothes, gambling and other vices.

For example, my first new car was a 1957 Bel Air, blue/white, sports sedan Chevrolet, with long tail fins. I bought it for about $2,500 from Fox Chevrolet on Hanover Street/Key Highway in South Baltimore. Think "Elvis on four wheels!" Back to the blacksmith shop! The front gate of it was usually open and you could see the furnace firing away in the back. It was a small building, darkish in color, like something out of Charles Dickens' London. The owner lived on the second floor of his shop. He was a very private person, short in stature, with a mostly dirty, unshaven face. One of the things the blacksmith made there was a "stevedore hook." It was about 8" long, with an "S" curve. It was connected to a very strong wooden handle. It was a useful tool for the longshoremen handling certain kinds of cargo. (The words stevedore and longshoreman were used interchangeably, although technically they have different meanings.) Movie buffs may recall the "stevedore hook" from that classic 1954 movie, "On The Waterfront," starring the late, great actor, Marlon Brando. You might remember Brando's famous line from that flick, delivered to Rod Steiger in the back of a car? "I coulda been a contender!" See: https://www.youtube.com/watch?v=uBiewQrpBBA

I recall buying a "hook" in 1955, from the shop. I was then eighteen-years old and I had just joined ILA Local 829. My dad, Richard Patrick "Dick" Hughes, Sr., a boss for the Alcoa Steamship Company, lent me the money to pay the initiation fee - about $180! (Bless your heart, Dad.) My grandfather, Martin Patrick Hughes, had started the family's ILA tradition back in the early 1890s. A native of County Mayo, Ireland, he had worked as a coal trimmer in Locust Point. He lived at 1309 Haubert St. The coal pier was squeezed between the P&G plant and the Domino Sugar terminal. My ILA Local 829 was located on Hull Street, opposite "Buck" Kreps' bar (nka "The Hull Street Blues"). We were then living a few doors away from from Kreps', at 1238 Hull Street, in a three-story house. It didn't take long for me to get my feet wet as a longshoreman. I was hanging out in the hall playing a friendly card game, when a gang carrier, "Reds" Burdinski, came rushing in. It was around noon time. Reds needed six extra men for his gang to start working at 1 PM, at Pier 8, N/S, Locust Point. It just so happened that there were six of us, including myself, at the card game. They were: Frank "Unk" Oswald, Steve "Eagle" Markowski, John "Hopit" Haspert, George Kelly and William "Duke" Brown. We were all hired on the spot. The cargo we were to work on was located on a barge tied to the ship. It was going to be loaded into the number one hatch of the vessel. The problem for us was getting onto the barge! It was positioned near the bow of ship. So, when you climbed down the "Jacob's ladder," (a rope ladder with wooden rungs), to get onto the barge, your body was literally swinging out there in the wind away from the vessel and over the water. It was a little scary, but we all made it safely aboard the barge. Once there, we had to carry the cargo, heavy wooden boxes of merchandise, onto a pallet. We paired up for the job. Kelly and I were partners. It was in the summer and I recall all of us were sweating our butts off. The jokes were also flying. "Unk" was a naturally funny guy, all five foot six inches of him. He was a confirmed bachelor who lived at home with his aging mother. On a good day, I could only understand every other word he spoke. "Unk" did a lot cursing under his breath, too, as he chewed away from the side of his mouth on his unlit cigar. "Eagle" and "Hopit" would dig the bejesus out of "Unk," but were smart enough not to overdo it. He had a hyper-sensitive fault line! "Unk" was notorious for quitting jobs and telling the boss, no matter how big or tough he was, a la Robert Di Niro, "go f... your self!" If he did quit, his partner "Duke" would be left on his own. Luckily, that didn't happen. The time flew by and soon the job, after about three or four hours, was over. Mercifully, we didn't have go back up that "Jacob's ladder." I was glad for that! A tug boat was there to take the empty barge back. First, it dropped us off at the head of the pier. Then we walked back to the hall, happy to have gotten the work and to have survived that "Jacob's ladder!"

There was another job on the docks that I won't soon forget. It was at the Davison Chemical Company's pier in Curtis Bay in South Baltimore. Davison is a division of the W.R. Grace Co. My buddy George Kelly and I were partners on that one, too. It was for Ed Swankie's gang. It was the middle of the summer on one of those God-awful humid Baltimore days. The cargo to be handled: 220 pound bags of chemicals - two men to a bag! Kelly and I, along with six other men were laboring in the hole of the ship. Think ultra-humid, like the heat you feel when you get off a plane in Phoenix, AZ. After working under those conditions for a while, I understood why those cowboys out West could be so bad-tempered and quick on the trigger of their gun. We started at 8 am. Somehow, I survived that grueling day, which ended around 5 pm. We did get an hour off for lunch. You are so exhausted by that kind of work, that even talking is cut to a bare minimum. Later, I would ride by that Davidson Chemical site and think to myself: "Thank you Lord for surviving that one!" Fast shift to the other extreme - a winter freeze! After a few years catching p/t jobs out of Local 829 and ILA Local 953 (the Checker's Union), I went to work for my dad, at pier 9, N/S, Locust Point, where the Alcoa Steamship Line vessels docked. It was a steady gig. I was a receiving clerk and had to join ILA Local 1429. My duties were checking the cargo that came into the pier by trucks or rail for loading onto the vessels. One winter night, we had to drive about 100 jeep vehicles onto the pier for the longshoremen to load on an Alcoa ship. The holding area for the jeeps was about a quarter a mile from the vessel. It was below freezing and windy and we were in an exposed area.

Paul Hutchins, now deceased, was one of my co-workers. I weighed then about 150 pounds soaking wet. While, Mr. Hutchins (his son by the same name was a noted "Baltimore Sun" photographer), came in around one hundred and twenty pounds. He was as thin as a rail. After about thirty minutes, I thought we're not going to last! Fortunately, wiser heads decided to re-assign some workers from another area to give us some relief. That saved the day and gave us a chance to "warm-up" between drives to and from the pier. I didn't realize until much later that my work experiences on the docks (1955-60), would mark the end of an era on the waterfront. The "stevedore's hook" would soon, too, become part of labor and maritime history. The highly automated process of intermodal containerization would take over much of the stevedoring work done on the waterfronts of America. The "Age of Containerization" had begun! This meant, too, that all of those colorful characters that I knew from my ILA Local 829 days would also soon recede into fond memories of that bygone period. I moved out of Locust Point in the late 70s. Baltimore City is still my home today.

36. Baltimore's HONfest 2017 Off to a Roaring Start in Hampden June 10, 2017

It was a sunny, Saturday afternoon, June 10, 2017, just right for the launching of the annual HONfest, in Hampden. Even at 11 a.m., "The Avenue," 36th Street, was packing up quickly with festival goers, many wearing their ubiquitous beehive hairdos. Oh, so Bawlmerish! This is the 23rd rendition of the popular event. Its purpose, according to the program notes, is to celebrate the "working women" of our fair city and their continuing contribution to its viability. I second that Motion.

The term "Hon" is one of endearment. I can personally vouch for that going back to my salad days as a Locust Point dude, who liked to also hang out in Highlandtown (Hon); and Up the Hill, on Webster Street at Fort Avenue.

This was just around the time that Bawlmer's own, John Waters, a filmmaking icon, was coming into his own. Yea, the same guy who gave the world in 1988 - "Hairspray," and later in 1990, "Cry-Baby."

Bring your dancing shoes to HONfest. There are three stages blasting out music of all descriptions, (& sound levels). Thirty-six live artists will be performing today and tomorrow right up till closing time.

HONfest will be open on Sunday, from noon to 6 pm. Check out the schedule for show times, especially for its main stage, which is located in front of the Bank of America. Go to: http://honfest.net/honfest-schedule/

You can view some of Hampden's working class origins at: http://honfest.net/hampden-history/. It was a mill town originally, along with its sister neighborhood - Woodberry.

There were plenty of vendors on hand selling their wares today. I think more than last year. And if you get hungry, don't worry, there are plenty of food vendors, hawking drinks, too, and sure to suit every taste.

As soon as I landed, I headed for the Art Under Ground Studio, to see if owner Rick Santiago, had any specials for sale. Indeed, he did.

One of my fave artists, Paul Mintz was out front of Rick's store drawing portraits for customers and selling some of his art. He did my portrait last year. So, I had Mr. Mintz draw one of my grandson, Matteo, age nine. He's visiting from LA. Indeed, it was a splendid job Mr. Mintz did on it.

Further down "The Avenue," I had a chance to chat with another pretty darn good artist, Matt Muirhead, who is also a popular Hampden resident.

Ms. Stacey Chambers, an entrepreneur, was on the scene. She's the owner of the popular "Gogo's," a large bus, filled with the latest ladies' clothing lines. It was parked for business at Elm & "The Avenue."

There was one music stage set up at Chestnut and then another way down at the Falls Road. There were plenty of families on hand, with their young children. The kids were having a great time. As soon as they heard the music, they were in dancing mode. It doesn't get any better than that!

It's fair to say, a good time was had my all. To learn more about this year's HONfest, go to: http://honfest.net/

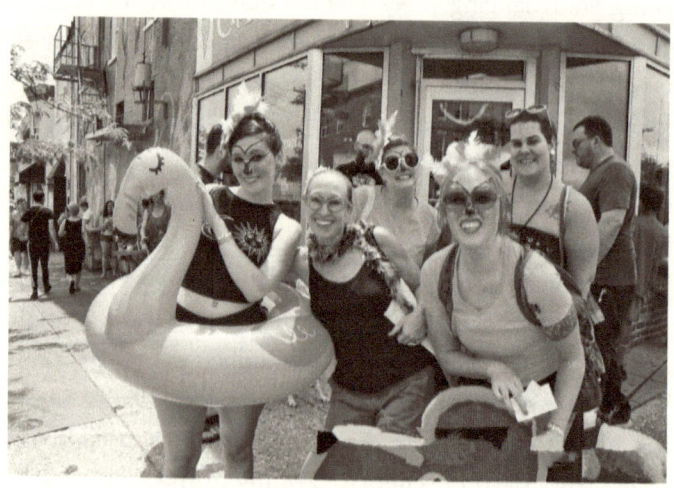

Celebrating HONfest in Hampden

37. A Son of Hampden: A Conversation with George Figgs October 3, 2017

On Saturday, September 16, 2017, I had a conversation with one of Hampden's unique sons - George Figgs. He's now residing across the Jones Falls in neighboring Woodberry. We sat down in his living room, filled with memorabilia of his days as the owner of the Orpheum Cinema in Fell's Point, (1991 to 1999), and chatted away about his colorful background.

Hampden is a neighborhood that, in its early days, was home for working class people who labored in the nearby mills along the Jones Falls Stream Valley. Today, its residents reflect a changing city, with a vibrant shopping area, popular restaurants, ice cream and art stores, and multiple festivals.

Figgs shared with me his fond memories of his childhood days, including schooling at St. Thomas Aquinas RC School on 37th Street, where he also served as an altar boy. He talked about his early family life. His mom was of Polish stock; and his dad of Welsh ancestry. His father was from a farming family originally from the Eastern Shore. Figgs' grandfather was a cobbler, who had a shop on the Avenue in Hampden.

In his early days, many of Figg's afternoons were spent enjoying the movies at the now-defunct "Ideal Theatre" on the Avenue. "Films," Figgs said, "engaged my imagination...and inspired my art work."

Figgs, born in 1947, was the oldest of seven children. He taught himself how to draw, sing, and to also play the guitar and the harmonica. Figgs explained: "I would do anything to make art."

As a young teenager, Figgs considered himself part of the counterculture scene and a "Beatnik." He hung out around Martick's, a restaurant and bar on Mulberry near Cathedral Streets in downtown Baltimore. It was during this period, that he met the Baltimore filmmaking legend: the one, the only - John Waters!

Figgs' relationship with Waters led to acting roles in some of his classic comedic flicks, such as: "Dorothy, the Kansas City Pot Head," "Eat Your Makeup," "Pink Flamingos," "Mondo Trasho," and one of my faves, "Multiple Maniacs." In the later flick, Figgs played the role of - Jesus Christ! In "Dorothy," he was the scarecrow.

Figgs was deeply impressed by the talented, late actor and singer, Divine, a drag queen, who was discovered by Waters in the 60s. "Divine was everything," Figgs said. "He had a global following way back then."

Divine (Harris Glenn Milstead), indeed, became a cult figure before dying at the young age of forty-two. He's buried in a small cemetery in Towson, Maryland. Since Figgs worked as an actor in many of Waters' early films, he is considered, along with Divine, and some others, as one of the "Dreamlanders."

Another Hampden neighbor of Figgs was the late Van Smith. He was the costume designer on many of John Waters' films.

Besides playing and singing in a band, along with Ben Syfu, also a Hampden boy, and school mate, Figgs found time to draw. One of his art works, "Baltimore Nocturne," will soon be on exhibit at the American Visionary Museum, located on the Key Highway, near Federal Hill.

Figgs also worked a stint as a ticket salesman at the Charles Theatre on North Charles Street during his meanderings before learning how to become a film projectionist. Figgs in to order to pay the bills also labored as a taxi driver.

After Figgs jointed the projectionist union, he worked as a "daily projectionist" on many of the Hollywood films that were being made in Baltimore and environs, including some of Barry Levinson's flicks. Unfortunately, this well-paying gig didn't last long (1993-94.) The digital age brought it to an abrupt end.

Once Waters talked with Figgs about what had happened to one of his earlier films, "Multiple Maniacs," which has been sent to a distributor in Canada. Waters tracked it down. The Canadians had rejected the film, but declined to send it back. They felt it was their duty to destroy it since it was such "trash." When Waters found out its miserable fate, "he loved it," said Figgs.

Figgs is proud of the fact that he participated, at age 16, in the "March on Washington," along with 300,000 other Civil Rights activists, back on August 28, 1963. He vividly recalls standing on the Mall, looking towards the Lincoln Memorial, and hearing Martin Luther King, Jr. make his famous "I Have a Dream" speech.

Figgs was also associated with the Walters Art Gallery in Baltimore City from about 2011 to 2014. He was in charge of visual presentations. He's been married twice, divorced twice and has two grown boys, Ivan and Oliver.

As a film historian, Figgs had nothing but high praise for Amy Davis' new book, "Flickering Treasures." He called her the "Priestess of the Cult." The book is about the old palatial movie houses that once dominated Baltimore's downtown area. Figgs added, "she doing a lot for the film industry."

Figgs, a genuine Renaissance Man, is currently writing a column on cinema for the publication, "Reveal Baltimore." He's known as the "Cinema Evangelist." He believes watching movies is "good for your soul." Check out a sample of his offerings from his Muse, at: http://revealbaltimore.com/kingofmarvingardens/

Asked if he had any general advice to film lovers, Figgs responded, accompanied by a huge laugh, "Yea, sure! They should start going out to the movies again. Get off the couch and get your face out of your I-phone!"

38. Annual Baltimore Pride Parade
& Block Party a Big Hit
June 18, 2017

Saturday afternoon, June 17, 2017, was the second day of this year's annual Baltimore Pride Festival. It was marked by a colorful parade, on a very sunny, hot day. The festival will finish up tomorrow, the 18th, with a full schedule of events. Druid Hill Park will be its main venue. Check this site for the latest information on it: http://baltimorepride.org/

Today, the marching, with flags and banners flying, started in the Mt. Vernon area, on Charles Street. There were bands, dancers galore and floats of various descriptions; and even a Michael Jackson lookalike. Corporations showed their support, such as the "UPS Company," by sponsoring an entry and displaying their corporate logo.

The parade, about two hours long, made its way up the city's main boulevard; pass my alma mater, the U. of Baltimore and historic Penn Station; and onward to North Avenue. A reviewing stand was located there at its intersection with Charles St.

Of course, Her Honor the Mayor, Catherine Pugh, participated in the parade, along with the City's Police Commissioner, Kevin Davis.

Rep. John Sarbanes (3rd District); U.S. Sen. Chris Van Hollen; Baltimore City Councilmen Bill Henry (District 4); Baltimore County Executive, Kevin Kamenetz; and one of my fave social justice activists, Hassan Giordano, also joined the festivities.

Mr. Giordano is running for the Office of Clerk of the Circuit Court for Baltimore City. All of the above are cary carrying Democrats.

Before the parade, there was a Pre-Pride Extravagance Show. It took place at North Ave. & Charles St, on the n/w corner close to the Wind-Up Space. After the parade, a good old-fashion Block Party was held on north Charles Street just above North Avenue. One of the scheduled performers was "Big Freedia." This area is known as the "Station North" community.

The Baltimore Pride Festival dates its origins back to 1975. According to its program notes, it is Maryland's largest "SGL/LGBTQ visibility event." An estimated "30,000 revelers" enjoy the festival each year.

This gala is also the GLCCB's largest "fundraiser." For this year's event, the theme was "Pride: Unleashed." Mr. Jaban M. Lyles is the President of GLCCB & Baltimore Pride.

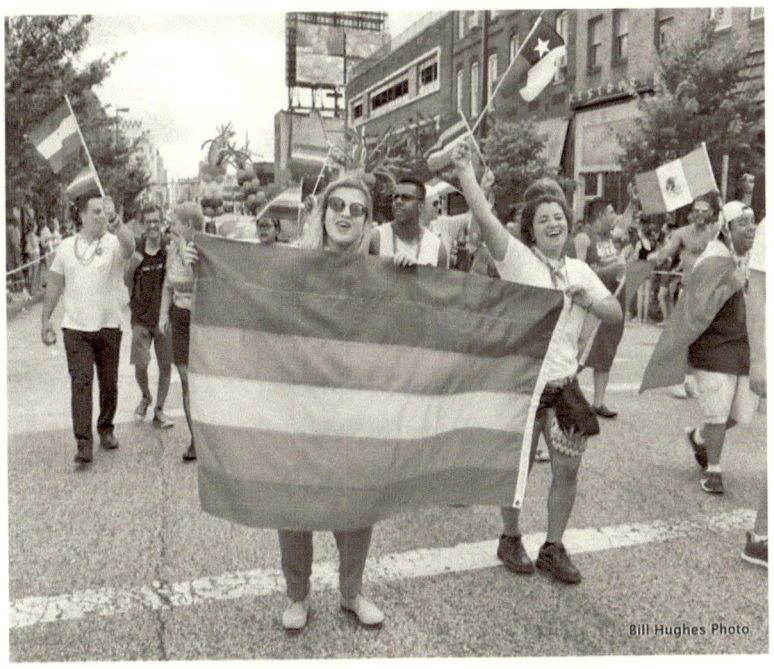

Celebrating Pride Day in Baltimore City

39. Author Ann Hornaday
at the Ivy Bookshop
July 22, 2017

On Friday evening, July 21, 2017, author and film critic, Ann Hornaday, currently the film critic for the "Washington Post," made an appearance at the Ivy Bookshop on the Falls Road. She read from her book, "Talking Pictures: How to Watch Movies."

Presently, a resident of Baltimore, Hornaday had, earlier in her career, worked reviewing movies for the "Baltimore Sun" and "New York Times." She is very fond of classic films, actors and playwrites from Hollywood's "Golden Era." In that category you will find legendary films, such as: "Citizen Kane," "On the Waterfront" and "Casablanca."

She recalled how she has gotten into doing movie reviews almost "by accident." Hornaday started off in journalism as a reporter. Part of her job was talking to the artists, who put the films togethers, such as the actors, directors and screen play creators. This is what led her into doing movie critiques.

One bit of advice, she would like to convey to the budding film critics is this: "Don't give too much away in your review of the film!" Don't be a "spoiler."

Hornaday underscored the importance of the screenplay and the acting to the making a good, memorable movie. She said one director told her: "If I cast it well, it's 90 percent done."

The director, of course, Hornaday underscored, plays a pivotal role. He/she can "make or break a film." Hornaday also gave a heads-up on the movie, "Dunkirk," which has just been released. She said it was a "visual" classic.

A capacity audience was in attendance for the program. A spirited Q&A session followed Hornaday's remarks. She was introduced by Emma Snider, co-owner of the Ivy Bookshop. At the end of the event, Snider presented her with an Ivy Bookshop cup.

My review of Hornaday's book, which I am highly recommending, can be found at: http://baltimorepostexaminer. com/book-critical-movie-watching/2017/07/05

40. Dedication of Amy Sherald's Mural, "Equilibrium" August 21, 2018

On Tuesday afternoon, August 21, 2018, at the Parkway Theatre in Baltimore, MD, artist Amy Sherald's mural, "Equilibrium," was dedicated. The ceremony was held inside the theatre. Her mural hangs on the wall outside the theatre.

Mayor Catherine Pugh of Baltimore spoke at the proceedings. She asked the audience "to continue to support the artists in our city." She added how proud she is of Ms. Sherald and her great work. Mayor Pugh also praised Station North and proprietors, like Kevin Brown, who owns a nearby restaurant. She ended by saying: "We hold you, Amy, as our own."

The artist, Amy Sherald, then added her remarks to the proceedings. She recently gain some notoriety as the artist who drew the official portrait of the former First Lady, Michele Obama.

The original painting of "Equilibrium" hangs in the United States Embassy, located in Dakar, Senegal. Ms. Sherald is a MICA graduate and a native of Columbus, Georgia.

Ms. Sherald's commented that she was "excited to unveil this mural" in Station North, close to the "electric nerve of our city." She added her paintings "celebrate the stories of light and love contained within the magical presence of the people who walk this stretch each day."

The Baltimore Office of Promotions & the Arts sponsored the event before a capacity audience inside the lobby of the Parkway Theatre. Kudos to the BOPA.

To see more of my photos go to my facebook page athttps://www.facebook.com/media/set/?set=a.102170085347 08953&type=1&l=c277f6df56.

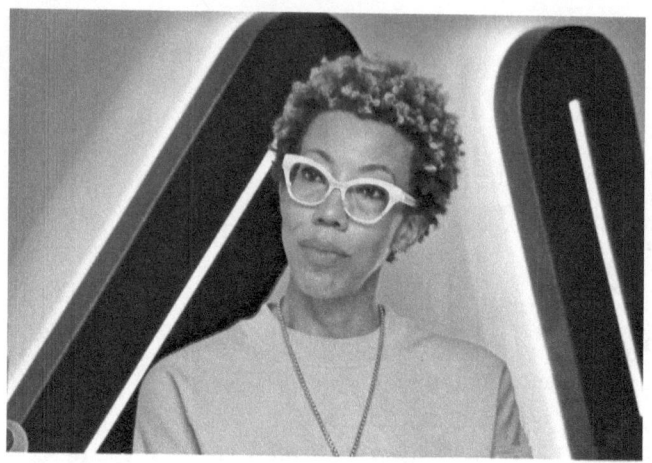

Amy Sherald

41. Mayor's Annual Christmas Parade Celebrates 43rd Birthday December 5, 2016

The weather was a little on the chilly side, but that didn't stop the many fans of the Mayor's Annual Christmas Parade from showing up for the event in Hampden, on Sunday (12.04.16).

Both sides of "The Avenue" (36th Street) were packed with parade lovers, especially children. The latter group were waiting for their favorite Christmas celebrity to make an appearance - Santa Claus!

According to parade officials, they expected about 160 marching units to participate in the festivities. And, you can't have a parade without a marching band. I spotted at least three dozen colorful bands, while I was out on "The Avenue" doing my canvassing.

The fabulous "Mummers" of Philadelphia made an appearance much to the delight of the parade watchers. There were the usual politicos; (Councilwoman Mary Pat Clarke & Rep. John Sarbanes to name just two); TV and radio personalities (WJZ's Ron Matz & crew); riding by waving to the crowd, while perched on the back seat of a limo. Dancing groups, Star Wars characters, an Elvis or two, a 1957 Chevy Bel Air, and floats with assorted themes also joined in the fun.

Plenty of motorcycles from various groups participated in the event. The Police Commissioner, Kevin Davis, was there, too, along with the incoming Mayor of Baltimore, the Hon. Catherine Pugh.

This would have been the current Mayor Stephanie Rawling-Blake's last parade of this type, but she was a no-show. She officially leaves office, at City Hall, on Tuesday, December 6th. She will be succeeded, in a 11 am ceremony, by Pugh, the Mayor-Elect, who will become Baltimore's 50th Mayor.

The parade route extended for an estimated 2.5 miles Beginning up on Falls Road, at Medfield/Cold Spring Lane; south to "The Avenue;" and then turning east on it over to Chestnut; finally, taking a left and finishing two blocks away on 37th Street.

The parade started at 1 pm and finished about three hours later.

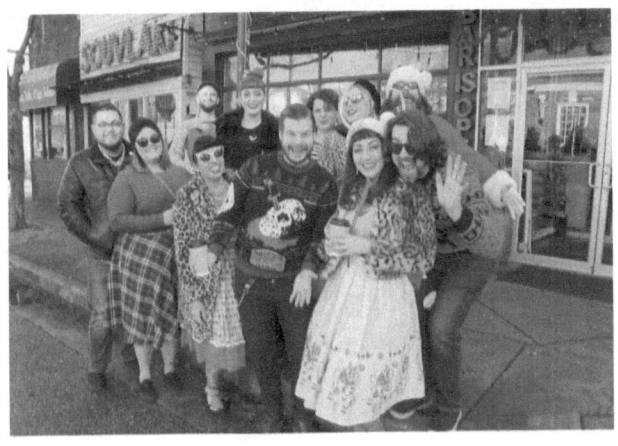

Celebrating Mayor's Annual Christmas Parade

42. NBC's Al Roker Does Weather Gig at Loyola University

Early Thursday morning, March 30, 2017, popular NBC-TV weatherman, Al Roker, from "The Today Show," took his "Rokerthon College Tour" to the campus of Loyola University in Baltimore. The tour involves a visit by Roker to selected colleges or universities around the country, who try to set a Guinness World Record while he's in attendance.

In between all of that fun, Roker did his regular national weather gig, in a live broadcast, before a huge turnout of cheering, dancing students. On hand for the event was the President of Loyola University, the Rev. Brian F. Linnane, S.J.

The location for the shoot was Loyola's "Quad" area, which is located on the Homewood campus, close to the McManus Theatre and the Humanities Building. The festivities ran from 5:15 am to 9: 45 am.

A large group of selected Loyola U. students, numbering in the hundreds, participated in the "crab walk." The walk involved, according to the program, "placing your hands on the ground, behind your back, and scuttle like a crustacean using all four limbs.

"You must start by sitting on the ground with your hands and feet shoulder-width apart and you must walk for two consecutive minutes. If you stop moving or touch the ground you will be disqualified from the record total."

Al Roker introduced an official from the Guinness company who was on hand to officially judge the contest. He stated that the old record was 376 crab walkers. He then announced: "Today, we have 494!" Bottom line: Loyola University students have set a new "Guinness World Record" for their crab walk and Al Roker couldn't have been happier.

To check out the video, go to: https://vimeo.com/210782901

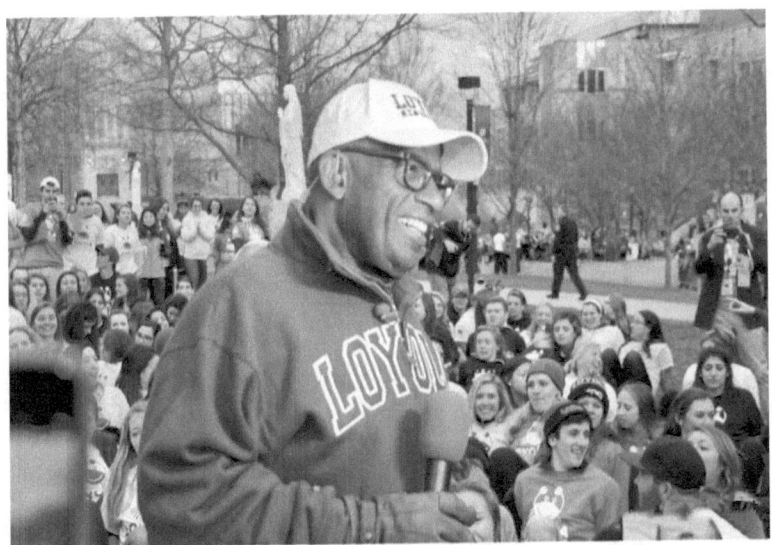

Al Roker

43. The Lights of 34th Street in Hampden December 1, 2016

You know it's getting close to celebrating a joy-filled Christmas when the display of lights goes up on the 700 block of 34th Street in Hampden. The block is located just south of "The Avenue," off of Chestnut (to the west), and Keswick (to the east).

This all takes place in one of Baltimore's favorite neighborhood, Hampden. And, it's becoming a bigger tourist attraction every year, plus a boon to local restaurants and ice cream stores.

The celebration of bright lights' history can be traced way back to 1947, according to one source. The displays on the front yards vary from Santa Clauses of all types (the kids just love them) to Christmas trees.

There are Santa's helpers, an Ode to Natty Boh, angels, movies/tv shows made in Maryland; nativity scenes, reindeers, and one home owner - this was my favorite - has made a Christmas tree out of a huge pile of shiny hubcaps and bicycle wheels.

Another neighbor puts out her "Peace" emblems, which I think is always timely, no matter the season of the year. They were all, and more, part of the colorful mix on 34th Street this year.

My wife Ann and I took in the festivities on Thursday evening, December 1st. The weather was cool and the crowd was off, but it's still very early in the season.

Suggestion: When the sun goes down in the days and weeks to come, grab the kids/grandkids and head over to enjoy the "Lights of 34th Street in Hampden." Trust me, your family will be in for a real treat. New Year's Eve is the final night for the 34th Street lights in Hampden to sparkle.

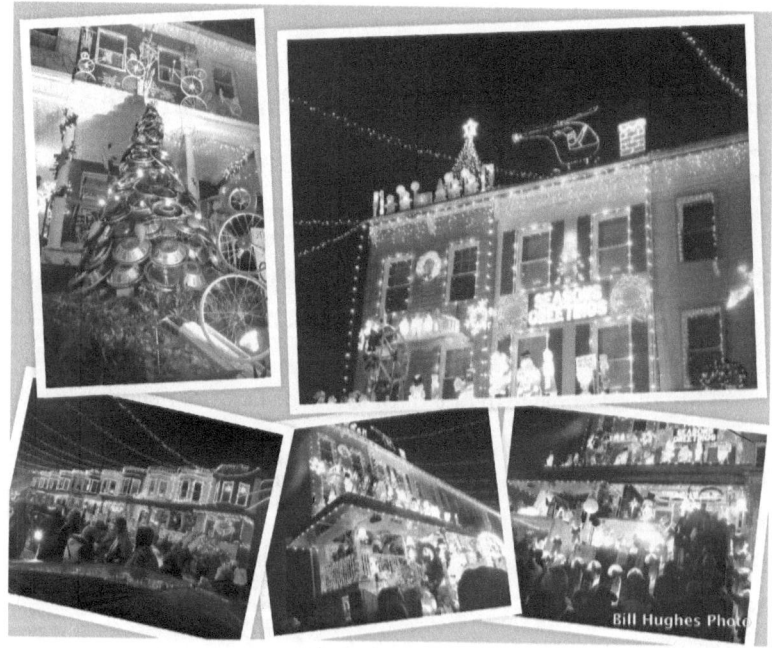

Lights of 34th Street in Hampden

44. One Man's Journey Into the Realm of Acting
March 5, 2017

As a subscriber to Baltimore's "Everyman Theatre," I and others were given an opportunity, in March, 2016, at a fun-filled event at their space, to give our renditions of the actor Marlon Brando's famous "Hey, Stellaaaaaaaaaaaa" line from the acclaimed play "Streetcar Named Desire." The judges - two of the actors in the play - scored participants on a scale of 1 to 10. One of them told me later, "I gave you a 13 for your effort." Hey man, that made my day!

By the way, there is a wonderful biography on Brando by Patricia Bosworth ("Marlon Brando"). Anyone seriously interested in the craft of acting needs to have her book in their library.

I came late to acting, it was in the 70s. I was in between marriages, working a day job, and needing to find something creative to fill up my spare time at night. (Read, how to stay the hell out of the bars!)

Somebody suggested doing a play at the Spotlighters Theatre on St. Paul Street. I was living downtown at the time, so that worked for me. The late, wonderful Audrey Herman was its artistic director.

Herman quickly cast me in some plays. One of them turned out to be my personal favorite - Agatha Christie's "Mousetrap." I was given the character role of "Major Metcalf," a retiree from the British Colonial Army. You know the type-pompous, with a huge white mustache which he's forever tweaking with his hand.

One of my lines in "Mousetrap," went like this: "Metcalf - Major. I read about the case in the paper at the time, I was stationed in 'Edinburgh' then. No personal knowledge." When my Irish mother came to see me perform, I changed the name of town to "Foxford," her old hometown located in the West of Ireland. She loved it!

After a while, I migrated over to professional acting. One of the first films I worked in, as an extra, was John Waters' "Cry-Baby." That was a lot of fun. It's a Waters' classic from 1990. I was in a court room scene (Northern Police District on Keswick Road), watching a trial. The shoot lasted a week. Johnny Depp (back in his salad days) had the lead and William Dafoe (who later portrayed Jesus in the "Last Temptation of Christ") played a "hateful guard."

A cameo role (speaking part) for me soon followed. This was also in 1990, in Steve Yeager's compelling film noir, "On the Block." Blaze Starr, the late, legendary "Queen of Burlesque," played herself. I was cast as "Barney" a pub owner. This was my first Screen Actors Guild movie. Check out the film's intriguing trailer at: https://www.youtube.com/watch?v=Eg5DtkamuPM

In 2004, John Waters' cast me a "coffee sex addict" in his laugh-a-thon film, "A Dirty Shame." I played opposite Big Ethel (Suzanne Shepherd). She was featured in the HBO series, "The Sopranos." My line to her is so vulgar that I can't repeat here in this family-oriented newspaper. Big Ethel, understandably, gets very upset with me and tosses a cup of hot coffee in my mug.

Naturally, to get it right, we had to shoot the scene three or four times, which required me to change my wet shirt each time. I recall Waters' repeated instructions - "don't blink!" Later, I thought they should have kept "his line" in the script. It was a winner!

Meanwhile, I was doing some acting work at Center Stage off and on. During most of that time Irene Lewis, a very talented artistic director, was running the show. I got enough playing time in there to get my "Equity" card. I also got a chance to work with some very talented actors, most of them were NYC-based, but included brilliant Baltimore-based actors, such as Wil Love.

A one-act play I did at Corner Theatre, then on St. Paul Street, way back when, has stuck with me over the years. It was called "The Dodo Bird." It was a very intense drama. I played the very flawed and damaged "Dodo Bird," the lead character. See: http://www.gate-theater.com/the-dodo-bird.html

Before taking on that task, I took an acting workshop ran by a local director and a true student of the art of acting - Barry Feinstein.

He was a big fan of a technique known as "method acting." It worked for me. I dove into the part.

The expert training I received from Feinstein helped me pull off the "Dodo" part. Trust me, it was a draining role and what I learned from him has stayed with me over the years.

There was another play in my amateur, learning-the-craft days I need to share. It was "Man for All Seasons." The St. Matthews Players put it on at St. Matthews R.C. Church Hall up on Loch Raven Blvd. I was cast as Sir Thomas More. In the movie by the same name, the celebrated actor Paul Scofield played the lead. There were a lot of lines to learn. Sir Thomas was on stage for most of the play. How did I do in that role?

Well, someone later told me that the night the local nuns from the grade school came to see the play, they all sat in the front row. At the end of that performance, after Sir Thomas makes his eloquent final and moving plea to the court and is sentenced to death, many of them - bless their kind hearts - broke down in tears! Is there a higher compliment?

Over the years, I have had cameo roles in "Homicide: Life on the Streets;" "Pecker," another John Waters' comedy; two episodes of "America's Most Wanted;" "Species Two", as a paparazzi; as an older man in 2015 in "House of Cards"; and, recently, in 2016, the TV movie, "East Coast Grow" and Matt Porterfield's film, "Sollers Point."

"Sollers Point" is in the post-production process. The flick stars McCaul Lombardi, Jim Belushi and Imani Hakim. It's about a small time drug dealer Keith (Lombardi) trying to find himself on a difficult reentry into his former working class neighborhood. It is Baltimore-native Porterfield's fourth film.

Finally, my acting journey has been mostly fun and also, at times, very challenging. It has left me with some wonderful memories. It has also given me a lot of respect for the talented and dedicated folks who make theatre and films such a joy for their audiences.

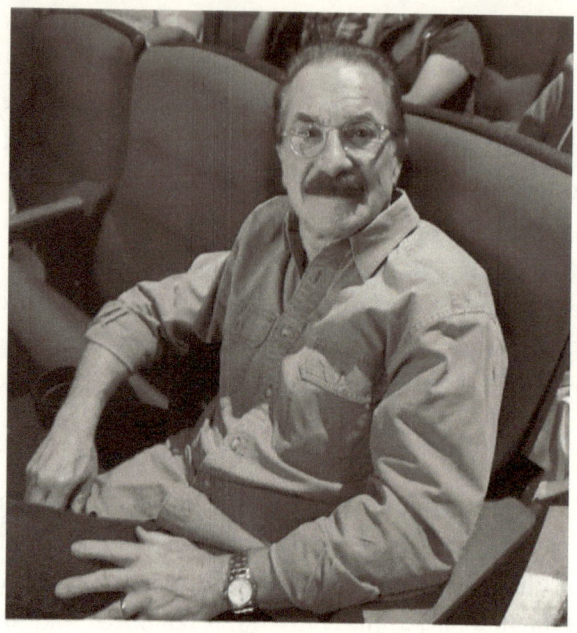

Director Steve Yeager

45. City Council President Jack Young & the Toys for Tots Program December 16, 2016

Thursday afternoon, December 15, 2016, at 5 pm, marked the official launching of the annual "Toys for Tots" program. It was marked, via a reception, at the Baltimore City Hall, with City Council President Jack Young, its chief local facilitator, presiding.

Also in attendance, were three members of the U.S. Marine Corps. The toys are collected by the Office of the City Council President and distributed to the community by the Corps.

The base of the City Hall rotunda was stacked high with toys. Included with the piles of gifts were row after row of colorful children's bicycles. In the center was a huge Christmas tree.

Amazon, bless its generous heart, donated $15,000 worth of toys. They arrived earlier today at City Hall. The U.S. Marines Toys for Tots' program is a nationwide effort.

In attendance besides the above, were the Mayor of Baltimore, the Honorable Catherine Pugh; City Councilwoman Mary Pat Clarke; City Councilman Eric Costello; and the Police Commissioner Kevin Davis.

Food, soft drinks and Zeke's coffee were available to the folks enjoying the event, along with some delicious-looking baked cakes.

Musical entertainment was provided by the "Swingin' Swamis." Trust me, they were right on the beat all evening long.

There were even three "giant" entertainers making the rounds. The trio, on stilts, call themselves the "Big Whimsy."

And, of course, you can't have a Toys for Tots program without the appearance of the big guy in the red outfit, with that bushy white beard and that ho-ho-ho accent - Santa Claus himself!

To learn more about this wonderful annual program, go to: http://toysfortots.org/about_toys_for_tots/toys_for_tots_program/default.aspx

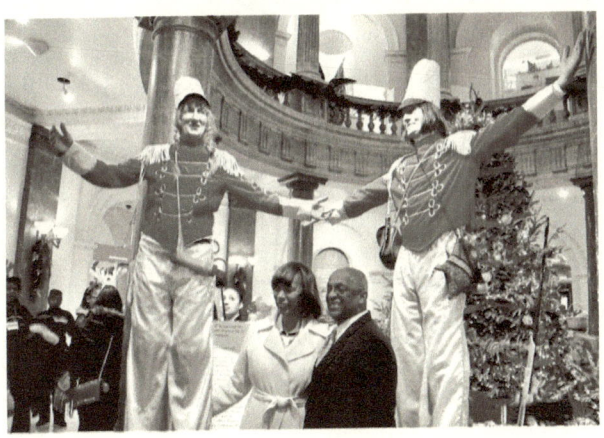

Toys for Tots Program at City Hall

46. Tracing My Irish Ethnic Trail VIA Ancestry DNA
April 3, 2017

My mother, Nora Thornton, was born in the village of Tavanaghmore, County Mayo, in the Wild West of Ireland, back around the turn of the last century. My father, Richard Patrick Hughes, Sr, was Baltimore-born, around the same time frame as my mother. His parents also hailed from Tavanaghmore.

When you look at this you have to say: Nothing could be more Irish. For about twenty years from the early 70s to the early 90s, I made regular trips to County Mayo to visit my mother's birthplace, my dad's relatives, and their surviving family members.

In fact, one of the trips was with my mother herself back in the early 70s. At that time her brother Mickey and sister Anne were still living. Mickey was holding up the fort in Tavanaghmore, the old family homestead. Anne was in the next village over - about a mile or so away - Stonepark.

One day Uncle Mickey took me to one of his local watering holes. It was a dark and dingy place with sweat coming off the ceiling. I thought I was in a James Joyce novel. Even though I had a hard time understanding my uncle, he was great company.

Tavanaghmore sits on a hill overlooking Loch Conn and the quaint village of Pontoon. In the distance, the northwest, you can see Mt. Nephin. It rises to 2646 feet. Uncle Mickey would insist - he fought in the Civil War in Ireland, 1921-22, on the Republican side - that his mountain was "higher" than Nephin's. Well, we'll let that one pass for the moment.

Tavanaghmore is only a few miles from the town of Foxford. It used to be home to a famous woolen mill. Foxford was also where the "First Admiral" of the Argentinian Navy, William Brown, aka Guillermo Brown, was born, in 1777.

I'm not sure in the 1970s exactly how many families called Tavanaghmore home. Just guessing, I would say no more than twenty. Lately, the real estate boom took over in County Mayo, so there has been a bit of a build-up near Loch Conn.

In any event, my impression was just about everyone in the village was somehow, someway related to each other. At least, it seemed that way to me. (Confession: I was drinking back then! Draft lager was my alcoholic beverage of choice.)

Let me put it another way, I believe without taking a scientific poll, that I was "related" to everyone living then in Tavanaghmore by some degree or other. "Kissing cousins" you could call us.

An idea was floated to check out the DNA Ancestry site and to see what it had to say about my Irish family tree. What came up next for me, however, was this: Why do I want to do that? I already know where I am from. And, I have tons of lovely Irish cousins to prove it.

But, here's the bigger issue. DNA Ancestry goes back much much farther in time using its technical data and sophisticated analysis, along with historical migratory trends. How far back? Try traveling back to the days of the legendary Celts!

Just when I was ready to say "yes," this scary thought popped into my head. Suppose I go the DNA route and find out that I'm related to some sinister character! Who will I find in my family line?

Alright - I recently got my courage up and for a modest fee sent a sample of my DNA to "AncestryDNA", at: https://www.ancestry.com/. After about a six weeks' wait, the results came back and here they are: "I'm 77 percent from Ireland, 21 percent from Great Britain and 2 percent from other regions."

Ancestry's model put my family, and its Tavanaghmore roots, right in the middle of "genetic community" that they call "Connacht Irish." Sounds right on to me.

Ancestry DNA said its "ethnicity estimates" show where my ancestors came from "hundreds of thousands years ago." Their origin profile shows my people coming out of mainland Europe, France (formerly known as Gaul in the days of the Caesar), and

Belgium (also once dominated by Celtic tribes), and heading north into the British Isles.

All of this conforms to a book that I consider to be an authority on this subject: "The Celtic World: An Illustrated History of the Celtic Race, Their Culture, Customs and Legends," by Barry Cunliffe. The Irish were Celts. The author, (I'm cutting to the chase here), suggests that some of the European Celts began migrating from (France) Gaul, and Belgian, too, to the British Isles as early as "second century B.C."

Keep in mind the Anglo/Saxon settlement in England came much later around the 6th Century, AD. The Normans didn't conquer England until the 11th Century. So, the British Celts' presence pre-dates both of those later dominating tribes. In fact, it is widely believed the Celts gave London its name: Londinon.

In any event, after conquering Gaul, Caesar moved on to Britain (Britannia) around 55 B.C. This campaign, along with his conquest of Gaul, made Caesar's reputation. Long after his death, the Celtic tribes were finally defeated by the Romans, around A.D. 84. The Irish Celts had also begun settling in Ireland around the first century B.C. Today, Ireland's population is about 8.4 million.

So, much of the above would strongly support the "21 percent Great Britain" found in my chart. The Celts were there very early on and many of them had stayed there throughout the centuries.

One of the puzzles left in my search for the deep state origins of my ethnic identity, is this one: What ethnic group is in that unknown "two percent" in my model? Stay tuned!

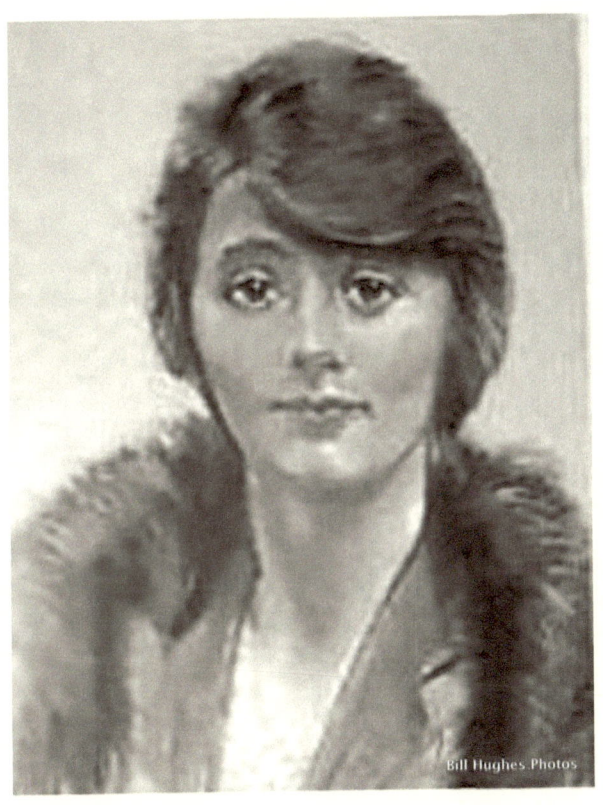

Portrait of Nora Thornton

REVIEWS

47. "Sollers Point" and "Sickies Making Films" Debut at Maryland Film Festival May 14, 2018

The 20th Maryland Film Festival (2018) runs from May 2nd to May 6th this year. It is centered again in Baltimore's up and coming Station North Arts and Entertainment District. It will feature 40 films and ten shorts programs, many with a distinct international flavor. To check out its outstanding program go to: https://mdfilmfest.com/about-the-festival/

The resurrected SNF Parkway Theatre at Charles & North Avenue is at the hub of the cinema-related activities. On Thursday, May 3rd, I had a chance to take in two of the festival's fine offerings before large, appreciative audiences: Joe Tropea's excellent documentary, "Sickies Making Films," and Matt Porterfield's riveting "Sollers Point."

"Sickies Making Films" dealt with the history of film censorship in America — particularly in Maryland, via the "Maryland Censor Board." In 1961, Mary Avara, a politico and also a bail bonds lady by profession from Southwest Baltimore, was appointed to the Board by then Maryland Governor, J. Millard Tawes. She served on it for two more decades and for much of that time she was also its controversial chairperson.

As the fates would have it, I knew Avara from politics. We belonged to the same organization, led by my mentor, the late City Councilman, Michael "Iron Mike" McHale, from Locust Point. The big boss was Julian "Fats" Carrick, aka "The Chicken Man." (Mr. Carrick, who was blind by then, liked to bring his gun to the club's meetings and place it on the table just before the reading of the Pledge of Allegiance." He would then ask me to read the minutes of the last meeting, which I would do in a shaky voice.")

Avara's rulings regularly ripped and railed against the films of Baltimore's own rising star, the comedic film director John Waters.

Of course, he is a big part of the documentary. Her repeated lashing out at Waters, in print and on television, had the salutary effect of making him into a national celebrity, and her as well! She would often rant that Walters' film deserved two kinds of ratings: "F" for filthy; and "R" for rotten!

Mr. Tropea looking to give his film some balance, asked me to share my views of Avara, which I was very happy to do. My postive recollections went back to around 1960, when I first met her at a political rally near the Hollins Street Market. The details are recounted in the film.

One of my other memories of that era is watching Avara doing her thing on the Johnny Carson, Dick Caveat, Merv Griffin and the Mike Douglas television talk shows, and laughing my a... off. She was a riot and the hosts and the audiences loved her.

Avara died in 1990, at the ripe old age of 90. Bless her memory. I attended her funeral in Southwest Baltimore at the now-defunct St. Peter the Apostle RC Church. The same church where the Baltimore immortal, George Herman "Babe" Ruth was baptized.

Getting back to the festival. There was a lively Q&A after the "Sickies" film with Tropea and Robert A. Emmons Jr. the film's editor/writer participating. Waters was in the audience and he had a lot film history and anecdotes to share. Here's the trailer for "Sickies." It features Waters with some hilarious comments - https://vimeo.com/149646713

The "Sickies" film recounts the history of film censorship and skillfully traces its evolutions from the founding of the movie industry right up till the present time. It's a treasure chest of information and done in a very entertaining way. Film buffs are going to love it.

Besides Waters, ex-State Senators Julian "Jack" Lapides and Howard Denis are in the flick, with some film historians from the local scene, and including the casting agent extraordinary, Pat Moran. Max Weiss of "Baltimore Magazine" gave the film "3 stars."

"Sollers Point" was also on my agenda yesterday. Its the fourth film from Baltimore's talented Matt Porterfield and stars McCaul

Lombardi, who attended Cardinal Gibbons H.S. He plays the role of an ex-con, (Keith) a former drug pusher, trying to get his life back together. It's a tough proposition for sure and the tensions from that struggle give the movie its energy.

The actor Jim Belushi plays Keith's father in the flick, set mostly in the Sollers Point area of Baltimore County. A critic for the "Baltimore Sun" called the film "another winner from Porterfield." I have a cameo in the movie as "Fred the bartender." My scene was shot in a tavern down in Curtis Bay off of Pennington Avenue.

Rotten Tomatoes gave Sollers Point a rating of "83%." Max Weiss of "Baltimore Magazine" tagged the movie with "3 stars." There was a Q&A after this film, too. And yes, Waters participated, much to the enjoyment of the audience. See the official trailer for the film at: https://www.youtube.com/watch?v=NqU6O4eYcso

Sollers Point opens for an extended run at the Parkway on May 11th. Check it out if you get a chance.

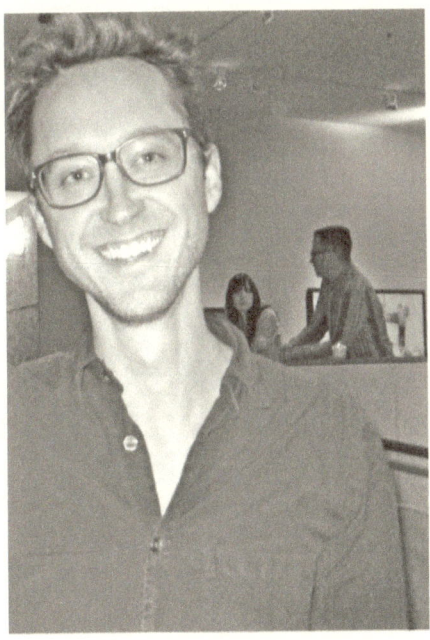

Director Matt Porterfield

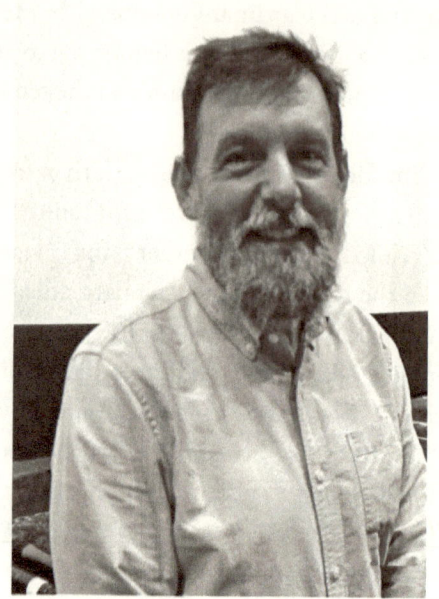

Producer Joe Tropea

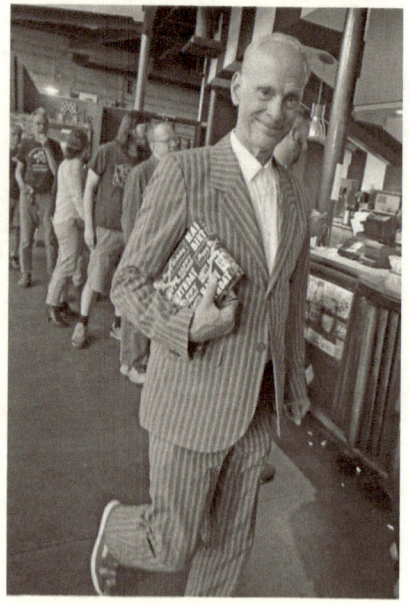

Filmmaker John Waters

48. Dorothy Kilgallen & Jack Ruby: A Toxic Mix January 16, 2017

In 1931, at the age of 17, she was a cub reporter for the "New York Evening Journal." At age 23, she was the first woman "to fly around the world on commercial airlines." In 1937, she wrote the screenplay for the film, "Fly Away Baby." She had a cameo role in the Hollywood flick, "Sinner Take All," and her moniker is enshrined on the Hollywood Walk of Fame. Her name is Dorothy Mae Kilgallen and she broke the glass ceiling for women in her chosen profession.

Kilgallen was born on July 3, 1913, in Chicago, Illinois. Her dad, James, was a highly-respected reporter for the Hearst newspaper chain. From her earliest days, "she yearned to be a reporter like her father."

In his book, "The Reporter Who Knew Too Much: The Mysterious Death of What's My Line TV and Media Icon Dorothy Kilgallen," author Mark Shaw tells her compelling story. He focuses on her work as a first class investigative reporter and more particularly on her highly suspicious death, on November 8, 1965, at her townhouse in Manhattan.

Kilgallen was very fond of President John F. Kennedy (JFK). She boosted him whenever she could in her "Journal-American" column. In 1962, thanks to "JFK's aide Pierre Salinger," she and her youngest son, Kerry, then eight years old, visited the White House and met the president. The meeting left a deep impression on Kilgallen.

When JFK was murdered in Dallas, Texas, on November 22, 1963, Kilgallen refused to accept the party line put out by the FBI's Director, J. Edgar Hoover. He insisted that the supposed assassin Harvey Lee Oswald "acted alone." His agency then took over all the files of the Dallas Police Department. When Oswald was shot and killed, on November 24, 1963, by Jack Ruby, Kilgallen made it her business to attend his trial. Like some Americans of my generation, I watched Ruby shoot and kill Oswald on live television. It was beyond shocking.

Author Shaw details Kilgallen's extensive journalism background. Her "Voice of Broadway" column, where she also covered Hollywood and politics, was syndicated in close to 200 papers. She attended and wrote about some of the biggest trials of her era: Bruno Hauptmann, Dr. Sam Sheppard, Dr. Bernard Finch, Wayne Lonergan, Anna Antonio and John Profumo.

In addition, Kilgallen was a regular panelist on the popular CBS TV game show, "What's My Line?" from 1950 until her death. She was known for having a "terrific sense of humor." The magazine, "Variety," praised Kilgallen as "The First Lady of Broadway."

Ernest Hemingway, himself, had labeled Kilgallen as one of the "greatest women writers in the world." She had become "a media icon" in her own time. Shaw wrote that Kilgallen was a feminist "before the word was coined."

For a while, Kilgallen also did a popular early morning program, called: "Breakfast with Dorothy and Dick," with her husband, Richard Kollmar, on WOR Radio, in NYC. He was an actor and producer. They had three children together. An Irish-Catholic, Kilgallen attended weekly Mass.

Investigating JFK's death became a passion for Kilgallen. She asked a lot of questions. Given that Ruby was the owner of a "strip tease honky tonk," she asked: How was he allowed to "stroll in and out of police headquarters in Dallas as if it were a health club?" She let Hoover and his cronies know that she was on the job. On November 29, 1963, she filed a column entitled, "Oswald File Must Not Close."

Not only did Kilgallen cover Ruby's trial, she got to interview him twice. She started to believe that he, like Oswald, might have been a "patsy." Kilgallen also made a trip to New Orleans to talk with sources. She was zeroing in on what Mob boss Ruby may have been working for at the time of the hit on the president. She began building an investigatory file on the case that she intended to turn into a book that would be the "scoop of the century."

The book, sorry to say, never happened. Kilgallen was found dead in her townhouse on the morning of November 8th. The police went along with the Medical Examiner's report that she most likely died from an "accidental" drug overdose of a prescription sleeping pills mixed with alcohol. There was no investigation of foul play.

Author Shaw rips that scenario apart. He states the death scene was "staged." The body was found in "the wrong bed" and in "the wrong bedroom." In addition, Kilgallen's "makeup, false eyelashes and hairpiece" were still on her. She was found in a blue bathrobe with nothing underneath. According to her hairdresser, she always wore "her favorite pajamas and old socks to bed."

Kilgallen had a prescription for the sleeping pills, "Seconal." A second drug, "Tuninal," however, was also found in her system. She had no prescription for that one. Was she slipped a "mickey?"

On top of all that, Kilgallen's file on the Ruby case was missing and it has never been found. Author Shaw, I must add, goes off the rails when he tries to show who may have done Kilgallen in. It's all speculation in my opinion and lacks any probative value. Also, in the book, I found it irritating that he was repetitive in places. Plus, he got Kilgallen's birthdate wrong.

Shaw also doesn't show much expertise with respect to the JFK assassination. My Bible on that crime of the century is "Deep Politics and the Death of JFK," by Peter Dale Scott.

If you want a quick overview on that complicated subject, with supposed who-done-it theories tossed in, check out, for educational purposes, the History Channel's You Tube videos, particularly this episode, #9, "The Guilty Men (2003)." See: https://www.youtube.com/watch?v=jgNfQYpS1gQ It's my favorite.

To his credit, Shaw has been trying to get the current District Attorney, in NYC, Cyrus R. Vance, Jr. to reopen the investigation into Kilgallen's death. Even though it has been fifty years, there is no statute of limitation with respect to murder. https://

Kilgallen was one of the finest journalists of her generation. Justice demands that the truth finally comes out about how this fearless reporter really died. Mark Shaw's book is a tribute to her distinguished career and legacy. It is long past the time for the stain on Kilgallen's memory to be removed.

49. Naming Jack the Ripper: Mystery Solved? LA Post-Examiner, August 16, 2016

You think finding someone criminally culpable for the death of Freddie Gray, in Baltimore, Maryland, in the spring of 2015, was difficult? ("Naming Jack the Ripper," Russell Edwards, 336 pages, Lyons Press, 2014, Book Review)

Well, try solving the blood-stained and grotesque murders, in 1888, of five prostitutes in and around the hellish slum k/a "Whitechapel," located in the "East End" of London. Over the years, there have been a lot of police investigations, theories and speculation, for sure, about those sordid crimes. Who was, really, the demented perpetrator? Up until now, however, there is no definitive answer to that query. The deranged serial killer of these five unfortunate women is known to history as "Jack the Ripper."

A recent book, "Naming Jack the Ripper," by author Russell Edwards, an Englishman, believes it has the final solution to this long-standing mystery. More about his intriguing tome, which features the latest in the arena of scientific DNA evidence, in just a moment. The website, casebook.org, is an excellent authority on Jack the Ripper. It names 34 suspects as the potential murderer. But then, it quickly adds that more "than 500 individuals," have been put forward as suspects some with little or no evidence to support the claims.

One of those suspected in the killings (can you believe this?) was a British Royal - Prince Albert Victor. He was known as "Prince Eddy." He was the grandson of Queen Victoria. The Prince had a reputation as a womanizer and for frequenting prostitutes, where he contracted gonorrhea. Around this time, there were 62 brothels and 1,200 women working in prostitution in the impoverished East End of London. I'm no big fan of the Royals, but talk about a stretch. Trying to nail Prince Eddy as the Ripper is way over the top.

There have been, according to casebook.org, close to 100 non-fiction books on this subject, movies galore and at least five documentaries. One of the films, "From Hell," (2001), featuring actor Johnny Depp, is relevant to this book review. In the film, Depp, played a police inspector who was investigating Jack the Ripper.

The author just happened to see the Depp's flick. It sparked his interest in the case. Edwards, a successful entrepreneur, felt a "deep affinity" for the East End. He knew that there was "a key" to answering the mystery of the Whitechapel murders by thinking about them in a "fresh way." Edwards put his detective cap on and began looking for "something that had been missed."

Since this is a family-oriented publication, I won't go into too much detail about the ritualistic style, the M.O. of the five killings. All the victims were "mutilated," their organs were taken out as "souvenirs," with a heavy "sexualized theme to the mutilations," wrote Edwards. The Ripper always "struck at night;" and, the victims, all street prostitutes and also heavily addicted to alcohol, were specifically "targeted" by the crazed predator.

For one of the five murders, victim #3, Elizabeth Stride, there was an eyewitness. His name was Israel Schwartz. He was able to identify a Polish Jew, Aaron Kosminski, as the man that he saw with Stride just before her body was found. Kosminski was then 23-years of age, working as a hairdresser/barber and residing in a neighborhood only blocks from where all of the crimes occurred.

Stride's throat had been slashed. Schwartz, a Hungarian Jew, however, refused to give evidence against Kosminski. By the time, he made his positive i.d., on July 12, 1890, the prime suspect was housed in the "Mile End Workhouse" under government control. He was even allowed to return home. The i.d. lacked legal efficacy since it wasn't done in a "line-up!" The cops however put him on a 24/7 watch. Just a few months later, however, Kosminski, at age 26, was confined on Feb. 6, 1891, to a mental institution by his family. He was declared "insane." He eventually died there in 1919. There were no more Ripper-like killings after Kosminski was taken off the streets of Whitechapel.

Prior to the publication of Edward's book, another author Robert House, an American, put his two cents into the mix. His book is entitled: "Jack the Ripper and the Case for Scotland Yard's Prime Suspect." House fingered Kosminski as the killer, too. His book underscored, as does Edward's, that Scotland Yard's then top cops thought Kosminski was the murderer. But - now this is important - they also felt that they "couldn't prove it in court!"

Feeling that someone is guilty, and deserved to be punished, is never enough. The bottom line is: where is the proof? Enter the science of DNA!

Cutting to the chase, this is where my hat goes off to author Edwards. He located a shawl that was found at the scene of Ripper murder victim #4 - Catherine Eddowes. Edwards then hired a renowned DNA expert, with international credentials, to examine it. Finally, after much effort, he located descendants of both Eddowes and Kosminski, in order to extract DNA from them. Conclusion: the expert's analysis showed a match. The DNA from Eddowes and Kosminski were both found on the shawl!

Hold off on the cheering! Before the ink was dry on Edwards' book, DNA experts were taking strong exceptions to his expert's findings. In addition, there is a huge problem with respect to the "chain of custody" of this key evidence and it's obvious contamination. The shawl is over 128 years old.

Do you remember the O.J. Simpson case and all the brouhaha about "contamination" of the evidence found at the scene of the murders of Nicole Brown Simpson and Ron Goldman?

In any event, Edwards' book will clearly not be the last word on the Ripper case. It is, however, a darn good summer read, well written and researched, but in places a little too chatty about the author himself. I'm giving it three out of five stars.

50. A Lovey Evening of Poetry Readings in Hampden (Hon) June 24, 2018

Saturday evening, June 23, 2018, was, indeed, a delightful time to enjoy some poetry readings. The event was held at the "Art Gallery of Fells Point on the Avenue." Previously located in historic Fells Point, its new location is 825 W. 36th Street. Participating in the readings were four talented poets; Christine Higgins, Ann LoLordo, Madeleine Mysko and Kathleen O'Toole.

The four are also the co-authors of a splendid book of poetry entitled: "In the Margins: A Conversation in Poetry." Critic Elisabeth Spires said about it: "Like voices in a choir, this beautifully modulated quartet can sing in harmony or rise to the demand of a solo, so that the collection, taken as a whole, is even larger, richer, and more resonant than its parts."

Most of the poetry that they read was from their book. A few were from newer works. The "Art Gallery" is a co-op run by 17 artists, including the four poets cited above. The shop has an outdoor patio.

"In the Margins: A Conversation in Poetry" is published by Cherry Grove Collections, Middletown, Delaware. As a sampling of the poetry presented, I have reprinted one of the 28 excellent poems in the book, "Thursday," by Madeleine Mysko.

"Thursday"
I have to kneel to wash my mother's feet.
Newly fragile from the surgery,
she trembles in the shower, holds on tight
to the towel bar. She's balanced slippery
as infants I have lathered in this tub.
I send a silent prayers through the steam:
Don't let me let her fall." I hardly scrub,
but ceremoniously overcome
the awkwardness, and move the sopping cloth
down my mother's legs, across her toes.
She thinks that she's a brother, but the truth
is I am stuck with piety and lose
myself in washing her, like one ordained
to take another's precious feet in hand.

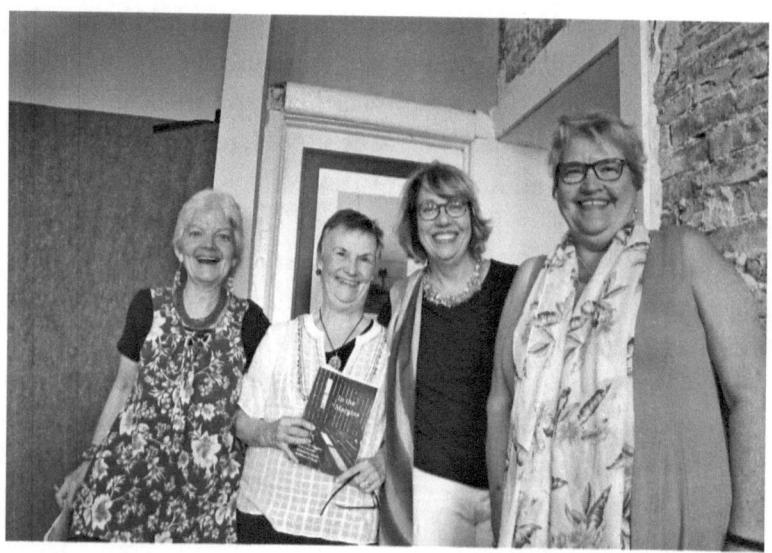

The Hampden Poets

51. Al Capone: His Life, Legacy and Legend
January 10, 2017

His mother, Theresa, attended daily Mass. His father, Gabriel, was a successful barber. His family and friends called him "Al." His detractors labeled him "Scarface," but never ever directly to him. He was the Brooklyn, New York-born Alfonse Capone - one of the most notorious and ruthless gangsters in American history. (Book Review: "Al Capone: His Life, Legacy and Legend," Deirdre Bair, 416 pages, Nan A. Talese, 2016)

In "Al Capone: His Life, Legacy and Legend," author Deirdre Bair recounts the story of this larger than life figure. He was to the world of the tough, violence-prone mobsters what Baltimore-born Babe Ruth was to the making of major league baseball. They both craved publicity, gained great success in their chosen fields, and went on to become legends in their own lifetimes.

It's all here: the machine guns, the bloody gang wars in Chicago, the St. Valentine Day's Massacre, the prohibition era, the roaring Twenties, prostitution galore, the Northside Gang, crooked politicos, the FBI, the Internal Revenue Service, hit men, the Outfit, Federal Court, the Income Tax evasion case, along with the multi-million dollar a year gambling, booze & vice empires.

Bair also does something different than most biographers of Capone have done in the past. What sets her biography apart is that she delves deeply into the private man who was a syphilis-ridden sociopath. Bair also reveals that Capone, born in 1899, was a loving family man behind the mystique of the "slick monster."

Capone was one of nine children. His parents were Italian immigrants from the "village of Castellammare di Stabia, just outside of Naples." By the time the Italian influx landed in America in the 1890s, the author said, "they had replaced the Irish at the bottom of the ethnic" ladder. When the city officials wanted someone to do the dirty work, "they gave it to the Italians."

Schooling for Capone ended "in the sixth grade." He then got a job in a candy store and later in a bowling alley setting up pins. At the age of 14, Capone worked as a "box cutter" along side his brother Ralph. Know as a "brawler" by then, and big for his age, Capone organized some of his cronies, known as the "South Brooklyn Rippers," to shake down small business owners.

All of this brought Capone to the attention of his first crime boss, and later mentor, Johnny Torrio, who was operating then out of lower Manhattan. He was an organizing genius, and Capone learned a lot from him. Torrio also never got his hands dirty. He knew how to delegate. The author suspects Capone, on Torrio's behalf, was involved in a "half dozen killing before he was eighteen."

Enter a pretty Irish girl - Mary Josephine Coughlin. She had "startling green eyes." Her nickname was "Mae." In late 1917, they began courting. Mae was "lace curtain Irish" and two years older than him. Capone got her pregnant. Their son was nicknamed "Sonny." They got married on December 30, 1919, in a Catholic ceremony. It was a "love affair" that lasted a lifetime. The author said he was truly "enchanted with her."

It was around this time in Brooklyn, when Capone began working as a bouncer for Frankie Yale (whom he later had murdered). Capone got his face gashed in a fight. The moniker "scarface" followed. Since he was hanging out in the brothels, he also contracted syphilis, which for some dumb reason, he declined to get treated. Whether this condition contributed to his homicidal tendencies is open to debate.

Capone soon left, at age 20, for Chicago, taking his young family with him. He was "an enforcer" for Torrio and knocked off crime boss "Big Jim" Colosimo at his request. He became Torrio's right hand man. He quickly began making some big bucks and bought a large house in the Park Manor Neighborhood of the city, where his mother and one of his sisters soon joined them.

Torrio survived an assassination attempt and soon retired from the rackets. Incredibly, at age 26, Capone became the boss of the outfit. From 1925 to 1932, when he went to federal prison for tax evasion, Capone was the kingpin of the Chicago gangland, hauling in multi-million dollars in illegal revenue a year.

Capone's family life was centered around his Chicago home. When the gang warfare got too intense, in 1927, he bought an estate in Palm Island, Miami Beach, Florida. It was a smart move, which gained him some measure of personal safety and gave his family a chance to breath freely as a unit.

His wife Mae and boy Sonny thrived in Florida. He bought his waterfront property for $40,000. Capone soon purchased a yacht and built himself a swimming pool. He had a wall built around the property. Sonny was enrolled in a "private Catholic school." Later on after his prison stint, and Sony's marriage, Capone also enjoyed the company of his four young granddaughters at his estate.

Capone, Bair insisted, didn't take the tax invasion case against him "seriously enough." Whatever could go wrong - did. He was found guilty and got 11 years in the slammer. Two of those years he served at Atlanta federal prison and five at the dreaded Alcatraz hell hole before being released for medical reasons. It was all hard time. The author covers the trial and his incarceration in great detail.

After Capone's release, in 1939, he was treated briefly at Baltimore's Union Memorial Hospital for "neurosyphilis." He then went to Florida, where he spent the rest of his days as "a blubbering invalid, who had deteriorated to the mental age of fourteen." In 1947, he died of cardiac arrest. He was forty-eight years old.

Finally, Bair's biography of the gangster Capone covers the waterfront. Her detailed portrait shows him warts and all. Nevertheless, in the end, the great Law of Karma caught up with Capone. It was a grim fate for his life of crime.

52. Anti-War Movement Film, "1971," at Charles Theatre May 21, 2018

On Monday evening, May 21, 2018, the antiwar film, "1971," was shown at the Charles Theatre before a large audience. The compelling documentary, which focused on a break-in by antiwar activists of an FBI office in Media, PA, on March 8, 1971, was produced by Johanna Hamilton. It will show only this one time in Baltimore. It was part of the "50th Anniversary of the Catonsville Nine's Resisting War Film Series."

For many reasons, the "Catonsville Nine" case became the "cause celebre" for the non-violent war and resistance movement. Two of its members, both Catholic priests, Dan Berrigan, a Jesuit, and his brother, Phil, became well-known public figures as a result of this daring action. https://wagingnonviolence.org/feature/how-the-catonsville-nine-survived-on-film/ Phil Berrigan later left the priesthood. He was a member of the Josephite Fathers and a WWII veteran who fought in the Battle of the Bulge.

Around that same time, the hierarchy of the Catholic Church in the U.S. was extremely conservative and mostly went along with the Vietnam War, as many of them did with the more recent Iraq conflict. The reactionary Cardinal Francis Spellman of NYC was their titular leader at that time of the Vietnam War. He never saw a war or weapon system he couldn't bless.

After the murder of President John F. Kennedy on Nov. 22, 1963, the U.S. build up of combat troops in Vietnam increased dramatically. First, under President Lyndon B. Johnson and then continuing under Richard M. Nixon's demented presidency (1969-74). The latter barely escaped impeachment before resigning his office.

The actor Martin Sheen, also an antiwar activist, was a colleague of Phil Berrigan. He attended his funeral in Baltimore, in 2002.

Sheen labeled the "Catonsville Nine" action, the "single most powerful antiwar act in American history." I'm inclined to agree with Sheen, but others - a minority - have seen it differently.

The backdrop for the "Draft Resistance Movement," especially on the Catholic Left, was the illegal and immoral Vietnam War (1963-1975). Over 58,000 of our finest sons and daughters died in that lethal conflict, with 303,000 more casualties. Congress had failed to "declare war," as required under the U.S. Constitution, instead the pro-war elements in the government, the Military-Industrial Complex, and in "Deep State," relied on the legally-suspect "Gulf of Tonkin Resolution" to justify their actions. The Resisters considered the war not only immoral, but illegal as well.

Getting back to the film, the "Washington Post," opened the floodgates by publishing most of the stolen files from the break-in, at Media, PA. Other newspapers, like the "New York Times," and a host of TV stations, soon joined in by also publishing the material seized. The FBI, under its then czar-like Director, J. Edgar Hoover, was also outraged by the newspapers' collective actions and threatened prosecutions. The highly-secret cache revealed the FBI was running a "a vast and illegal regime of spying and intimidation of Americans, who were exercising their First Amendment rights." The FBI's name for its patently illegal operation: "COINTELPRO."

Media, PA is a town located on the outskirts of Philadelphia. The activists revealed in the film that they chose it as a site for a break-in because this particular FBI office was located in a building with little or no security. They carefully planned the break-in. They were never caught or prosecuted for their offenses. Nobody squealed either. They were careful to wear gloves and left no fingerprints. The statute of limitation has long since passed for any criminal prosecution of the defendants to take place.

One of the participants in the Media action was Keith Forsyth who actually "broke the lock," to get into the building. He was present at the viewing of the documentary at the Charles. Forsyth, also a member of the "Camden 28", action, took part in the lively Q&A session that followed the film's presentation. Steve Sachs, former U.S. Attorney for Maryland, (1967-70), joined in the post-movie discussion as well.

Mr. Sachs was the federal prosecutor in charge of the Catonsville Nine case, although he wasn't one of its "trial attorneys." He did however, personally prosecute another case, the "Baltimore Four," (10.27.67), which did involved destruction of government draft records by "pouring blood on them" at the Customs House. One of the "Baltimore Four" was in the audience, the poet, David Eberhardt. Another defendant in that case was the late Phil Berrigan.

Moderating the Q&A session was Joe Tropea, who co-produced the popular documentary, "Hit & Stay," which covered not only the Catonsville Nine case, but other antiwar actions during that same period. There were reportedly 271 draft board raids in the U.S. between 1968-71. "Hit & Stay" was also shown at the Maryland Film Festival, along with Tropea's "Sickies Making Films," which dealt with film censorship in Maryland. The spirited Q&A session went on for about an hour. Folks in the audience, like local peace activist, Max Obuszewski, had more than one question to ask, as did others from the Peace Community.

Sachs said, with respect to the break-ins and destruction of draft records cases, that you "open the door to a lawless society," if you pick and choose what case to prosecute based on the motives, no matter how honorable, of the defendants. Motives, he added, are important only at sentencing for the court to consider, however, they have no role to play in the bringing of a criminal action.

Forsyth countered by saying, it all comes down to what is the "right or the wrong" thing to do for an individual under the circumstances. A person has to decide for him or herself: "Am I on the right or wrong side of humanity on this issue?"

Citing the desperate situation that the Jews found themselves in WWII, in France, under the "Vichy Regime" (1940-45). Forsyth said the democratically sourced government in that country had decided "to round up" its Jewish population for deportation back to Nazi Germany. An individual back then, Forsyth underscored, had to decide for himself either to "resist those laws," or to go along with them. Were those laws - right or wrong? "It was that simple," concluded Forsyth.

The "Camden 28" case also came under discussion. This anti-draft board action took place in 1971, in Camden, NJ. All 28 defendants were found "not guilty" by a jury in 1973. Forsyth said that a few of the jury members told him after the acquittal, that they decided on a "not guilty" verdict because they believed the "Vietnam War was wrong."

It also turned out that one of the 28 defendants was "an informant" for the FBI and that he had been involved in the "planning and training perspective" of the action. That was more than enough to convince the jury to acquit the defendants. Some have called the verdict in the "Camden 28" case, a classic example of "jury nullification!"

Finally, the presentation of the film, "1971," at the Charles, in light of the current political situation in this country, was, indeed, a fitting way to round out the 50th anniversary of the "resisting war films series."

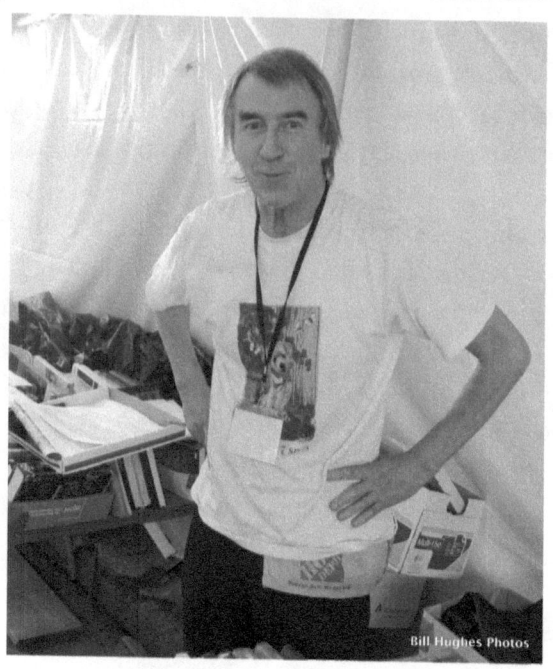

Activist Max Obuszewski

53. Dashiell Hammett: A Man of Mystery
August 25, 2016

His family roots ran deep in the "Old Line State." Dashiell Hammett, aka Samuel "Dash" Dashiell Hammett, was born on a tobacco farm in 1894, in Saint Mary's County, Maryland. Before Hammett died in 1961, in New York City, at age 66, he had become one of America's most famous detective/mystery novelists.

("Dashiell Hammett: Man of Mystery," Sally Cline, 272 pages, Arcade Publishing, 2016)

When Hammett was seven years old, his family moved to 212 North Stricker Street, in Southwest Baltimore. He even attended Poly H.S. for one semester. Only "six blocks away" from him on

Hollins Street resided the "Bard of Baltimore," the incomparable, H.L. Mencken. Their literary paths would soon cross as Hammett began to find his life's calling.

Hammett's mom, Annie Bond, was a nurse, but "sickly." His "bad-tempered father," Richard, was a loser. He couldn't hold a job and was also a "drinker and a womanizer." His father was related to the prominent Briscoe Clan of Southern Maryland. Father and son were "not friends," wrote author Sally Cline. Whose off-the-wall conduct to you think Hammett would emulate as he matured into adulthood? Try - his father's!

In "Dashiell Hammett: Man of Mystery," Cline brilliantly captures the life and times of this often private, enigmatic and talented man. By all accounts, he took pulp fiction yarns - about hard-boiled private eyes, such as his popular creation, Sam Spade, in "The Maltese Falcon" - to new, and higher, literary heights. Edgar Allan Poe and Arthur Conan Doyle would be proud.

When I was growing up in the post-WWII era, I vividly recall enjoying the Spade character in the movie version of "The Maltese Falcon." He was portrayed by the splendid actor, Humphrey Bogart. The film is a classic in that genre. The book went on to become the "best known American crime novel of all time." Also in the film were some of the iconic actors of that black/white film era: Mary Astor, Peter Lorre, Sydney Greenstreet and Ward Bond.

"The Maltese Falcon," according to Cline, included some of Hammett's darker, philosophical views on life. She wrote: "Its primary theme is how appearance belies reality, nothing is ever as it seems, how order and meaning are mere human fabrications, and blind chance is the only thing on which we can count."

The 1941 movie, directed by the legendary John Huston, helped to make the book "a massive best seller." Whether or not Hammett appreciated the fact that his "most famous and meaningful passage" about life, was left out of the film, isn't known.

Getting back to Hammett's formative years. Like his dad, he had a hard time holding onto a job until age 21. Then, in 1915, he went to work for the Pinkerton Detective Agency in Baltimore. One of his assignments was in Butte, Montana, to spy on the Wobblies, a radical union group. That chore turned his stomach. He left the agency in 1918, to join the U.S. Army at Fort Meade, MD.

Hammett served stateside, during WWI, and rose to the rank of sergeant. In the process, however, he caught the "Spanish Flu," which led to tuberculosis. While recuperating out in Tacoma, WA, he met his future wife, an attractive VA nurse, Josephine "Josie" Dolan. In July of 1921, they were married. Before long, they added two lovely daughters, Mary Jane and Josephine, to their household. To say that their relationship was complicated, is an understatement.

While living in San Francisco, CA, in 1922, with his family, Hammett's literary career began to flourish. Mencken published his story, "The Parthian Shot," in his magazine "The Smart Set." Four more short fiction pieces soon followed.

When, in 1923, Mencken took over the "Black Mask" magazine that featured pulp fiction, it published Hammett's first pulp fiction novel, "Arson Plus." The rest, as they say, is history. "Five groundbreaking novels, one novella, and more than sixty short stories" were his lifetime output, Cline tells us. Hammett concluded his fiction output with "The Thin Man," in 1934. Then, "writer's block for twenty-seven years" intervened!

In 1931, in Hollywood, Lillian "Lilly" Hellman entered his life. She was then 25 years old, short, plain-looking, high energy, Jewish, with red-hair, and a wannabe playwright. Hammett was then a 6 ft.-plus, suave, 36 years old, a successful novelist and a lapsed Catholic. They were both married. They also both loved sex, booze, life in the fast lane and literature. The connection was made. Their often rocky relationship was to last for 30 more years until Hammett's death.

When WWII started, Hammett, age 48, joined the U.S. Army in September, 1942, despite his serious medical problems. He spent two of the next three years assigned to the Aleutian Islands and loved every minute of it. He again made the rank of sergeant.

During Hammett's Hollywood days in the 1930s, he had been busy doing screenwriting. As "The Great Depression" sunk in, he was also a political "Lefty." Many of the unions and groups, including the Communist Party that Hammett joined, supported the revolution in the Soviet Union and opposed the rise of Adolf Hitler in Germany. During WWII, the Soviet Union was America's ally. Soon after it ended, however, the "Cold War" began, along with the rise of McCarthyism. Red-baiting then became fashionable on Capitol Hill.

Cutting to the chase, Hammett was targeted by the FBI's J. Edgar Hoover and right-wind politicos in Washington, D.C. He once told Hellman: "I don't let cops or judges tell me what democracy is."

His anti-fascist beliefs, and refusal to "name names," led in 1951, to a six-month's confinement in a federal slammer for "criminal contempt of court."

By then, Hammett was a broken man - physically and financially - and also blacklisted in the film industry. He owed hundred of thousands in back taxes. Despite making over one million dollars from his books and screenplay work, he died living off his VA disability pension and the charity of Hellman.

In death, however, Hammett, a veteran of both WWI and WWII, scored a telling blow against the Right Wing creeps that had so viciously hounded him in life. He is buried in sacred ground among America's most honored dead: Arlington National Cemetery!

Summing up, I'm giving Sally Cline five out of five stars for her first-rate, well-researched and compelling biography on Dashiell Hammett. It is a gem of a book, very entertaining, and it belongs in the library of all lovers of American literature.

54. Elvis Presley and Me

March 3, 2017

He was a momma's boy. Born piss poor in the poverty-stricken Deep South (Tupelo, MS). He was also shy and fearful. His twin brother, Jesse Garon, was delivered stillborn. About a half hour later, he made his appearance on the world stage. His name was Elvis Aaron Presley. The date was January 8, 1935.

(Book Review: "Elvis Presley, A Life," Bobbie Ann Mason, 192 pages, Penguin Lives, 2002)

I, too, was a twin, but my entry into the world wasn't quite that dramatic. I appeared a few years after Elvis, at the South Baltimore General Hospital, on Light near West Streets. Brother Jim said "hi" first to everyone. Then, after surviving a sharp kick from him to my right shoulder, (which he continues to deny to this day), I was able, slightly bruised, to introduce myself.

It was the middle of "The Great Depression" and my Irish-born mom told the treating physician, Dr. Aaron Sollod, to put his bill "on the ticket." That wasn't a problem with the good doctor. He knew that when work picked up on the waterfront for my father, a member of Local 953 of the ILA, his bill would be paid in full.

When Elvis emerged as the "King of Rock & Roll" in the late 50s, I, too, was working on the waterfront as a longshoreman out of ILA Local 829 on Hull Street in South Baltimore's Locust Point. My prime dance buddies, William "Duke" Brown and George Washington Kelly, also neighbors and fellow longshoremen, like myself, didn't quite know what to make of the dude with that funny accent and wild gyrations. We wondered: "Is he for real?"

Also in the 50s, Bill Haley & his Comets were then dominating the music scene for the younger set with their popular fast dancing tune, "Rock Around the Clock." Chuck Berry was in this mix, along with Little Richard, the off-the-wall Jerry Lee Lewis and the rhythm and blues man himself, the incomparable Fats Domino.

In fact, I recall how we Locust Point boyohs went out to hear Fats and Little Richard, performing in a concert on April 5, 1956, at the now-defunct Baltimore Coliseum. These legendary recording artists were then at the top of their game. The arena, also used for sports events, was located at 2201 North Monroe Street.

When we first heard Elvis' rendition of "That's All Right (Mama)," everything started to change for us. It was clear a new star was being born, especially for jitterbug aficionados like us. When he came out with with his hip-jarring hit "Jailhouse Rock," we were sold on the phenomenon that was Elvis. In between, he had released that haunting single, "Heartbreak Hotel." Elvis followed up that success quickly by releasing his acclaimed recordings of "Don't Be Cruel," "Hound Dog," and "All Shook Up."

Growing up in the 50s, our favorite jitterbug dancing venue was called the "Advent." It was located on south Charles Street, near Ostend. It was a church hall, and the younger crowds from both Locust Point and neighborhoods around the "Advent" enjoyed it. The music was played on a juke box. The hall on Friday nights was always packed with high-energy teenagers.

Duke was the best jitterbug dancer of the three of us, Kelly was second and I came in a close third. But, I had my niche: I had mastered the cha cha. I loved to dance it to Paul Anka's "Diana." The best jitterbug dancer out of that ILA Local 829 hall was a gang carrier, Larry "Perch" Holman. He liked to show off his talent around town, particularly in taverns that had a dancing space. One of his fave stops, as well as ours, was Sledge's Bar in Locust Point.

Getting back to Elvis. In the area of popular rock and roll, blues, country and gospel music, I submit there was no single entertainer - before and since - who embodied so creatively all four of these styles like he did. This brings me to this question: "Who was Elvis?"

One of his biographers, Bobbie Ann Mason, ("Elvis Presley, a Life"), also a Southerner, said that he had become a "super star like the world had never seen before." She added: that his "style of music" would dominate the world for the rest of the century." Elvis helped, she continued, to launch the "youth culture."

Elvis' dad, Vernon was a share cropper and had a "strong mellow voice." His mom, Gladys, who had some Cherokee blood in her, was known as a good "buck" dancer. They were from the wrong side of the tracks in East Tupelo. Life was centered around the church. Mason said that they didn't "have a pot to piss in."

Vernon did a stint in prison for forging a check. When Elvis was eleven, Gladys bought him a guitar. (He was angling for a .22 rifle.) When they moved to Memphis, Elvis was thirteen. Elvis loved gospel music and idealized black musicians, such as Muddy Waters, Sleepy John Estes and Arthur Crudup. They were his prime inspirations.

Mason said that because of his background, Elvis ended up "making music that was the voice of the Southern poor - both black and white working class..." She said that they shared a common heritage that "stamped them as outsiders."

Before stardom arrived, Mason explained Elvis was "self-conscious, awkward, nervous and often mumbled." One day in the summer of 1954, he went into the office of Sun Records in Memphis to make a record for his mom.

By a quirk of fate, the gal who manage the session, Marion Keisker, liked what she heard. She let her boss, Sam Phillips know about Elvis. This opened the door to his performing "That's All Right (Mama)." The rest, as they say, is history.

Elvis's blazing star burned out in Memphis, TN, on August 16, 1977, at his beloved "Graceland." He died much too young. He was only forty-two years old. Elvis' daughter, Lisa Marie, was nine years old at the time of her dad's tragic passing.

In any event, Elvis's tremendous, and often brilliant musical legacy, continues to live on in the memory of tens of millions of his grateful admirers around the globe, including me, and many of my boyhood friends from my Locust Point days.

So, I leave you with these words from one of Elvis' earliest and finest ballads - "Heartbreak Hotel":

"Well, since my baby left me,
I found a new place to dwell.
It's down at the end of lonely street
at Heartbreak Hotel."

55. Fireworks Follow the Release of "I, Tonya" and "The Post"
January 13, 2018

"I, Tonya" was one of the newly-released movies that I really enjoyed over the holidays. It dealt with the controversial U.S. figure skater, Tonya Harding. You might recall how, in 1994, she was allegedly involved in the vicious assault on her main competition, Nancy Kerrigan, a fellow Olympian. She later pleaded guilty to "hindering the investigation."

Well, the flick painted Harding, born in Portland, OR, and played by Margo Robbie, as more a victim of her scheming ex-husband and one of his dim-witted cronies. She also had a Mother from Hell, marvelously portrayed by Allison Janney. Mommy dearest came off on the screen as the epitome of white trash, if there is such a thing. Her mother's response to the film: "Tonya is a liar."

Watching the flick, I was hoping Tonya would hit her mother over the head with a frying pan and rip that mustache off her ex-hubby's face. No such luck. I couldn't help but think after viewing this movie: Hey, maybe Tonya was given a bad deal in the first place by the Media. Wrong!

Enter feisty pundit Maureen Callahan of the "New York Post" - one of my fave tabloids (01.12.18). She insisted that the movie, in a scathing rebuttal, retells the scandal - "untruthfully." Callahan pointed to solid police and FBI evidence that showed that Tonya was definitely in on the plot. Callahan is convinced dear little, supposedly naive Tonya, deserved the jibe - "pariah!"

Next up is "All the Money in the World," another well-done movie. It also created some post-production fireworks of its own. You might remember how parts of this Ridley Scott movie had to be reshot after the lead actor, Kevin Spacey, suddenly, had to be replaced by Christopher Plummer. Spacey, also a fixture in Netflix's

"House of Cards' program," had badly slid off the runway in sexual harassment scandals from his past.

Plummer, age 88, took over the lead in the film, playing the emotionally-stunted zillionaire, Jean Paul Getty. It turned out that Mark Wahlberg, who had a featured supporting part in the flick, refused to go along with the reshoot unless the producers "payed up." His agent, and rightly so, insisted on a pay day of $1.5 million for the ten day shoot, according to the Dailymail.com, 01.12.18) And, guess what? Wahlberg got what he demanded!

Meanwhile, Michelle Williams, a co-star on the production, received only $80-a-day for the reshoot even though she had more screen time than Wahlberg! So, her pay day amounted to only $800, if these reports are true. How Ridley Scott and his boy-ohs got away with this one warrants some explaining. I have never heard of a SAG-featured performer getting only $80 a day for a shoot. This is what they pay extras in a film!

Bottom line: Wahlberg deserves credit for being savvy enough to demand more money for the reshoot. Reportedly, he had a clause in his contract protecting his interest in this kind of unusual situation. Unfortunately, Ms. Williams didn't. If you want to be paid what you're worth in a sexist Hollywood, you need to cover your bases. I'm sure Ms. Williams, and her fellow actresses, have learned a valuable lesson from this Made-in-Hollywood experience.

Finally the political movie, "The Post," which concerned the release of the controversial "Pentagon Papers," in 1971, needs to be addressed. The film focused on how the "Washington Post" newspaper published the "secret documents" after a federal court injunction had stopped the "New York Times" from doing so.

Writer Norman Solomon believed that the above was "the high point of the Washington Post's record in relation to the Vietnam War. The newspaper strongly supported the war for many years." ("The Real Story Behind Katherine Graham and 'The Post,'" Counterpunch.org, 12.27.17)

Katherine Graham, the "Post's" publisher, played capably by Meryl Streep in the film, had a "cozy relationship" over the years with senior national security figures, such as the shadowy Henry Kissinger and slippery Robert McNamara, Solomon reported. You have to wonder has anything really changed with that paper since the death of Mrs. Graham? Graham, Solomon added, also had a vindictive streak as far as respecting the rights of union workers.

U.S. involvement in Vietnam lasted from around the early 60s to 1975. Our country sacrificed 58,200 of its finest sons and daughters in that bloodbath. The "Post" did little or nothing to stop the conflict and/or to bring to justice those who had deceived the people, a la the "Gulf of Tonkin Resolution," into getting us into the war in the first place.

Daniel Ellsberg is the real hero of "The Post" movie, but he is hardly mentioned in the film. He risked serious jail time for his daring conduct. The actor Matthew Rhys portrayed him in the movie. See, http://www.history.com/topics/vietnam-war/pentagon-papers

Now, eighty-six years old, Ellsberg has continued to be a strong anti-war activist, speaking out at pro-peace rallies across the country, no matter who is sitting in the White House.

It's true "The Post" is an entertaining movie. Tom Hanks as Ben Bradlee does a credible job as the editor of the paper. But, the flick doesn't deserve all the applause it is receiving. Keep in mind that, "The Post," is only a Hollywood version of what really happened with respect to the Pentagon Papers, the Vietnam War, the Washington Post and the late Katherine Graham.

56. Gerry Sandusky Scores Winning Touchdown with his Book, "Forgotten Sundays" July 5, 2014

Gerry Sandusky's book, "Forgotten Sundays: A Son's Story of Life, Loss, and Love from the Sidelines of the NFL," is one darn good read. Baltimoreans know Gerry primarily from his sports' commentator post at WBAL-TV. Lately, he's branched out to do the play-by-play accounts on radio for the Baltimore Ravens, a National Football League team. In both sports-related personas, Gerry is known as a highly-competent professional.

When Gerry was at the Barnes & Noble's bookshop in Baltimore, on June 15, 2014, discussing and signing his book, I got the distinct impression that this guy really knows his NFL stuff, like a genuine insider. I also had a chance to see his softer side, especially when he recalled his evolving relationship over the years with his late father, John Sandusky. He died in a nursing home in Florida, age 80, in 2006. John had been ravished for the last five years of his life by the terrible disease of alzheimer.

Gerry's tome is essentially a father-son story, but it is much more. Think family, work, church and life. There's plenty of football in this book, but it's mostly utilized as a back drop. Gerry's dad, John, played and/or coached in the NFL for forty-three seasons. He started his playing career with the legendary Cleveland Browns. They won three NFL titles in the 50s, under the great coach/manager Paul Brown. John coached in the NFL for thirty-five of those 43 years as an assistant, except for one year, 1972, he served as the head coach for the Baltimore Colts.

If you know anything about pro football, then your know that "Sunday," game day, is the day of the week that really counts. On many of those Sundays, Gerry was with his dad at the ball park;

whether it was in Philadelphia, Baltimore and/or Miami. He filled roles for the team, such as the "ball boy." This means he made sure that if a foot ball went out of bounds on his side of the field, that he had to have another ready to give to the referee.

Gerry, during this period, saw a lot of his dad. This included witnessing many of the highs and lows of his coaching career, which covered his sacking as head coach when he was in Baltimore by a dork head of a general manager, Joe Thomas. Trust me, nobody in Baltimore liked Thomas. Most wanted to run him out of town on a rail or worse!

Parts of Gerry's book even made me cry. It brought back memories of my relationship with my father, Richard "Dick" Hughes, long dead now. He was a boss on the Baltimore docks for the Alcoa Steamship Company. I worked with him for five years on the piers in Locust Point and got a chance to see up close what made him tick. He was a strong, silent type. One day as a ship we had loaded with cargo was leaving its berth, he suddenly put his arm around my shoulder, as if to say: "Good job, Bill!" What a special moment that was!

Getting back to Gerry. When his older brother Joe died, it was a very hard blow to the family. It caused a rift between his parents, which never truly healed. Later after his mother, Ruth died, and his father remarried, that situation didn't set well with Gerry either.

What's clear from Gerry's telling of the family history is that bringing up sensitive subjects to air wasn't a strong suit for any of the players. John could easily fly off the handle, like my dad, on almost any subject, especially religion. The default conduct in the Sandusky home, as in many households of that day, was just to muddle along, keeping the strong emotions covered and deeply buried.

I remember John's first year, 1959, with the Colts as an assistant coach. It ended well. Baltimore won the championship, beating the New York Giants, Dec. 27th, 31-16, in the title game at fabled Memorial Stadium on 33rd St. I was there that day as was my cousin, Herman Krueger. Some thug stabbed Herman for no good reason. Fortunately, a pretty tough longshoreman, he survived.

Some of Gerry's book is by necessity focused on the convicted sex pervert and ex-assistant coach at Penn State University, Jerry Sandusky. No relation to Gerry at all. The pain this similarity in names has caused Gerry and his family borders on a horror story. After the scandal broke, he became an "instant pariah." Gerry reserves a whole chapter, "The Meaning of a Name," to how he and his young family found the fortitude to stand-up to this controversy. Indeed, it's an inspiring tale how they did it.

There is so much more in this book to take in. Coach John, all 300 pounds of him, originally out of South Philly, and the University of Villanova, sang in the church choir and loved to belt out Irish tunes, such as "Dandy Boy!" Hell, that's enough to make him a huge fave of mine.

In conclusion, let me confess, I'm and I always will be a diehard Baltimore Colts' fan. So, I will end this review of Gerry's wonderful tome by quoting a line of his that stands out for me. He wrote: "I only saw or heard my father cry three times in my my life, when my brother died, when my mother died, and when John Unitas died!"

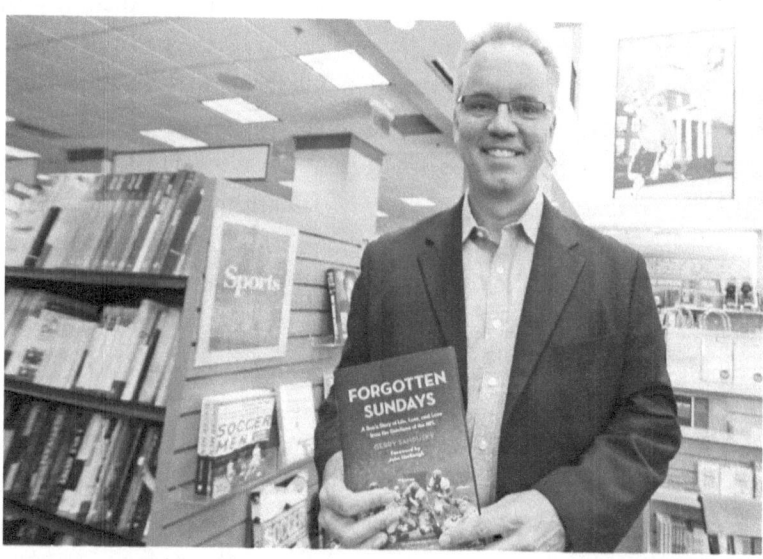

Author Gerry Sandusky

57. Alexander Hamilton Vs. Aaron Burr: A Deadly Feud November 16, 2016

Alexander Hamilton was one of the primary architects of the American Republic. At the moment, he's never been more popular. The play about him, "Hamilton," a rap musical, is currently a smash hit on Broadway. It has won all kinds of awards. Hamilton's spirit - he's buried in the graveyard of Trinity Church in lower Manhattan - is, I'm sure, pleased with this happy turn of events.

By the end of his life, however, Hamilton's political star was in a free fall. He was a protege of the legendary General George Washington, serving as his aide-to-camp. As an artillery officer in the Continental Army, Hamilton fired the first shot at the battle of Trenton. He ended his army career participating in the American victory at Yorktown, VA, over the British troops, in October, 1781.

Hamilton was also the creator of the Federalist Party and contributed in a major way to the making of the U.S. Constitution. Washington appointed him as the first Secretary of the Treasury. His achievements in that arena are monumental in scope.

When Washington retired to his farm in Virginia, in December, 1797, after serving two terms as president, Hamilton's national political influence began to fade. The Republican Party led by Thomas Jefferson and James Madison had taken center stage.

Hamilton, age 47, died tragically, on July 12, 1804, as a result of a duel, with a fellow patriot, who was also an attorney - Aaron Burr. It took place in Weehawken, NJ. Burr was charged with Hamilton's murder. Rather than contest the case, he stayed out of New York and New Jersey. Burr eventually fled to Europe from 1808 to 1812. The charges were later dropped. Burr died in 1836.

Washington never took to Burr and refused him any sinecures. Whether Burr blamed Hamilton for the rebuffs is not known for sure.

To say that Burr was seriously jealous of Hamilton would be an understatement. He comes off as suffering from delusions of grandeur. Burr's reckless conduct, as he aged, bordered on treason.

Hamilton was a resident of Manhattan. He left behind a grieving widow and seven children, one of whom was adopted. (His oldest child, Philip, had also tragically, died in a duel, in 1801.) The then-young American nation was shocked by Hamilton's death. NYC was "consumed with grief." A state funeral, with the militia marching and "church bells ringing out sorrowfully," was held with the patriot, Gouverneur Morris, giving "a stirring eulogy."

A new book, "War of Two: Alexander Hamilton, Aaron Burr and the Duel That Stunned a Nation," penned by author John Sedgwick, brilliantly captures events leading up to the fatal clash between the feuding duo. The author, in a breezy, scholarly style, traces the origins of Hamilton and Burr: their early family histories; schooling at Princeton; war years exploits; and, their days practicing law in New York state. Sedgwick fills in their backstories with many interesting anecdotes along the way.

Burr came from "a nearly divine American lineage," Sedgwick wrote, while Hamilton, on the other hand, was a "solitary immigrant of unknown ancestry." He was born on the island of Nevis in the Caribbean. His mother was of French Huguenot stock. Hamilton was born out of wedlock. His father was supposedly a Scottish sea Captain. But, Sedgwick speculates that a man named Thomas Stevens, formerly of St. Croix. was his real father.

Thomas Stevens was Hamilton's major patron when he landed in NYC, at age 16, in 1773. Stevens also had a son, named Ned, who was two years older than Hamilton. Their resemblance was striking. Hamilton's friend, Timothy Pickering, "thought they must be brothers." Question: Why would Stevens extend "guardianship to a non-relation," absent a closer kind of bond?

Burr's main claim to military fame was his involvement in the expedition to take Quebec from the British. The daring campaign, in 1775, up through 600 miles of Maine's freezing Kennebec River, was led by none other than Benedict Arnold. The weather was harsh, the terrain difficult and food was in short supply. "Only 650 of the original 1,100" brave soldiers survived the passage. Arnold was wounded in the attack. The Americans were roundly defeated, but Burr emerged from the hellish ordeal as a "man of honor."

Burr did have a very successful political and legal career. He served two terms in the NY Assembly; one term as the state's Attorney General, one term as a U.S. Senator; and one term as Vice-President, with Jefferson as President (1801-05). Some of the Burr's legal cases were against Hamilton; a few were, oddly enough, when they both served as co-counsel for a client.

The pretext for the duel was a comment Hamilton made at a dinner party. He referred to Burr as "a dangerous man." History has surely proved him right on that score.

There is so much more in this book that I'm sure the readers will find highly entertaining. The vicious political backstabbing at that time makes the Clinton/Trump campaign battle look like a grade school picnic. The print media at the time behaved very badly, too. Hamilton and Burr, both had dirty hands for sure in this realm of cut throat politics, as did the supposedly saintly Jefferson.

Finally, John Sedgwick has written a winner of a book. I am recommending it to America history buffs and political aficionados.

58. John Waters' "Multiple Maniacs" Returns to the Scene of the Crime! September 12, 2016

The iconic filmmaker John Waters told the capacity audience at Baltimore's Charles Theatre, in Baltimore, Maryland, that in 1969, he had to borrow money from his dad to make the trashy cult classic, "Multiple Maniacs." It didn't go over that big with moviegoers when it was released in 1970, but it did somehow slide by the Maryland Censor Board.

Waters then had a running feud over censorship with the Board and its then chairlady, the late Mary Avara. How this film, with its scenes of sickening depravity, serial murders and shocking blasphemy, got pass her could be the making of yet another flick. But, "Multiple Maniacs," has always had its niche audience with comedy/horror lovers. In any event, the movie featuring the late Divine has been restored and is headed for national re-circulation, via Janus Films.

Divine was played superbly by the actor Harris Glenn Milstead. He was a boyhood buddy of Waters. He died on March 7, 1986. Milstead was known not only as an actor but also as a singer and drag queen. Before launching his acting career, he had been a hairdresser in Baltimore. He's buried in Prospect Hill Cemetery in Towson, Maryland.

The movie was filmed mostly in and around the Baltimore area. Fell's Point, a wee bit trashy itself in that bygone era, was in a lot of the shots. It brought in just over $25,000 at the box office. Some of the opening scenes, Waters said, were filmed in his back of his parents' home in Baltimore County.

At the showing on Monday, September 12th, there were some talented folks, like Pat Moran, Susan Lowe, Mink Stole, Vincent Peranio and George Figgs, in the audience. They had worked on the film in various capacities and were known as the "Dreamland" acting troupe.

George Figgs took on the role of Jesus Christ - a high calling - under any circumstances. He was more than adequate. And, Mink Stole nailed it as the Religious Whore. While, Divine carried the flick in the demanding, hilarious role of Lady Divine.

As for Peranio, he also designed the giant lobster, known as "Lobstora," for the movie. They said it cost about $20 for the material. It looked real to me and that's the bottom line.

Waters introduced each of actors present to warm rounds of applause. To learn more about the film's restoration, check out the article in "Variety" dated, August 6, 2016, at: http://variety.com/2016/film/columns/multiple-maniacs-john-waters-divine-1201831560/

Rotten Tomatoes, a movie review website, Walters reminded the audience, has given "Multiple Maniacs," a hundred percent rating. It is his "highest rated film." Who knew? The restored version will carry the tagline, "Restored! Reviled! Revolting." It opened in early August of this year at one of the Waters' fave hangouts, the Provincetown Film Festival.

This is your final warning!

What kind of reaction did "Multiple Maniacs" get on September 12th? Let me put it this way: It was a non-stop laughathon!

(By way of full disclosure, this writer has had cameo roles in two of Waters' films, "Dirty Shame" and "Pecker.")

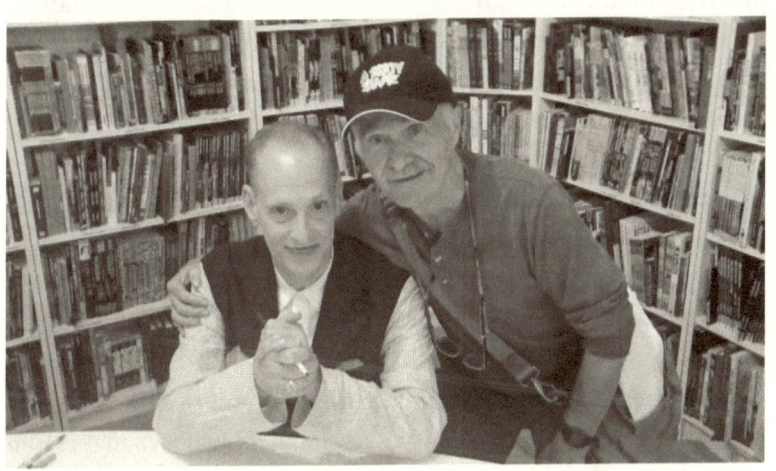

John Waters, with the author Bill Hughes
aka the "Wild Man of 22nd Street"

59. Netflix's "The Keepers" Series Is Compelling TV Drama
May 24, 2017

"The evil in man is of gigantic proportions." - Carl Jung

Did the Archdiocese of Baltimore (AOB) lie about Father Joseph Maskell's crimes? This is one of the key questions that came up in Netflix's "The Keepers" docu-series, ("Justice for Sister Cathy"), a program launched on May 19th of this year.

More on the background of Sister Cathy's murder in just a moment. But first, let's look at this key issue. The AOB claimed it didn't know that Father Maskell (now deceased) was a sexual pervert, who we now know was viciously preying on school children, male and female alike. The AOB claimed that it wasn't until the early 90s, that it knew of his criminal activity.

The credible evidence in this series, however, strongly challenges the AOB's version of history. In the late 60s, the mother of a one of Maskell's victims told church officials about Maskall sexual abusing her altar boy son, Charles Franz.

Franz said that at first, Maskell treated him as a "golden boy" - then the abuse began. Franz eventually became a successful dentist, but he also battled with alcoholism and low self-esteem for nine years as a result of his abuse. His courageous contribution to truth-finding, along with his late mother's, (bless her memory), makes him a true "golden boy" in my eyes.

How did the AOB's respond to the charges brought by Mrs. Franz? In 1967, it moved Maskell from St. Clement RC parish in Landsdowne (where young Franz was as an altar boy), to Archbishop Keough, an all-girls, Catholic high school, in Baltimore City, run by the School Sisters of Notre Dame (SSND). This change gave Father Maskell a whole new crop of victims.

Franz commented: "If the Catholic Church had dealt with this properly in 1967, there would be no murder. We wouldn't be here."

This case reminded me of what happened in the Archdiocese of Boston a few years back. In Boston, the church's wrongdoings were later exposed by the "Boston Globe" in their "Spotlight" series.

We now know that the "Spotlight" disclosures weren't the end of the Catholic Church's troubles. It was only the beginning! Ryan White is the producer of "The Keepers." His work deserves an award. The questions that come up after watching "The Keepers" are endless.

Investigative reporter, Tom Nugent's role, is pivotal in this drama. He has been working on the case of Sister Cathy since the early 90s. In episode one, you see him moving around his attic checking out boxes of old files, with articles and notes on the case. This setting is a perfect place to start telling this saga. One of his sources, "Deep Throat," was a police official familiar with the case.

This is a case nearly fifty years old. Some key players were priests, policemen and neighbors, but many memories have faded and some of the main characters have died. Nugent is in all seven episodes. His narration and questioning is a road map through the tangled web/murder mystery on the killing of Sister Cathy. Check out Nugent's article, in 2013, on Sister Cathy, at: https://whokilledsistercathy.wordpress.com

The prime keepers of the memory of what happened to Sister Cathy are two of her former students at Keough - Abbie Schaub and Gemma Hoskins. They remind me of those amateur detectives on the British TV shows who go sleuthing around looking to solving mysteries.

Sister Catherine Ann Cesnik, (Sister Cathy), age 26, who was a faculty member at Keough, was prepared to blow the whistle on Father Maskell's wrongdoing. Before she could act, however she was murdered by party or parties unknown on November 7, 1969. She was last seen leaving her apartment to do some shopping. Her badly-battered body was found on January 3, 1970, by two hunters in a landfill, off Monumental Avenue, in Baltimore County.

Sister Cathy shared her apartment with another nun, Sister Russell Philips, now deceased. Sister Russell has always refused to talk about the case. Why? I have to wonder: Was she also in fear of Father Maskell? Could she have set Sister Cathy up?

Father Maskell was a suspect in Sister Cathy's killing, but never charged. He fled to Ireland and later died in 2001, in Baltimore County. Recently, his body was exhumed, but no DNA could be found that matched the crime scene. Some insiders theorize that Maskell probably had one of his cronies kill Sister Cathy.

Around the same time, that Sister Cathy was murdered, Joyce Malecki's body was found. She was only 20 years of age. She lived close to Sister Cathy. There are similarities in these two unsolved cases that have intrigued investigators. Her throat was slashed and her hands tied behind her back. She was a parishioner at St. Clement at the same time Father Maskall was a pastor there. Could the killer or killers of Malecki be the same ones who were in on the murder of Sister Cathy?

The FBI investigated Malecki's murder. Her body was found on federal property. The agency has a file on her case, that supposedly contains forensic evidence. If true, it needs to share that file with both the Baltimore City and County police and do it - now!

An attempt to have Father Maskell indicted as a sexual predator in Baltimore City, back in the 90s, was unsuccessful. The Assistant D.A., Sharon A.H. May, said the case wasn't strong enough to bring to trial.

Two of the heroes of this saga are Jean Hargadon Wehner and Theresa Lancaster. They were the plaintiffs in a civil case against Maskell and the AOB in the early 90s. The case, however, was tossed out by the trial judge because it ran afoul of the statute of limitations. The duo have continued to fearlessly speak out for justice in this matter. Four other students from Keough have also joined them in going public about their stories of abuse.

Mrs. Wehner told the police that Father Maskell took her to the place where Sister Cathy's body was dumped soon after she went missing. Her memory on this issue is very credible. She added that Maskell, at the site, threatened her by saying that she could end up dead like Sister Cathy if she got out of line.

The AOB has paid out, without admitting fault, $472,000 to the victims of Father Maskell.

Thanks to "The Keepers" series, the unsolved murders of Sister Cathy and Joyce Malecki are getting more attention than ever from the police, the media and those intrepid daughters of Keough who have refused to let this matter go. Let's hope it leads to justice for all of the victims of this deplorable saga.

60. "My Life As a Mermaid"
Amazon.com, July 13, 2015

Over the last few years, I've been taking photographs at some of the literary events happening around Baltimore City. Jen Grow was one of the readers that I often heard. I recall her sharing her stories at sites hosted by authors such as Jen Michalski, Rafael Alvarez and Michael Kimball, and others.

Jen Grow is the editor of the "Little Patuxent Review." And on June 15, 2015, she launched her debut book at the popular Ivy Bookshop before a standing room only audience It's entitled: "My Life as a Mermaid," a collection of twelve short stories. They are excellent and resonate with often vivid images of the human condition with all of its often dreary, dark, boozy and gloomy circumstances. The author is sympathetic in her deft portraits of the subjects, but without going overboard.

One of her tales, a very moving one, indeed, is about death itself. It's called: "Small Deaths." The narrator is the daughter. Her mother is "so frail," that she can hardly stand-up. The author makes you feel that you are in the room with these two gallant souls as they bravely embrace, "the clumsiness of death."

Shifting gears! There's Vivie stumbling through her days in an alcoholic daze. Her neighbors are packing-up and leaving town. Vivie desperately wants to do the same in, "OK, Goodbye." She suspects her anger-filled husband, Don, is screwing around on her. Vivie is forever losing her keys, perhaps a metaphor for her perpetual floundering through her shots of whiskey and mountains of tears.

There is a water theme in many of these stories, none more so than in the title piece itself, "My Life as a Mermaid." It contrast two sisters. Kay is off on a dangerous and adventure-filled excursion in Honduras, Central America, as a "relief worker." The narrator, the other sister, sits home with her three small kids and recalls the fun times that they had growing-up together and going often to the local swimming pool. How to give her boring existence some meaning is her main quest. It's not easy. She labels her predicament as the "land of marriage, motherhood (and) matching socks."

"Joe Blow" is one of my fave stories in this collection. It's populated by characters, colorfully created, who remind me of my days growing up in Locust Point. Back then, it was a bastion of the working class, many of whom belonged in a Hollywood movie. Here's one of Jen Grow's best lines in her book: "Winter is a bastard that beats his wife." It's mouthed by a hapless street person named Larry. He lives in a truck, parked on a street in a residential area, with his drinking crony, Roger. They are juxtaposed with Joe Blow! He's a "clean freak," who always has a "broom with him." The narrator has an upstairs apartment with a wide view of the human carnival below.

"What Girls Left Behind" is a pain-filled cry for help! A lonely housewife, the narrator, with kids long gone and an ex-husband out of the house, bemoans her dismal fate. Regularly saucing-up at the corner bar helps her through the day. The next door neighbor, Evelyn, another pitiful loser, is her companion. There is plenty of anger in the tortured soul of this housewife.

There is so much more in this gem of a new book. Jen Grow digs deep into the human psyche in her selected stories. So deep, at times, that the despair and hopeless rise to the surface and spill over. The author's prose dances across the pages. "My Life as a Mermaid" is highly recommended. It will make for a terrific summer read.

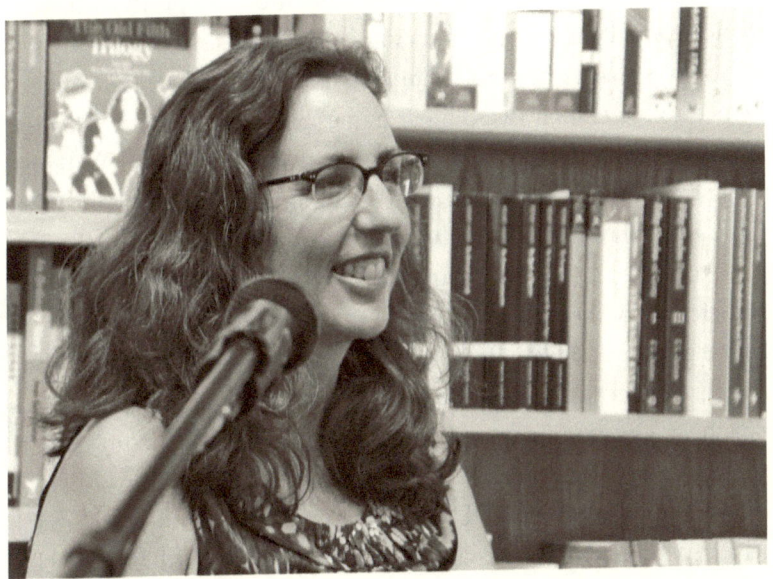

Author Jen Grow

61. The Boys of Dunbar
September 29, 2016

I know it's a cliche, but I found it hard to put down this book: "The Boys of Dunbar: A Story of Love, Hope, and Basketball." I discovered it was not only well written by its Brooklyn, NY-born author, Alejandro Danois, but captivating on a number of levels. (Book Review: "The Boys of Dunbar: A Story of Love, Hope, and Basketball," Alejandro Danois, 288 pages, Simon & Schuster, 2016)

It is surely more than simply a book about the Dunbar Poets - a winning and acclaimed public high school basketball team - from the hard streets of black East Baltimore. At a deeper level, it's an inspiring tale about the magnificence of the human spirit played out in the lives of young people. They had to learn to survive, struggling to do their best daily in the crime-ridden housing projects, in very difficult, challenging and often dangerous times.

Sports, basketball and Paul Lawrence Dunbar High School helped to focus their lives. Their names: Tyrone "Muggsy" Bogues, Gary Graham, David "Gate" Wingate, Reggie "Russ" Willams, Reggie "Truck" Lewis and Tim Dawson, along with nine other darn good players, will long be associated with this celebrated team.

At center stage in their story is Dunbar's 1981-82 (29-0), undefeated basketball season. The team was led by its stellar, 5'3" point guard, Muggsy. Its head coach, and father figure, was Bob Wade. Wade had earlier learned his craft serving as an assistant coach at Dunbar under the incomparable, late William "Sugar" Cain, whose reign as head coach lasted 32 successful years.

Wade, also an ex-NFL cornerback, comes across in the book as a mix of a brilliant basketball strategist and a hard-as-nails U.S. Marine Corp drill instructor! Wade once played under NFL's legendary coach Vince Lombardi, (then, with the "Washington Redskins"). So, you can see where he may have inherited some of that tough guy, take-another-lap-around-the-field persona.

The 1980-81 season ended on a bummer note for the Poets. They lost to my alma mater, the Calvert Hall Cardinals, coached by the Catholic League legend, Mark Amatucci, (94-91), at the Towson Center before a capacity audience. The game went into triple overtime. The Poets were "actually winning by nine points with less than two minutes to play in regulation," wrote Danois.

After that bitter defeat, Wade & his team, were committed to the 81-82 season - not only for it to be a winning one, but to also extract some sweet revenge on the boy-ohs from Towson, who wore the Cardinal & Gold uniforms. From the first practice session - (incidentally they usually lasted about four hours) - Wade pushed hard to create a mindset of victory, no matter how high the price.

Author Danois take you game by important game through the season. He also tells you, at time, poignantly, what was going on inside the sometimes difficult families lives of the players. It rings with the pain-filled truth. But, despite the roadblocks, the setbacks, the players (and their family supporters) soldiered onward.

Lurking on the perimeter of this story are the ubiquitous drug dealers who have been ravaging, and causing havoc in the black neighborhoods. The 81-82 Dunbar team knew what had happened to one of the schools' greatest basketball stars, Allen "Skip" Wise. He was "The Man" on its team in the early 70s.

Wise only lasted one year at the U. of Clemson, turned pro and then became a serious drug user. He also served time for drug related offenses. Wade's players knew that this could be their fate too, if they hung around with the "wrong characters." Besides drugs, Danois also mentions another curse, that had seriously impacted on all the blue collar neighborhoods in the city - in the "late 70s and early 80s," particularly in black East Baltimore - "deindustrialization." The globalist schemers pushed through unfair Trade Agreements, like NAFTA, that robbed our country of many of its steel mills, shipyards and booming manufacturing plants, such as the Bethlehem Steel's Sparrows Point plant. To learn more, go to: http://economyincrisis.org)

After the breadwinner lost his job, Danois underscores, in some of the cases, "these teenage drug dealers became their family's main wage earners." As the years progress, he writes ominously, the drug dealers have become "younger and younger."

As a former soccer player who went to the University of Baltimore on a sports scholarship, I could identify with the importance of basketball in the lives of the Dunbar players.

Like in many stories of this kind, there are a host of unsung heroes. One of them is Leon Howard. He ran the Lafayette Projects' Rec center. He was Muggsy's first mentor. Another hero was the long time principal of Dunbar, the late Mrs. Julia B. Woodland. She was a first class motivator, who insisted on the surrounding communities being an "integral part of the school community."

I'm not going to tell you if Wade's Dunbar team got its revenge on Calvert Hall. You will have to read the book to get the answer to that one. He does write, however, about each of the team's players and how they faired after Dunbar, including that "eighth wonder of the world" - Tyrone "Muggsy" Bogues.

Summing up, Alejandro Danois has written a gem of a sports story. It belongs in the library of all lovers of high school athletics. Bottom line: The book, "The Boys of Dunbar," is a winner!

62. The Cult of Aleister Crowley Lives On July 20, 2014

"It was sex that rotted him. It was sex, sex, sex, sex, sex all the way with Crowley. He was a sex maniac!" - Vittoria Cremers

John Lennon, Timothy Leary, Iggy Pop, the Jonas Brothers and the Rolling Stones' rock group, among others, were all influenced in one way or another by him. He was into sex, ceremonial magic, yoga and the occult, like no other so-called "spiritual seeker" of his time. His name was Aleister Crowley and he was British to the core. His motto was: "Do What Thou Wilt shall be the whole of the law. Love is the law, love under will."

Crowley followed his own mantra right to the very end of his Christianity-hating, drug-abusing and higher consciousness-seeking life. If you want to know what Crowley looked like in his prime, check out that famous cover of the Beatles' best-selling album - "Sgt. Pepper's Lonely Hearts Club Band." He's the dude with the shaven head and bulging eyes. Crowley, a hero then to many in the "Pop Culture," is swished in between two other fabled icons of the 60s, Marilyn Monroe and Che Guevara.

Author Gary Lachman has done an excellent job profiling Crowley, aka "The Great Beast 666." He came by his interest in this unusual man with a monstrous ego via an interesting route. Back in the 70s, Lachman was playing in a rock and roll band in NYC. One of his bandmates had a thing for the occult. The musician also had a copy of one of Crowley's novels, "The Diary of a Drug Fiend." This led Lachman to lodge onto another of Crowley's literary efforts, "Moonchild." It's "roman a clef" showing members of the London-based "Hermetic Order of the Golden Dawn," in a very negative way. William Butler Yeats and Crowley were members of that group, even so, Crowley despised the Irish poet.

The title of Lachman's book is: "Aleister Crowley: Magick, Rock and Roll, the Wickedest Man in the World." Crowley's huge mug is on the cover. He was born in England in 1875, and despite a life of extreme excess, including lots of booze, drugs, hookers and sex, and later on a serious addiction to heroin, Crowley managed to live till 1947. At one time, he was even into serious mountaineering and proved himself very adept at it. The Alpine mountaineering community held him in the highest esteem.

Crowley loved women and he was also an active homosexual. He married twice and had three children. He wrote poems, novels and books. Much of his work, because of its shocking nature, was self-published. He may even have been a spy for the Brits and/or the Nazis. Who knows?

Like William S. Burroughs of American notoriety, (think "Naked Lunch,") who emerged during the post-WWII "Beat Generation," Crowley came from wealth. He never had to work a day in his life. Crowley also got a solid education, which included the best prep schools and a degree from Cambridge University. As a result, Crowley was able to dedicate his life to his "religion." He called it, "Thelema." A religion/philosophy needs a sacred text. So, Crowley made one up by way of his contact with a "Higher Power." He then bestowed on it the moniker - "The Book of the Law."

Talking about addictions, I'm into the forensic crime shows on the cable networks. I couldn't help but noticed on several programs, that when relating the bio on an individual who suddenly went way off the tracks into a life of crime, the turning point was when the father of the bad guy unexpectedly died. Is this what happened in Crowley's case, too?

Crowley's father was out of the upper class and a fervent evangelical, bible-belting Christian. He died of "cancer of the tongue," when Crowley was only eleven. The young Crowley scorned his mother. Of that transformative period, he recalled, "I simply went over to Satan's side; and to this hour I cannot tell why... and I felt passionately eager to serve my new master. I was anxious to distinguish myself by committing sin."

Well, Crowley, often an arrogant character, sure did dedicate his life to the goal of sinning. Traveling widely, there were few major cities on the globe, where he hadn't left a sample of his sperm. And, author Lachman captures just about every one of his sins, including disgusting acts of sadomasochism, in every awful, smelly detail. Crowley also made several visits to the U.S. New Orleans was "his favorite city." I wonder why?

Crowley was into documenting, too, via letter-writing, books and pamphlets his often weird ideas, outrageous behavior and quest for hedonistic thrills. This was particularly so when he formed an Abbey of Thelemalites at Cefalu, Sicily. Eventually, Italy's then-dictator, Benito Mussolini was offended. He gave Crowley and his groupies the boot. By the way, author Lachman was a founding member of the rock group, "Blondie." He also wrote the excellent book, "Jung, the Mystic."

In this well-researched tome, Lachman also does a masterful job demonstrating Crowley's far-reaching legacy. It extends today into many areas of our counter-culture, such as magic, painting, mysticism, esotericism, filmmaking, punk and rock music, heavy metal, death-loving goths and the occult.

With respect to filmmaking, I think some of the iconic director John Waters' bad taste flicks have a noticeable Crowley influence. Take his "Dirty Shame" movie for instance, in which I had a cameo role. The plot centers around a city neighborhood, that is divided between the "puritans" and the "sex perverts." The latter clique of crazies engage shamelessly in their "unique fetishes." (Think, "Do What Thou Wilt!").

Waters, now a best-selling author, thanks to the popularity of his tome, "Carsick," just happens to keep an electric chair in his Tudor-styled house in Baltimore. So Crowleyish! Back to Lachman's book. It's a terrific read containing a wealth of credible information on what caused the British's tabloid, "John Bull," to tag the want-a-be prophet Crowley as the "wickedest man in the world!"

Finally, whatever the final word on the controversial Crowley will be, his portrait today does hang in London's prestigious National Gallery. His cult, for better or worse, lives on.

63. Washington's Immortals: The Untold Story of an Elite Regiment from Maryland Who Changed the Course of the Revolution June 24, 2016

When the Pride of Baltimore II, "America's Star-Spangled Ambassador," sails into the waters of Baltimore's outer harbor, it passes two land-based forts. On its portside is Fort (William) Smallwood; and on the starboard, Fort (John Eager) Howard. ("Washington's Immortals: The Untold Story of an Elite Regiment Who Changed the Course of the Revolution," by Patrick K. O'Donnell, 463 pages, Atlantic Monthly Press, 2016)

Both of these sites, now popular public parks, were named in honor of two distinguished Revolutionary War heroes. They, with many other gutsy citizens/soldiers, were associated with the fabled "Maryland Regiment," and America's noble cause for Independence.

In its formative year, 1774, the regiment was called "The Baltimore Independent Company." Its founding leader was the patriot, Mordecai Gist, a local merchant, then 32 years of age.

The Maryland Regiment gained its enduring fame in August, 1776, at the "Battle of Long Island," aka the "Battle of Brooklyn." There, American troops, the Continentals, about 6,000 strong, under General George Washington, were outflanked, and badly outnumbered by the British and Hessian forces of 20,000.

In order for the Continentals to gain time to safely retreat from the battlefield and to fight another day, the Maryland Line, with Gist commanding, not only held its position, but valiantly charged, with fixed bayonets, their foe's fortress-like position. Many died in the daring effort and/or ended up as prisoners of war.

General Washington watching the courageous display with a spyglass, commented, "Good God! What brave fellows I must this day lose." Those soldiers later became known at the "Immortal 400." Their actions allowed Washington "to pull off one of the greatest military retreats in history."

Today, marking the Marylanders' sacrifice is a rusted metal sign. It hangs from the American Legion Post #1636, in Brooklyn, New York. The Legion's hall is surrounded by garages and auto repair shops. The sign reads: "Maryland Heroes. Here lie buried 256 Maryland soldiers Who Fell in the Battle of Brooklyn. August 27, 1776." If there is such a thing as "Hallowed Ground," their mass grave, is believed to be located nearby, surely is.

We live in an era of monuments galore, but, shamefully, there isn't one to honor these fallen heroes from Maryland. Hopefully, Patrick K. O' Donnell's latest book will correct this glaring oversight.

The name of O'Donnell's well-written, and superbly researched tome, is "Washington's Immortals: The Untold Story of an Elite Regiment Who Changed the Course of the Revolution." It's told from the point of view of the on-the-march citizen/soldier, the daring rebel. He's fighting the good fight against the British Imperialists.

Members of the Maryland Regiment were paid by the state government. It was never much and they had to also in the beginning buy/create their own uniforms and weapons. As the war dragged on for over eight years, "many Marylanders starved, wore rags and went barefoot."

If captured, chances were a soldier would have ended up dead, sooner on later, on one of the 16 British prison vessels berthed in New York Harbor. An estimated 11,500 American POWs died in those filthy hell holes. Their bodies were then tossed overboard. Of the 30,000 Americans captured during the war, "some eighteen thousand died while being held prisoner" by the British.

O'Donnell wrote that 1,444 troops, in December, 1775, were formed to constitute the Maryland Regiment. "It was a battalion of 9 companies, 2 independent companies, and 2 companies of artillery. All the men were volunteers."

Placed in charge was Colonel William Smallwood, a native of Charles County, who was educated at Eton. Gist became a Major in the unit. Also joining the battalion were the likes of Cecil County's Nathaniel Ramsay and Edward Veazey; Somerset County's John Gunby; James Peale, brother of the artist, Charles Wilson Peale; Baltimore's Bryan Philpot Jr., William Sterrett and James Fernandis; Kent County's John Bantham; Frederick County's John Hughes; and Anne Arundel County's Jack Steward and Ben Ford.

O'Donell underscored, "Free African Americans also joined the ranks of Smallwood's Battalion…This was not only America's first army, but America's first integrated army." Later, hooking up with the regiment, on Manhattan, was another legend, Major Otho Holland Williams. He had participated in the siege of Boston and would later distinguish himself in many of the battles to follow.

In a companion Maryland unit, labeled, "The Flying Column," was found the iconic Captain John Eager Howard. The Flying Column command was given to General Rezin Beall. Unfortunately, no overall leader of Maryland forces was named between the two. This created an ongoing "dispute" over authority.

The Maryland Regiment would see action not only in Brooklyn, but in major key battles throughout the war: Trenton, Stony Point,

Camden, Cowpens, Guilford Court House and Yorktown. Over and over again General Washington came to rely on this elite unit.

Author O'Donnell has a military background and is considered an expert on elite units. He served as a "combat historian in a Marine rifle platoon during the battle of Fallujah." As a result, O'Donnell was able to tell the compelling story of the Maryland Regiment by spotlighting the struggles and aspirations of the citizen/soldier in a very intimate and often inspiring fashion.

In his book, O'Donnell covered a lot of ground in over an eight year period of combat. Two of my favorite battles related by him, involved the strategic actions utilized in the defense of Fort Mifflin (Mud Island), and at Cowpens. In the first, Lt. Colonel Samuel Smith is featured; and at Cowpens, it's Commander John Eager Howard.

As the fates would have it, Smith and Howard had political careers after their outstanding tours of duty in the Continental Army. A monument to Smith stands on Federal Hill, while an equestrian statue to Howard can be found on the north quadrant of Mt. Vernon Place. Smith served in both the U.S. Congress and as Mayor of Baltimore (1835-38). Howard served in the Congress, too, and was later elected as Governor of Maryland (1788-90).

Author O'Donnell is at the top of his game in "Washington's Immortal." It's a must-read for Revolutionary War and Maryland history buffs alike.

64. "The Year That Made Hitler: 1924" March 7, 2016

In the 2016 U.S. presidential campaign from hell, the name of Adolf Hitler has been repeatedly invoked. Hysterical comparisons have been made between the German dictator (from 1934-45) and the billionaire real estate magnate, Donald Trump, one of the

Republican candidates for president. ("The Year That Made Hitler: 1924", Peter Ross Range, 363 pages, Little Brown and Company, 2016)

Nothing could be further from the truth. Again, the evil genius that was Hitler is grossly underestimated by the pundits - while a windbag, and political lightweight, such as Trump, who was born into the lap of luxury, is given an unwarranted status. "The Donald" is simply feeding off the emotions/fears of the royally-pissed-off electorate. It's a below-the-belt tactic well known to political aficionados.

The wise guys pundits have short memories. They've forgotten how George H.W. Bush, (Dubya's daddy), played the race card - to wit: the notorious Willie Horton TV ads - to bring down his presidential opponent Democrat Michael Dukakis in 1988 election. Dirty tricks in politics in the U.S. have takes many forms and have a long, despicable history.

In the book, "The Year That Made Hitler: 1924," the author, Peter Ross Range, focuses on a critical time in the political life of Hitler. This was the year he spent as a prisoner in Landsberg Prison, just outside of Munich (November 11, 1923 to December 20, 1924.) In fact, it was a make or break time for him and his revenge-seeking Nazi party.

The setting is post World War I, in Bavaria, in the south of Germany. It's a heavily Catholic area with a population reeling from the harmful effects of the war. The economy had collapsed and hyperinflation had reached epic levels. Try this: "a loaf of bread cost 200 billion marks. Savings were destroyed and food shortages had sparked riots."

(As an aside, one of the Nazi concentration camps located in Germany, after the brutal Nazis took power in 1934, was at Dachau, near Munich. It wasn't a death camp, no gas chambers, but thousands of inmates nevertheless died there, including "621 Catholic priests, 477 of them of Polish heritage." See, Bedrich Hoffmann, "And, Who Will Kill You.")

Getting back to post-WWI, the French occupied parts of the Ruhr region as a result of the Treaty of Versailles, they had also had seized the Alsace-Lorraine area. The German people were hit, too, with a $12.5 billion reparation obligation and "humiliated by the 'sole guilt' clause of the treaty." Bavaria was a hotbed of "nationalistic parties and groups." It was then known as the "putsch (coup d'etat) capital" of the federated German state.

Political violence was endemic and irrational hatred of Jews common place. The big lie/myth, repeated ad nauseam, that enflamed the German populace was that WWI was lost not on the battlefield. It was lost because of a conspiracy of political hacks, "The November Criminals," with Jews predominating, that had "stabbed the country in the back."

Communist leaders in Berlin, Karl Liebknecht and Rosa Luxemburg, both Jews, in 1919, were assassinated, along with Matthias Erzberger, who had signed the WWI armistice. A right-wing hit squad took credit for "more than 350 political murders," during this reign of terror. This included the killing of Walther Rathenau, "a German foreign minister and a Jew."

The hatred of the Jews by right-wingers was fueled also by their fears of Marxism. Around this same time, the Bolsheviks had came to power in Russia. The Czar and his family were slaughtered. Jews, because of past bloody pogroms, had played a minor part in the upheaval and its aftermath. See, "Stalin and His Hangmen: The Tyrant and Those Who Killed for Him," Donald Rayfield. The Nazi propagandists, however, ignored the real facts, and blamed "a Jewish conspiracy" for the Russian Revolution.

Enter in late 1923, Adolf Hitler! The former private from WWI was living in a cheap sublet in Munich. A native of Austria, he was viewed as "a failed artist and drifter." Hitler generally awoke late in the day and haunted the "raucous beer halls of the city at night." But, he did a have a job of sorts. Hitler was a spy for the German Army (Reichswehr)! He was hired in 1919, to place under surveillance workers' political clubs for any pro-Marxist activities, and to also "promote German nationalism."

In September, 1919, Hitler was assigned to check out a small group, then called the "German Workers' Party." He spoke at their meeting and the "demagogue" was born. The power of his voice and his talent for speaking were evident to all. The clique that was dominating this organization were all raving "anti-Semites." Hitler soon became their messiah. The German Workers' Party morphed into National Socialist Party of the Nazis.

Fast cut to November 8, 1923. This was the date of the failed coup in Munich against the national government. Hitler was its leader. The author Range captures brilliantly every move and counter-move of this history-shattering event. It starts in a beer hall and ends up on the blood-stained streets of Munich. Fifteen Nazis were killed and Hitler was injured. Two days later, he was hauled off to Landsberg Prison. The coup had failed. Hitler had failed miserably and the nascent Nazis Party was shattered.

Yet, a remarkable rebirth, a transformation, was soon coming. Within a decade, it would shake the world to its roots. Hitler, and his Nazis Party (NSDAP), would then be at center stage. How could that be?

Hitler was able to turn his trial for "High Treason" into a smashing victory. He acted mostly as his own lawyer, brilliantly at times, and got away with blaming everybody but himself for the failed coup. In the process, he gained national and global notoriety and "political martydom." Author Range brings you inside the Munich courtroom with his detailed account of this compelling legal drama.

Even Hitler's conviction was turned into a positive for Hitler and his gang of vipers. His sentence was reduced, via a pardon, from five years to 13 months. The prison at Landsberg couldn't have been cozier for him and his adoring cronies. It was more like a vacation lodge, only with guards. Instead of "disgrace and obscurity," imprisonment ended up for Hitler as "springboard for success."

Landsberg Prison was utilized by Hitler as a time for him of "learning, self-reflection and clarification of his views." It is while housed in cell #7, that he composed his political manifesto, "Mein Kampf/My Struggle." It is not true, the author wrote, that he dictated his book to fellow prisoner, Rudolf Hess. Hitler typed it himself on a portable Remington, which was given to him by a female devotee. The rest as they say is history. It was indeed a dark, lethal one, filled with massive crimes against Humanity.

There were just so many times during these early tumultuous days that the sinister Hitler could have been stopped. A good stiff jail sentence would have done the trick and/or deportation to Austria and obscurity. Most, however, didn't see just how dangerous Hitler was, until it was too late.

Author Range deserves credit for brilliantly and concisely bringing this important slice of history to visability. Hitler's life in 1924, changed him, and because few were paying attention, it changed the world, too, forever.

65. The Screening of "Bonhoeffer," a One-Man Play March 26, 2017

On Saturday evening, March 25, 2017, "Bonhoeffer," a film of a one-man play, was screened in the sanctuary at Bolton Hill's Memorial Episcopal Church, in Baltimore, MD.

The film starred the late actor Peter Krummeck, who also produced the play. He was born, in 1947, in Johannesburg, South Africa. He died in 2013, in St. Luke's Hospice, Cape Town, South Africa. Archbishop Desmond Tutu was one of the patrons of Krummeck's Cape Town-based African Community Theatre Service.

"Bonhoeffer," the play, originally debuted in Washington, D.C. in the early 2000's. It also was performed in Canada, South Africa and at Baltimore's "Theater Project." It was televised in Canada.

Backstory on Dietrich Bonhoeffer (1906-45). He was a German Lutheran pastor, theologian and author, who opposed the Nazi regime. He was active in the resistance movement and in a plot to kill Adolf Hitler, the German dictator. Bonhoeffer was arrested in April, 1943, and jailed at Tegel prison. He was subsequently hanged by the Nazis - at Flossenburg - just weeks before WWII ended.

Tonight's program was hosted by Rev. Grey Maggiano of Memorial Episcopal. After the presentation of the film, Professor John Kiess of the Theology Department at Loyola College, the Rev. Dr. C. Anthony Hunt of United Methodist Church, Senior Pastor, and Ms. Judith Krummeck of classical radio station WBJC, participated in a panel discussion.

They each shared their views on Bonhoeffer. A spirited Q&A from the audience followed.

In her remarks, Ms. Krummeck, a sister of Peter Krummeck, talked about the "background" of her brother's work, especially in the area of the role of theater, and the church, too, in "promoting social justice and reconciliation." She has been the popular "evening drive time host" for WBJC, since 1998. Ms. Krummeck is a native of South Africa. She is also an actress, educator and author. Her latest book, "Beyond the Baobab," is a collection of essays about her immigrant experience. Check out: https://judithkrummeck.com

I must add that I thought Peter Krummeck's portrayal of Bonhoeffer in the 45 minute edited film version of the play was simply riveting. He captured the essence of the doomed, but courageous cleric.

There were two co-sponsors for the event: the Memorial Episcopal Church and "The Samaritan Community."

Bonhoeffer's martyrdom was also depicted in a well-received documentary on his life and death. It was produced, in 2003, by writer/director Martin Dobimeier. See, http://www.imdb.com/title/tt0371583/.

A lively discussion of the importance of Bonhoeffer to our contemporary era came up. Rev. Hunt mentioned Martin Luther King Jr. and Bishop Oscar Romero as just two of the modern day spiritual leaders/martyrs, who were guided in their struggle for Justice by their abiding Christian faith. He added there were also many more "unsung heroes" for the cause of Civil Rights in America. Dr. King was murdered in 1968.

Bishop Romero of El Salvador was a champion of the poor in his beleaguered country. Siding with the poor, however, was considered a "subversive act" by the blood-stained Oligarchy running the regime. He was murdered, in San Salvador, by the death squads, in 1980, while serving Mass.

Professor Kiess, who is an expert of the writings of the Jewish intellectual and historian Hannah Arendt, raised some relevant comments about the moral duties of an individual, when facing "evil." Arendt penned, in 1963, the controversial book, "Eichmann In Jerusalem: A Report on the Banality of Evil." Kiess's book, published in 2016, is entitled: "Hannah Arendt and Theology."

It needs repeating that the widespread resistance by many heroic Christian clergy to the Nazi regime, during the blood-stained days of the German Reich, isn't well known. The records, however, of the Dachau concentration camp, located in the South of Germany, near Munich, tell, in a compelling fashion, some of their story.

According to a finely-detailed book, "And Who Will Kill You," by Bedrich Hoffmann, Pallottinum, (1994), the author revealed that "2,670 members of the clergy" passed through the Dachau hell hole during WWII. Of that number, "621 died" there for reasons that aren't disclosed. Roman Catholic priests, 598 to be exact, made up the majority of the 621 clerics who perished at Dachau from 1934-45.

Finally, I think one of the consensus from tonight's viewing of "Bonhoeffer," was that the play, and the important moral issues that it raised, is just as relevant today as it has ever been.

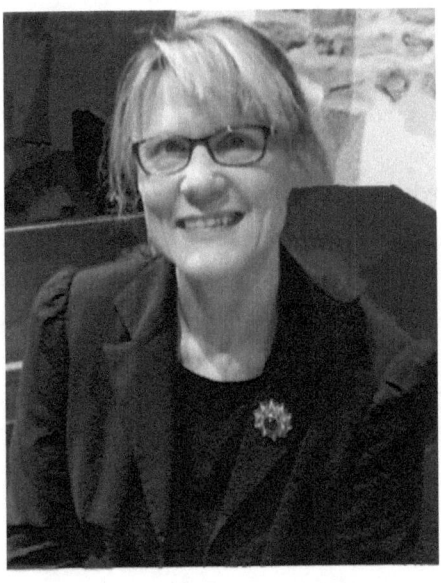

Judith Krummeck, Author and Radio Personality

66. Flickering Treasures: Rediscovering Baltimore's Forgotten Movie Theaters October 29, 2017

Author/Photographer Amy Davis has written a delightful book about Baltimore's Movie Palaces from yesteryear, with plenty of riveting photos to bring it to life. It's called: "Flickering Treasures: Rediscovering Baltimore's Forgotten Movie Theaters."

On Saturday afternoon, October 28, 2017, Ms. Davis gave a talk about her literary effort at the Gallery CA, 440 E. Oliver St., at the corner of Greenmount Ave. The event featured 19 of the hundreds of photos she took for the book. The exhibit is entitled, "Home Movies: Portraits of neighborhood movie houses." (This gallery presentation will end on November 12th.)

Naturally, I got very excited when I saw the Deluxe my old neighborhood (Locust Point) movie house included. More about the Deluxe in a moment.

Ms. Davis mentioned that there were once 240 theaters in Baltimore. Over nine years, she did some remarkable research, then selected 74 movie houses to feature in her 300 plus page book.

The book, which is also a history of the great movie house era, opens with a foreword by Baltimore's own Barry Levinson. He chats about his earliest movie experiences as youngster - probably "seven or eight years old." Levinson was captivated by the movies he attended, seeing them as "perhaps step one to my future."

The preface is a must-read. The author sets up the challenges she encountered in writing the book. Ms. Davis mentions there are "300 interviews" in her tome. West Baltimore theaters get equal billing with South, East and North Baltimore movie houses. The anecdotes, she continues, "reveal the powerful connections we all experience in a darkened theater."

The first movie house lauded is the "Electric House," it dates back to before Larry King was born - 1896. The author finishes up with the Parkway and the CineBistro. They were the latest jewels to come on board in - 2017. One of Ms. Davis' lines from the preface cuts to the chase with respect to the changing movie scene over the years. She writes: "The only certainty is that nothing stays the same."

Ralph Moore, popular community activist, shared his memories of the "Harlem" theater in West Baltimore. He said: "The only worry was that a rat could come scurrying across your feet. The Harlem was a true adventure, a true competition for any action on the screen."

George Figgs, artist, film historian, actor and the former operator of the Orpheum Theatre in Fells Point, gets a lot of deserved ink in the book. I recall seeing a movie there a few years back. It was one of my faves, "LA Confidential." Figgs developed his movie habit growing up in Hampden (Hon).

In his salad day, Figgs was a projectionist at the Charles Theater. Later, he worked for about two years as a "daily projectionist" on some of the Hollywood movies being made in Baltimore. Figgs is a true Renaissance Man. Ms. Davis rightly titled him: "The high priest of celluloid."

Getting back to my home base, the Deluxe movie house on Fort Avenue - Ms. Davis was kind enough to include my anecdote about it on page 112.

I feel compelled, however, to add another: I remember going to an early show at the movie when I was about 12 years old. After I left, I needed to relieve myself, I went around to the back of the Deluxe. Just as I was finishing up my business, a cop car pulled up and put a flashlight on me. Out of the car stepped one Sergeant Frank Battaglia.

My heart stopped! Battaglia was "Mr. Law & Order" himself. Later on, he devised the controversial "Battaglia Plan" and became the Police Commissioner of Baltimore City. He roughly snapped at me. I thought, oh Lord, I'm going to spend the night in the lock-up at the Southern District. Battaglia gave me the "third degree." I suspect he knew my dad who was a boss on the waterfront. In any event, to my relief he just barked at me: "Go on home and behave yourself." I responded meekly: "Thank you, sir!"

Ms. Davis also highlighted the Patterson Theater in her book. Now, it's the home of "Creative Alliance," located in heart of East Baltimore's Highlandtown. Back in the late 50s, I was dating a "Hon" from Highlandtown. She became wife No.1. This is what our typical date night looked like: Movie at the Patterson, a pizza at Matthews across the street, and then a draft beer at a pub close to her Fait Avenue address. Cost, seriously: try around $10.

I attended Calvert Hall High School, when it was located at Mulberry and Cathedral Street, across from the Pratt (1951-55). So, I got a chance to attend many of the downtown theaters, like: the

Mayfair, the Town (now Everyman), the Hippodrome, the Stanley and the Century.

On a date with my Highlandtown Hon at the Century, located at 18 W. Lexington Street, I recall seeing a Baltimore Colts football player. It was Alan "The Horse" Ameche. This was probably around 1957. On Dec. 28, 1958, I would be in Yankee Stadium, watching Ameche (now deceased) scoring the winning TD in overtime against the New York Giants in an NFL championship game. Yes, the Hon was with me.

At the end of the book, there are two full pages, listing all 74 of the movie houses included in the volume. Plus, there is an excellent map which reveals where they were located in the city.

Before I go, I must mention some other movies houses that were within striking distance of my Locust Point base. There was the Echo on Fort Avenue near Light St., the Beacon and the McHenry also on Light, near the Cross Street Market. And just opposite the Market on Charles Street was the Garden Theater. My father said there was once a bowling alley on that site, where as a teenager, he would work setting up the pins.

Well, on that note, I going to say good-bye to my fond memories and Ms. Davis' classic book of "Flickering Treasures." This book belongs in the library of every Baltimorean that loves movies and their city's history.

I'm giving "Flickering Treasures" Five Stars and the highest recommendation.

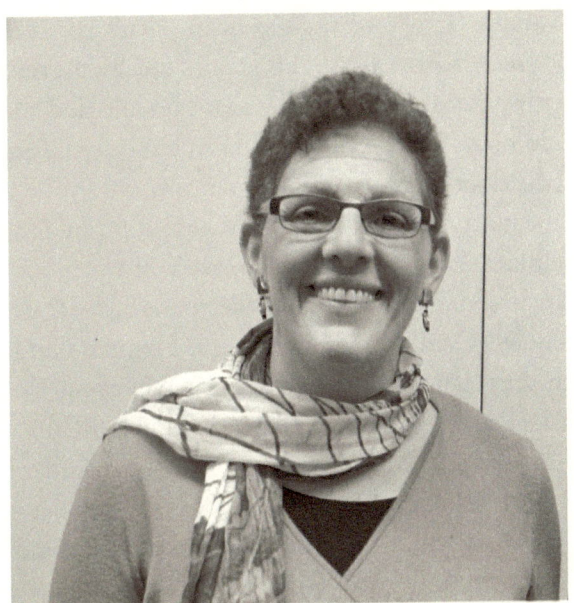

Author and Photojournalist, Amy Davis

67. "American Pastoral" Captures the Vietnam War Era
October 24, 2016

With the 2016 Presidential Election from Hell, mercifully, running out of gas, there's a new movie out that reminds us that things could always be worse. "American Pastoral," a film about the turbulent-Vietnam War era, reveals in suspense-filled details the conflict's damning effects on one, middle-class family.

It stars (Ewan McGregor) as Seymour Levov, Jewish, a Newark, NJ-based entrepreneur, high school star athlete and WWII veteran. He's contently married to a Catholic girl, Dawn Dwyer (Jennifer Connelly.) She's a pretty, former "Miss New Jersey." He's a happy go-lucky political liberal. His friends call him "Swede."

The Swede's factory makes gloves in what's left of Newark's industrial base. After the assassination of MLK, Jr., the riots of 1968 strike the town hard. It's fair to say that Newark, and the Swede's business and home life, were badly shaken by the experience.

Nevertheless, the Swede's family, residing out in the patrician-dominated countryside, soldier on. They are enjoying the good life out on their farm/home, in suburbia New Jersey.

The Levovs have one daughter, Merry. As a child, she's played impressively by (Ocean James, age 8; and Hannah Nordberg, age 12). When she reaches that late teenage time of open rebellion, the fine actress, (Dakota Fanning), enters the frame. Merry, a blonde, is a little on the spoiled side growing up. She also has a serious stuttering, and "dad problem."

The movie is based on a popular novel of the same name, authored by the controversial Philip Roth. In 2012, he declared, a la J.D. Salinger, that he was going to fade from the literary scene. (Oh, my, these testy writers! Sometimes they can be worse than those larger-than-life egos on the TV show, "The View!")

The novel, "American Pastoral," came out in 1997. I haven't read it. I prefer to review a movie without forever comparing it to how the book portrayed this or that subject, which can be so distracting. I understand the film is true to the spirit of the book.

In any event, the screenplay for the flick was written by John Romano, and he gets the job done. It's McGregor, himself, (the Swede), who very skillfully, directs the movie. His acting is compelling, too.

The Levov family is soon shaken again. As the Vietnam War heated up in the 60/70s, their daughter Merry, now age 16, is pulled into the most extreme antiwar politics of the day. She starts associating with violence-prone antiwar radicals in New York City.

The generation gap in families is all too familiar. But, when you toss in a very unpopular war, the mix can be toxic. The Swede and his wife try, but have a tough time dealing with Merry. Meanwhile, she has developed a smart-ass, know-it-all attitude.

Backstory: The Vietnam War (1964-1975) literally ripped the country apart. After the murder of President John F. Kennedy, his successor, the shadowy Lyndon B. Johnson, launched the conflict based on a false flag op, k/a "The Gulf of Tonkin Resolution." Close to 58,000 of our finest sons and daughters died; many more were wounded. The Vietnamese casualties ran into the millions.

Protesters in the U.S. hit the streets. Vietnam birthed the modern day, "Antiwar Movement." It also brought out the crazies, the ultra-militant, "Weathermen," aka "The Weather Underground."

The chant, "Hey, Hey, LBJ! How many kids did you kill today?" regularly rang out at demonstrations across the county. The torching of the American flag was also a frequent occurrence at these demonstrations.

Matters begin to speed up in the film when a bomb goes off in the Swede's local Post Office. It brings the war home for him and his family. The postmaster is killed in the blast. Merry is implicated in the act of terrorism and suddenly goes missing. The FBI is on her trail. Her devastated father tries to track her down, too, which takes up about the last half of the movie.

Much of the story is told in a narrative form by an ex-classmate of the Swede, Nathan Zuckerman, ably played by (David Strathairn). A sounding board for Zuckerman is the Swede's brother Jerry (Rupert Evans), a doctor. They relate how the years had burst the bubble of Swede, the one-time high school jock.

The Swede's search for Merry brings him into the mean streets of Newark's ghetto. One day at the glove factory, he visited by a young woman, Rita Cohen (Valorie Curry). She purports to be a friend of Merry's from the underground movement. Is this a setup? Is she just looking to shake him down and then do him harm?

In any event, some of Roth's views on the Vietnam War period come off as too far removed from the struggle itself. It's like he relied mostly on headlines, and stereotypes, from that period to craft two of his most important characters: the Swede's daughter, Merry; and the extremist radical, Rita Cohen.

For one, Merry's evolving, so quickly, into a full fledged bomb maker doesn't compute. The mysterious Cohen character, I must add, is totally incredulous. Despite those objections, the movie, still works as first-rate entertainment. The film was shot in Pittsburgh, PA.

It's the superb acting, which keeps "American Pastoral" together. It sustained your interest throughout. This sad film recreates, at times, insightfully, via the highly-fictionalized history of one impacted family in suburbia New Jersey, the trauma, anxiety and grief of that horrific Vietnam War era.

I'm not only recommending "American Pastoral," I'm giving it three out of five stars.

68. Barry Levinson's "Wizard of Lies" Rocks!
May 18, 2017

Hollywood iconic film director, Barry Levinson, was recently back in his hometown of Baltimore, Maryland. On Thursday afternoon, May 4, 2017, he made an appearance at the newly renovated Parkway Theatre located on North Avenue at Charles Street, near Penn Station. Levinson currently calls New York City home.

The last time I saw the Oscar-winning director was way back in 1990. He was in town then to direct his film, "Avalon." I was deep background as an extra in two of its scenes. One was shot at Druid Hill park at dusk and another was inside a railroad station. (I'm pretty sure that my right elbow made it into the final cut of "Avalon.")

Getting back to the Parkway. It is older than Larry King! Try 102 years. It has been brilliantly restored with a few spray paint touches more to go. It took $18.2 million to make it operational. It is now the official home for the Maryland Film Festival (MDFF). Years ago, the Parkway was known as the "5 West Art Theatre." I recall attending movies there back in the late 50s, early 60s.

To learn more about the MDFF and the Parkway's history and funding as a non-profit, go to: http://mdfilmfest.com Levinson's riveting docudrama, "The Wizard of Lies," was having it premier on May 4th, as part of the annual MDFF event. It's an HBO-movie which will debut on cable for the rest of the globe on Saturday, May 20th. More about that flick in a moment. The MDFF is now in his 19th very successful year.

My wife Ann and I attended the 4 pm showing of the "The Wizard of Lies" - after which, Levinson and Jed Dietz, the top honcho for the MDFF, engaged in a Q&A with the capacity audience. The main theatre seats 420. The other two of its screen rooms will each have 100 seats.

Dietz is a gem of a guy. He is the founding director of the MDFF. He deserves a lot of credit for bringing the Parkway back to life and for his significant ongoing contributions to reinvigorating the theatre life of Baltimore. Think Charles and Senator Theatres.

Also, I would like to give a plug to all those unsung volunteers who worked at the four day MDFF this year. Each of them deserves a pat on the back for a job well done. During the Q&A, Levinson was asked by an audience member if he wanted to be a "filmmaker" when he was growing up in the Park Heights area of Crabtown. Levinson's answer caused a wave of laughter from the audience when he replied: "My greatest ambition in life was to not work in my father's appliance store."

I'd be remiss if I didn't mention that Levinson was also the executive producer for 122 episodes of the very popular "Homicide: Life on the Street" TV series. It ran from 1993-99. All the shooting was done in Baltimore and vicinity. The headquarters for the production was the historic Broadway Pier down on Thames Street, in Fell's Point.

Broadway Pier was the place you went to audition for a role in "Homicide." The very capable Pat Moran had an office there. She was in charge of casting for "Homicide," as well as for all of John Waters' legendary movies, including two of my favorites - "Pecker" and "Dirty Shame."

(I had a cameo role, as a "Homeless Man," in one of the "Homicide" shows, on July 12, 1995. I also worked as a union/SAG extra in many, many others. I now look back on the '90s as the Golden Era for employment for professional actors from Baltimore.)

Returning to Levinson's compelling "The Wizard of Lies." Two of Hollywoods finest actors star in it. Robert De Niro plays the mega-fraudster, Bernie Madoff; and Michelle Pfeiffer portrays his wife, Ruth. They were both at the top of their acting game in this drama. See the trailer for "The Wizard of Lies" at: http://www.slashfilm.com/wizard-of-lies-trailer/

Madoff was a master of the Ponzi scheme to the tune of billions of dollars. He was convicted for his crimes and will spend the rest of life behind bars in a federal slammer. Madoff was so contemptibly evil, that he even defrauded the revered Holocaust survivor, Elie Wiesel, of his life savings.

What's so special about this docudrama is that it focuses on Madoff as a person without a conscience - a genuine sociopath - and only in a broader sense about his massive wrongdoings. It also shows how his crimes catastrophically effected his own family whom he thought he could protect.

The book by financial reporter Diana B. Henriques, entitled: "The Wizard of Lies: Bernie Madoff and the Death of Trust," was used as a basis for the film. It works in telling this gripping story about this much-despised felon for a movie audience.

The Oscar-winner director Levinson has done it again. "The Wizard of Lies" is a classic.

69. "The Girl on the Train" is a Bumpy Ride
LA Post Examiner, October 11, 2016

British-born actress, Emily Blunt is on a role. I thought she was terrific in the 2015 crime-thriller film, "Sicario." She played an FBI agent, Kate Macer, a difficult part to pull off. It gave her some considerable attention in the U.S. for her acting ability. Blunt has experience in both stage and film work and is also known as a pretty good alto. She will be filming in 2018, "Mary Poppins Returns," a sequel to the 1964 musical classic.

Enter the 2016 bumpy ride, "The Girl on the Train."

First, this is not an easy film to sit through. I hate seeing a fragile, complex woman, in this case (Rachel), played superbly by Blunt, get sloppy drunk and then act out of top of it by smashing mirrors and tossing cupcakes around. It's hard to sympathize with such a character. So, in my situation, I had to just stay with it and let the movie play itself out, one long, train ride; one quick flashback, after another. Meanwhile, Rachel narrates her solo parts.

As the title suggest: a train ride is central to the shaky plot in this movie. It's a commuter train which riders, such as Rachel, a divorcee, take daily into and from Manhattan for work, and back to the suburbs at night. The scenic Hudson River is often a backdrop. (In Rachel's case, we find out much later that this typical scenario didn't really apply to her.)

Rachel's ex-husband, Tom (Justin Theroux), lives along the train route in a very nice single family home. His new wife's name is (Anna), Rebecca Ferguson. She's a blond. Rachel, with her dark hair, enjoys spying on them from the train. She also gets off by stalking them, and their young infant.

Why don't Tom and Anna have Rachel prosecuted for her threatening behavior? This would be the logical thing to do. They don't and this makes the contrived plot even harder to accept.

To complicate matters, Rachel's also zeroes in on another home, which is within spitting distance of Tom and Anna's. The gal who lives there is a blond-headed hottie, Megan (Haley Bennett.) Her husband is Scott (Luke Evans), whose's built like a halfback for the LA Rams. Like Rachel, Megan narrates her solo part.

Megan works p/t as a nanny for Tom and Anna. Tom is also screwing the hell out of her every chance he gets. Then, Megan becomes pregnant! (You see how darn complicated all of this is?) Most of the time, however, the depressed Rachel is walking around NYC City lit up with booze, or slouched deep down in her train widow seat, or sticking her mug up against the glass pane, or simply sitting there mumbling to herself.

Rachel usually appears badly hung over, the result of a huge bender the night before. Some of her alcoholic-induced flashbacks border on the incredulous. It's difficult to take her rants seriously.

It's about eighty-five percent through the movie, when it, mercifully picks up steam, with some consistent logic. Megan, the hottie, goes missing! Where is she? Did she runs off with a new lover? What about that shrink she's been seeing? Can he be trusted? Did her hot-headed hubby, Scott, find out that she was cheating on him behind his back and stuff her down some deep well? Scott becomes a person of interest, and, so does our gal - Rachel!

It's time for the New York City police to make a dramatic appearance. The suspense really begins to build after that happens, as more revealing flashbacks come zooming by. Blunt carries the movie in a performance worthy of a rising Hollywood starlet. She has a lot of help, too, from a very strong supporting cast. Keep an eye out for Ms. Haley Bennett. She is very easy to look at and has stardom written all over her.

I was also very taken by the compelling performance of character actor, Allison Janney (Officer Riley). As a former Baltimore city prosecutor, with a cameo on Barry Levinson's TV classic, "Homicide: Life on the Street," I can tell you that Riley comes off as the real, let's get-to-the-bottom-of-this-mess detective.

Summing up, It's the powerful acting, not the flawed script, that makes "The Girl on the Train" worth seeing. I'm giving it three out of five stars.

70. 17 Carnations: The Royals, The Nazis, and the Biggest Cover-up in History September 8, 2016

They are just a memory now. But in their day, the Duke & Duchess of Windsor were world class celebrities. Their stars blazed so brightly that they would have made the crude Kardashians of today's Lalaland look like rusted soda cans on an abandoned lot.

(Book Review, Andrew Morton, Grand Central Publishing, 384 pages, 2015.)

He was formerly King Edward VIII of the United Kingdom. She, Bessie Wallis Warfield, was a twice-divorced socialite (first a Spencer and later a Simpson). The Duchess was born in 1894, in Blue Ridge Summit, PA., a summer home for Baltimore's blue bloods. She resided for a time, at 212 E. Biddle Street, in the Monumental City, only blocks from today's Belvedere Hotel, which opened in 1903.

In December, 1936, the emotionally immature King, then age 40, gave up his throne after a reign of only 325 days to "marry the women he loved." He then accepted the title of Duke of Windsor. Wallis was 42 years of age at that time. The Duke was given a stipend of 25,000 pounds a year from the British Royal Family's treasury. He needed it, since he had never held a real job before. And, the London-based Palace crowd never wanted to see him again! He had "badly miscalculated" the situation.

The Royal Family resented the Duke for bailing out on them, and they deeply despised Ms. Simpson also. She was referred to as "that woman." How much of that hatred was inspired by class distinctions and/or the fact she was an American, is difficult to discern. The Duchess divorced her second husband and the Royal love birds married in 1937, living mostly in France, during those pre-WWII years. They even made time, later in 1937, to visit Adolf Hitler in Germany. That set the Duke/Duchess-bashing tongues wagging.

Keep in mind, that back then, most Americans, and many of the British elite, too, considered Joseph Stalin's Godless Soviet Union/Communist regime to be the "Evil Empire," and the Fascist Nazis were seen as a bulwark against any encroachment from the "Barbarian East." Plus, the Duke was of German stock and darn proud of it.

Also, the Duke hated Stalin, and his butchers, the Bolsheviks, for murdering, in 1918, his Godfather Czar Nicholas II, and his family. This included his wife and three innocent, young children. In 1938, no less an iconic figure than Winston Churchill had this to say about the German dictator: "I have always said that if Great Britain were ever defeated in war, I hope we should find a Hitler to lead us back to our rightful position among the nations."

Enter British author Andrew Morton! He covers celebrities, a la "Enquirer Magazine," and had previously penned a best-selling book on the ill-fated Lady Diana. Well, in "17 Carnations: The Royals, The Nazis and the Biggest Cover-Up in History," he works hard to sell the notion that the Duke and Duchess were conscious "Nazis sympathizers... and had collaborated with the enemy in wartime." Question: Where is the hard evidence?

Morton can't have it both ways. He portrays the royal duo as mostly hapless, shallow and narcissistic, interested primarily in accumulating jewelry, fancy clothes; and traveling to exotic locations, and hanging out with other members of the aristocratic set. If anything, Morton's Duke and Duchess come off as pathetic figures, given to silly gossip, attending endless parties, and talking through their cocktails. They were more to be pitied than feared.

The idea that these two poor, often boozed-up souls plotted with the Germans for the Duke to be set up as the King of England if the Nazis prevailed with their war against the Brits, just doesn't fly. You can't build a solid case against this spacey duo based on rumors, gossip and party-time buzz.

The Duke's closest confidant, Lord Louis Mountbatten, described him as a "lonely person and sad." To his credit, the Duke did visit the front line in WWI in France. Later, he recalled witnessing "the ground gray with corpses." Before getting hooked up with Ms. Simpson, he also enjoyed a series of attractive socialite mistresses. Morton's strongly suggest that, in 1934, the Duchess had an affair with the then-German envoy to the UK, "the pompous former champagne salesman, Joachim Von Ribbentrop." The supposed proof: He sent her "17 carnations!" The truth: There is no evidence to support this slur against the Duchess at all. Ribbentrop, a congenital liar, was hanged in 1945, at Nuremberg, for his role in starting WWII.

After WWII, Morton spotlights the manic chase to secure the "secret documents" of the Third Reich. The British were fearful the records might "embarrass" the Clan Royals, including the Duke, re: their supposed Nazis ties. This is all much ado about nothing. To show the popularity of the Duke and Duchess outside of the Royal circle, Morton described a visit that they made to the U.S. in November, 1941. On the agenda was Baltimore - the Duchess's home town. He writes: "Over 250,000 people lined the streets to catch a glimpse of the homecoming duchess." Can you imagine 250,000 people lining up to see the (double gasp) Kardashians?

Back in London, the notorious Soviet spy, Sir Anthony Blunt, was operating, for years, right under the blue-colored noses of the Wallis-Simpson-bashing British Royals, their Palace guards, and their intelligence services. To complete the WWII saga, after the U.S. got into the war, the "Godless" Soviet Union joined forces with the U.S. and the UK, in the Allies' winning fight to smash Nazi German. Go figure.

Finally, Andrew Morton is a very good writer and has penned a highly entertaining book. He's also went to great lengths to document his sources. I, however, respectfully disagree with his conclusions, which are based too much on hearsay and scuttlebutt. I'm giving his tome three out of five stars.

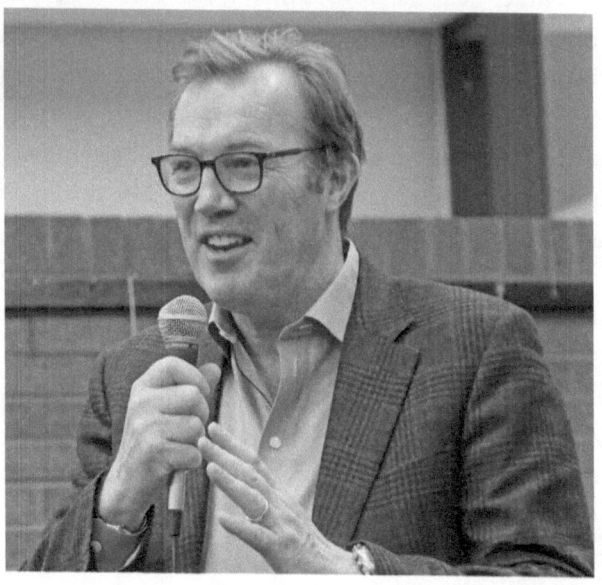

Author, Andrew Morton

TRAVEL

71. It's "Mardi Gras," the Mother of All Celebrations, in New Orleans February 13, 2018

It was the thick of "Mardi Gras" season when I landed in New Orleans, Louisiana, on Saturday morning, February 3, 2018. It's a celebration, a festival, a carnival, like no other that I have ever witnessed. Its origins date back to pagan days. The French Catholic settlers can take credit for bringing it to the New World.

By tradition, it is launched after the Christian feast of the Epiphany and continues right up until the day before Ash Wednesday - aka "Fat Tuesday." Now, that's a lot of opportunity for serious partying, with countless beads and other trinkets also getting tossed around in a friendly fashion.

If you come to Mardi Gras, bring your walking shoes and an umbrella. Trust me, you will get plenty of exercise taking in all the fun-makings. The weather is tricky. It can pivot from a sunny day to a hard rain in minutes. Bottom line, however is this - the revelers won't be stopped!

My first-class hotel, Homewood Suites by Hilton, was centrally located and only blocks from the fabled French Quarter. It is there where the carnival atmosphere is mostly played out in non-stop fashion. On top of its being Mardi Gras season, the "Crescent City," on the Mississippi River was also celebrating its 300th birthday this year.

Around town - I was there for a week - there were endless street parties going on, with plenty of dancing; lavish dinners, masked balls, colorful costumes, marching bands, huge rolling floats with exotic themes; parade horses; and serious looking dudes carrying torches. I also saw, here and there, particularly in the "Quarter," a few unfortunates, perhaps on drugs and/or alcohol, sleeping off their "high" in a doorway saturated with their own urine.

By tradition, purple, green and gold are settled as the Mardi Gras colors. A lot of the shirts sold to the tourists were in those colors. Artists selling their paintings/drawings were endemic. The food is special and sumptuous. There was also a strong police presence. I did witness one arrest for a non-violent offense. Supposedly, the suspect was shooting a video "up a woman's skirt!"

In 2005, the City of New Orleans took a hard blow from the horrific effects of Hurricane Katrina. It has continued to fight back gallantly from that major disaster. Recovery has been slow, very expensive and in some areas - substantial. But some, especially in the black community, complain about being left behind.

New Orleans has a black majority, currently about 60 to 40 percent. The Catholic influence is still heavy. The current mayor is Mitch Landrieu of French ancestry. He will be replaced on May 7, 2018, by LaToya Cantrell, the mayor-elect, who is black.

In between taking pleasure in the festivities, I toured the historic battlefield at Chalmette. It's located outside of town and to get there I boarded the paddlewheel vessel, "Creole Queen," for the journey.

On January 8, 1815, the invading British imperial forces, with superior numbers, suffered a stunning defeat at Chalmette at the hand of US troops, including free blacks, under the command of Maj. Gen. Andrew Jackson. He labeled the British the "common enemy of mankind." That magnificent victory launched Jackson on the path to the White House (1829-1837). It also eventually led to this popular ballad about the battle by Johnny Horton at https://www.youtube.com/watch?v=V-rNnIXJmZs

Enter the National WWII War Museum. Put this one on your "Don't Miss" list. It's located down on the waterfront. Actor Tom Hanks brilliantly narrated a film, "Beyond all Boundaries," on the conflict. It made my day. Next door, at the Audubon Museum, Meryl Streep, narrated a documentary on the the vanishing wetlands that surround New Orleans. Climate change and some poor planning, continue to put the fast-fading wetlands at risk.

I also enjoyed a walking tour of the Quarter with a guide. We checked out Jackson Square and the St. Louis Cathedral, along with the background on many of the Quarter's historic buildings. I was surprised to find a store in the Quarter - the Cigar Factory - that actually "makes cigars." It's at 415 Decatur Street. When you walk in you will find workers hand-rolling the cigars. The last time I saw a site like that was on my visit to Havana, Cuba, back in 2016.

The walking tour also included a visit to "St. Louis Cemetery #1." Buried there, among others, is the architect of U.S. Capitol and the Catholic Basilica of the Assumption in Baltimore - Benjamin Henry Latrobe. He died in the yellow fever epidemic of 1820, along with his son. Latrobe was born in England, but his mother was of Pennsylvania-German stock. See, https://vexillog.wordpress.com/antes-family/william-hughes-benjamin-h-latrobes-german-connections/

Close to the Latrobe's final resting place is a pyramid-sized tomb. It is owned by the actor - Nicolas Cage! At one time, he also owned a number of mansions in New Orleans. The tomb is a nine-foot-tall stone monument. Not all the locals are happy about Cage's pyramid in a beloved cemetery which is held sacred by so many.

I just loved walking on Canal Street. It is the widest roadway in America. It forms the upriver boundary for the city between the Quarter and its uptown. In its middle, "the neutral ground," street cars run in a east and west directions.

One day while in the Quarter, I witnessed a "grease poll" contest held at a hotel. Four young ladies participated. There was a band, of course, to give it some drama, and an emcee, with plenty of champagne passed around to lift everyone "spirit." The crowd loved it and gave the winner a huge round of applause.

Wherever I went on my strolls, music was in the air. On just about every street corner, particularly in the Quarter, you will find energetic music-makers; doing jazz, rock & roll, playing bag pipes, fiddles, drums, whatever; some solo performers, but most playing in a group. Indeed, music is the soul of New Orleans.

You will also find monuments in the city to its great performers of yesteryear, such as: "Fats" Domino, Al "Jumbo" Hirt and Pete Fountain. When I was younger, I saw "Fats" perform at the Coliseum in Baltimore. His ballad, "On Blueberry Hill," still rings in my ear.

No visit to New Orleans would be complete without taking in a swamp boat tour. They are found just a short hop from the city in Cajun country. In fact, my guide on this trip was of Cajun stock and he was a story-teller par excellence. I enjoyed the beauty of bayou, learning the history of the marshlands and the folks who live nearby and seeing lots of alligators, snakes, turtles and birds.

On New Orleans' Riverside is found a "Monument to Immigrants." This city is "Exhibit A" in its rich experience with growing into a major metropolitan hub, thanks to its evolving immigrant populations. Take the Irish for example. They have a rich history in New Orleans, dating back to the late 1700s, up till the present day. Check out: http://www.neworleansonline.com/neworleans/multicultural/multiculturalhistory/irish.html

Finally, New Orleans is a one-of-a-kind experience. If you haven't already done so - put "The Big Easy" on your bucket list!

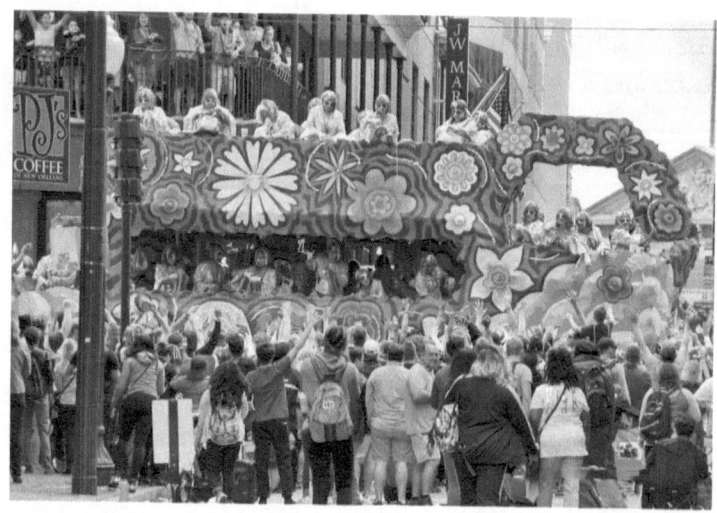

Enjoying Mardi Gras

72. Argentina, Chile & the End
of the World - 'Cape Horn'
December 15, 2013

My earliest memory, around age ten, of a personality from South America, is not of any politician, artist, or explorer. It is of the heavyweight boxer, Luis Angel Firpo - "The Wild Bull of the Pampas!" His nickname enthralled me! Firpo is buried in "La Recoleta Cemetery" in Buenos Aires, where I got a chance to pay my respects on November 24th of this year.

It was the beginning of my wife Ann's and my memorable two week trip to Argentina, Chile and fabled "Cape Horn" - the end of the world. We finished our journey on December 7, 2013.

As the fates would have it, in that same Buenos Aires' cemetery is buried Admiral William (Guillermo) Brown (1777-1857), a native of Ireland. He briefly lived in America as a young man, became a sea captain on merchant vessels and made his way to Argentina where he became a national hero. He is known as the "Father of the Argentinian Navy."

Admiral Brown's hometown in Ireland was Foxford, located in County Mayo. My mother, the late Nora Thornton, was born in the village of Tavanaghmore, only a few miles away. There is a monument to Admiral Brown in Foxford, in the town's square, which I saw on my first in visit to the wild west of Ireland in the early 1970s. I never dreamt that I would one day visit his grave in Argentina. Go figure.

As for Cape Horn, my wife Ann's great-grandfather on her mother's side, William Walton Freed, did travel around the feared promontory as a seaman on the British bark, "Iron Crag," on November 15, 1878. His account, "Before the Mast," is reprinted in the family's history book. It reveals a harrowing experience. So, a visit to celebrated Cape Horn, has been on Ann's agenda for a good while.

Although we have been to many countries in Central America over the years, and once to Venezuela together, and Ann alone to

Peru, this was our first trip to the deep south of the continent - Argentina and Chile. They share a common border that runs roughly for 3,300 miles along the majestic, snow-covered Andes Mountains.

At the moment, the most popular tourist attraction in all of South America, Pope Francis, isn't there! He was elevated to the Pontificate on March 13, 2013. We did get a chance to check out the facade of the "Metropolitan Cathedral of Buenos Aires."

As the then-Archbishop of Buenos Aires, this was his last residence before moving to the Vatican. He is very popular in both Argentina and Chile. One woman told me: "Pope Francis is a breath of fresh air. I'm thinking seriously," as she laughed out loud, "of coming 'back' to the church!" Me too!

Over all, we spent four days in Buenos Aires and environs. Imagine traffic, like in the flick "Rush Hour!" The Plaza de Mayo, rich in the nation's history, was our starting point. Sadly, there's some evil-doing lately associated with it. From 1976 to 1983, the country was engaged in a "Dirty War," a time of blood-filled "state terrorism." There may have been as many as 30,000 innocent victims. To learn more about this grim subject, and the participation in the protest over the missing, led by the brave mothers, check out: "Madras de Plaza de Mayo."

I also recommend, on a much lighter note, a visit to Buenos Aires' artsy, working class neighborhood, the charming - "La Boca" - located in the old waterfront district.

Leaving Buenos Aires, we took a plane ride to a boomtown, Calafate, found on the great windswept plains of the Patagonian steppes. Think film director John Ford and his fave cowboy, John Wayne. The flight took five hours, as we inched closer to Chile. We visited by bus some of "Los Glaciares National Park." Is it big? Try 1,700 square miles! The highlight for us was a close-up view of the Perito Moreno Glacier.

Along the way, we crossed the border with Chile and headed towards Punta Arenas - a bustling port city. Passing through the Torres del Paine, we saw a spectacular waterfall. There were also a wide variety of bird species, guanacos, Andean condors and gray foxes to admire. We even worked in a visit to a delightful sheep farm.

From Punta Arenas, we boarded our expeditionary vessel, the Chilean "Stella Australis." The accommodations and the food were first-class. This was our home for the next four days and nights as we sailed the pristine waters of the Strait of Magellan, Beagle Channel, Ainsworth Bay, Glacier Alley, Wulia Bay and eventually around Cape Horn, where the mighty Atlantic and Pacific Oceans meet.

I did encounter one Chilean, in Punta Arenas, who was willing to speak, off the record, about the ex-dictator General Augusto Pinochet's lethal 17-year legacy in his country (1973-90). He told me: "At the end of the day, Democracy prevailed. But, it was a very heavy price to pay. We're glad to now say: Pinochet is gone! And yet we know the Far Right is till very strong in our country and it can come back with a murderous fury." As an American, I am sorry to note the late President Richard M. Nixon and his Iago-like hatchet man, Henry Kissinger's, reputed roles as accomplices in that reign of terror.

Getting back to the tour. Our delightful cruise continued on Dec. 1, 2013, into Ainsworth Bay, where our vessel moored close to the 120-foot-high Marinelli Glacier. Later, our expedition ship sailed to Tucker Islet, where we made an excursion near the shore, via our zodiac life raft boats, to catch sight of the famed Magellanic penguins. The skua galls and the cormorant birds like to hang out here, too, along with other Fuegian birds.

I could have sworn I saw one of my fave actors, Danny "The Penguin" DeVito, hopping around on that island, while squawking his little head off. Check out his "Penguin" role in the popular flick, "Batman Returns" (1992).

We had a lovely excursion, too, one day to "Glacier Alley," where sits fabled "Pia Glacier." Again, we used the ship's zodiac life rafts boats to transport us to the shoreline. As a passenger on it, I felt like I was a member of a U.S. Navy Seal team. Once there, we checked out the glacier from its origins in the Darwin Mountain Range, (the background in some of my photos linked below), to where it meets the sea. By way of a cautionary note, a 2003 study by researchers from the U.S. Jet Propulsion Laboratory has documented the fact that the Pantagonian ice fields of both Chile and Argentina, due to the effects of global warming, are "the fastest area of glacial retreat on Earth!"

I'd be remise if I didn't say a word about the tour's sponsor, "Overseas Adventure Travel;" our tour leader, Ms. Gracieala Rubin; and the Captain and the crew of the vessel, "Stella Australis." Well, here is that word: "Bravissimo!" As for the people of Argentina and Chile, they couldn't have been nicer to us. It's true that their lands, lakes and rivers are very beautiful. And, so is something else that goes mostly unsung - the beauty of their women!

All of the above brings us to the apex of our journey - Cape Horn. On December 3, 2013, we reached it - "the world's southernmost point." At times on our climb up the promontory, the wind speed hit around 60 mph. The rain felt, often, like it was cutting my face. While moving towards the "Albatross" monument, we were able to take refuge in a chapel and also a lighthouse, which is maintained by the Chilean Navy.

Finally, magnificent Cape Horn, steeped in global maritime history, deserves a poem. Therefore, in closing, I offer one from a Chilean poet, Ms. Sara Vial. It is entitled: "Cape Horn Memorial."

> "I am the albatross that awaits you
> At the end of the world.
> I am the forgotten souls of dead mariners
> Who passed Cape Horn
> From all the oceans of the world.
> But they did not die
> In the furious waves.
> Today they sail on my wings
> Toward eternity,
> In the last crack
> Of the Antarctic winds."

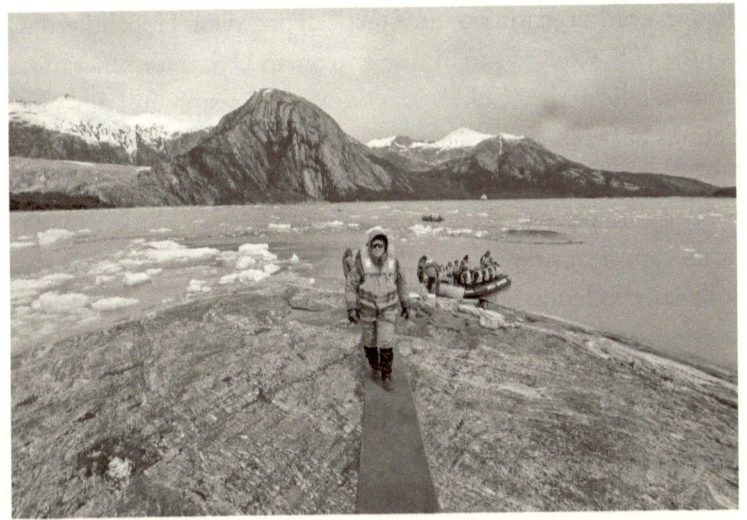

Stepping Ashore at Pia Glacier, Chile

73. Havana, Cuba: A Spirited City in Transition May 15, 2016

Try forty-three minutes! This is the time it took, on May 9, 2016, for our chartered jet plane to fly 228 miles from Miami, Florida, to Havana, Cuba. As it approached the island, I saw so much green, I thought we were landing in the West of Ireland.

The airport is located just southwest of the bustling capital city of 2.2 million. Havana is steeped in the history of colonial Spain.

The five day tour, entitled "Discover Havana," was put together with an educational and cultural focus, in order meet the current strict U.S. standards for obtaining a visa to visit. Our experienced tour guides, I am pleased to say, were all first-rate in every respect.

Just about every Cuban I met on my brief trip saluted President Barack Obama for his March, 2016, visit to the island/nation. It was a first in nearly a century by an American president. Hopefully, it will lead the U.S. Congress to lift the draconian U.S. trade sanctions on Cuba - a relic of the "Cold War,"(1960) - and restore full diplomatic relations between the two countries.

The iconic Hotel Nacional was our home base. What a national treasure this place is. It dates to the 1930s. Just blocks from the Caribbean, it is simply marvelous. Back in the post-WWII days, Hollywood celebrities loved to hang out there, along with some of the Mobsters from Chicago, Los Angeles and New York.

The lobby of the Nacional is filled with photographs of Fidel Castro, the former Cuban President. It showed him with visiting statesmen and celebrities, like the actor Robert Redford. It reminded me of the Belvedere Hotel in Baltimore, where the late Victor Frenkil, its then owner, got a kick out of filling the walls of its lobby with his mug shot beside that of a movie star and/or a politico.

I got the distinct impression, however, that it's the late Che Guevara, one of the heroes of the Cuban Revolution, who is the most revered figure in Havana. He wasn't even a Cuban! Guevara was a native of Argentina and of Irish and Basque descent. His image is featured in Revolutionary Square, among other sites.

The streets of Havana are packed with restored American cars, many from the 1950s era. Some are used as taxicabs. It is such a wondrous sight to take in. I felt as if I, a former owner of the 1957 Bel Air Chevy, blue and white, were a passenger in a time machine.

When the so-called "Russian Bloc" collapsed in 1991, it was a hard blow to Cuba's national economy. New investors from China, Europe and Canada had to be pursued. An economic professor told our tour group that "private investors now make-up about 29 percent" of the economy for Cuba.

Tourism is helping to grow those private investor numbers and to renew its capital city in a fast-changing economy. I asked one Havana cabbie what he thought his country needed most. He quickly fired back: "More capitalism!"

I fell in love with the section of the town known as "Old Havana." It's where the city originally started. I could have hung out there every day. I enjoyed watching the workers fixing up the streets, the boys kicking the soccer ball around, a child chasing after the pigeons, and the young girls practicing their dance steps.

At night, "Old Havana" is even more intriguing with its small streets filled with children playing, musicians of all stripes belting out Latin tunes, and craftsmen selling their wares. The restaurants in "Old Havana" are filled with the finest seafood caught daily from the waters surrounding Cuba.

"Old Havana" is also like an ongoing Baltimore-based "HonFest." There are so many charming characters out on its streets/plazas doing their unique thing. And, of course, when the senoritas are all dressed up in their colorful and traditional native dress, they rock. Rides through the district in a horse-drawn carriage are a regular occurrence, too.

I need to underscore this fact: Havana is a very safe, big city. Cuba ranks third in public safety in all of the Americas after Canada and Chile. In my travels, I did not see any military personnel and the police were a rare presence, except occasionally for directing traffic.

One day, we checked out the local cemetery, "Cristobal Colon," named after Christopher Columbus. It is huge, and its monuments are more luxurious than even fabled "Recoleta Cemetery" in Buenos Aires, Argentina. This demonstrated how much wealth was once based in Havana. There is even have a monument to a man who was known as "Ernest Hemingway's favorite bartender!"

Talking about the much-loved Hemingway, we took a trip about fifteen miles outside of Havana one afternoon to visit his former estate, "Finca La Vigia." It was featured in the newly-released film: "Papa: Hemingway in Cuba." It was easy to understand after viewing the property, why the great novelist was so enamored of it.

Hemingway was fond, too, of the quaint fishing village, Cojimar, just east of Havana. A statue to Hemingway is now located there, along with a 17th century fort. Cojimar was also on our tour.

In my five day visit, I also got a chance to check out, among other interesting places: a large factory that made cigars; a day care center; a print-making shop; art, dance and music schools; and, a small village that featured flamboyant mural-making.

I'm please to say that many of the locals spoke English and we were able to exchange views on a variety of subjects. One thing they didn't like about America was (you guessed it) - Donald Trump!

As a socialist nation, Cuba's extends to all of its citizens free health care (Bernie Sanders, please copy); free schooling, including college; free housing and no income tax on its wage earners. Elections, however, aren't free. Cuba is a Communist Party-controlled state.

Our return flight to Miami was on May 13th. I would be remiss if I didn't give a "highly recommended" plug to "Friendly Planet Travel," located just outside of Philadelphia. It put together this excellent, memorable and reasonably-priced "Discover Havana" tour. I feel fortunate to have been a part of it.

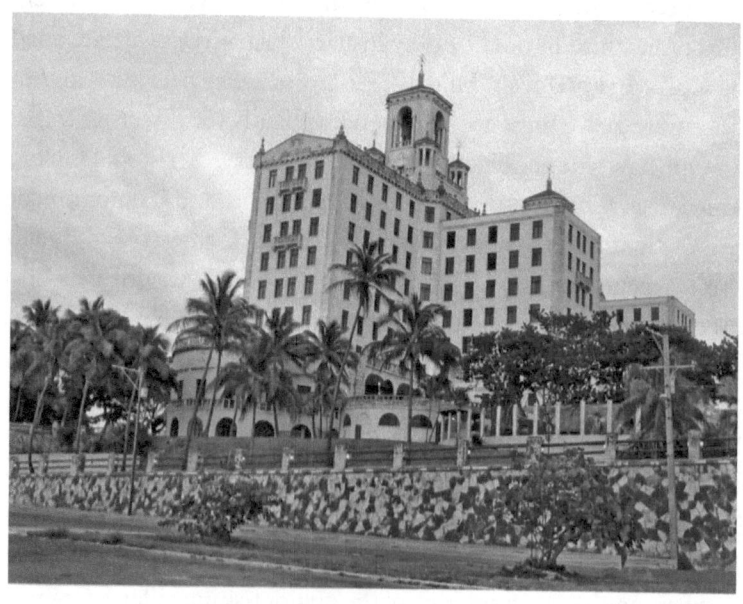

Hotel Nacional in Havana

74. O Canada! A Train Trip from Toronto to Vancouver with a Stop Over in the Town of Jasper
August 2, 2018

We took a plane ride on Air Canada, from Baltimore's BWI to Toronto, early Tuesday morning, July 25, 2017. Would you believe, it only took sixty-five minutes?

We got into Toronto early enough to check out some of the sites in and around its Union Station, located in the city center. Their major league baseball park, home of the Toronto Blue Jays, was just around the corner.

The venerable railway hub was the starting point for our journey, entitled: "VIA Rail Canada," westward across five provinces of Canada, a huge stretch of the country. Try about 2,100 miles. See: https://www.facebook.com/viarailcanada/

After Ontario, we would travel through Manitoba, Saskatchewan, and Alberta provinces, ending up on the west coast, in British Columbia, and the city of Vancouver. More about this jewel of a city later.

When passing through Manitoba, you will see a lot of flat lands - prairies. Very green - kind of like Kansas and Nebraska, and even parts of Missouri in the summertime.

On our trip, after three days riding, we had a two-night stay in the charming town of Jasper, in Alberta province. It is located in the fabled Canadian Rockies. Jasper reminded me a lot of our America's Wild West. Think Virginia City, Montana, once Mark Twain's fave hangout.

Getting back to Toronto. It's the capital of Ontario province, and it is big. It has a population of 2.7 million. Its Union Station has, appropriately, been designated as a National Historic site.

Our neighbor to the north is currently celebrating its 150th anniversary. An express train took us from the Toronto airport, Pearson International, to Union station. It was only a short hop away.

We boarded our train, "VIA Rail," around 9 p.m. Our accommodations in a sleeper car were cozy and comfortable, with a double bunk. There was a wash basin and reading lights in our private room. A shower facility was located at that end of our car. I didn't have any problem sleeping on the train. When you come from a family a nine, you can sleep anywhere.

There was an observation car found just passed the dining car, only a car or two from our sleeper. It had large windows with terrific views of the expansive countryside, the winding rivers and lovely lakes, the tunnels, and in some cases, the cities we were passing through, such as Edmonton and Winnipeg.

Our "VIA Rail," when it got underway, had three engines, hauling 29 cars with about 450 passengers. In Canada, the freight trains have the right of way. So, there was some "waiting time" for our passenger train. Don't get upset about it, it comes with the territory. Just roll with the punch is my advice.

The freight trains were carrying thousands of shipping containers ready to be trans-loaded onto a vessel or a truck. They were also plenty of tank cars carrying fuel and chemicals of all descriptions.

I need to mention that the city of Edmonton, in Alberta province, had the largest train yard I have ever seen! It just went on and on. It was much larger than the train yards I have passed through in Washington, D.C. and even in New York City.

Keep in mind, I was raised on Locust Point in South Baltimore, once one of the busiest marine terminals for freight carriers of the Baltimore & Ohio Railroad, now part of the CSX Network. But, Edmonton, Canada, takes the prize for the biggest rail yard in my opinion.

The dining car set four guests to a table for a meal. The service was first-rate and the cuisine was, too. There were three meals a day and you usually had a choice of four types of food to select from. Alcoholic beverages were available, too, at an extra charge.

Just about everyone we met on our train journey was friendly and interesting. There were travelers from the UK, France, Germany, India, Australia, Canada, of course, and the U.S., onboard. We had different dining partners for every meal. When they found out we were Americans, the first question to us was often: "What do you think of Donald Trump?" That made for a lively discussion.

It wasn't until the last day of our rail trip that we finally met a couple who not only knew all about Baltimore, but also were rabid fans of John Waters. They just loved "Divine," and were glad to hear that Waters was continuing to recreate himself as a comedian on the international lecture circuit.

Jasper, as I mentioned up front, is an old railroad town. It was a lot of fun. We spent two nights in that area. It's a small town and its train station sits on its main street in the middle of Jasper National Park. It's surrounded by a protected forest and the gorgeous Canadian Rocky Mountains.

We checked out some of the beautiful waterfalls that surround the town and took a ride on the Jasper Sky Tram. You can see six different mountain ranges from it. Its upper alpine station rises to 7,500 feet. It's a seven minute ride to the top with a great view below of Jasper and the Athabasca River, and also of the snow-capped Whistlers Mountain on which the tram is located. The latter stands at 8,100 feet.

When we left Jasper, we boarded another "VIA Rail" train, for our 17 hour, overnight trip, to Vancouver. On this part of our journey, there was musical entertainment, which was simply delightful, presented by Michele Ackerman (flute) and Kevin Ackerman (nylon string guitar). One of the tunes they performed was - "Mr. Bojangles."

I am giving our VIA Rail experience in Canada, which ended for us on July 31st, the highest recommendation. Put it on your bucket list!

We stayed three nights in charming Vancouver, only blocks from the beach. While there, we took in Stanley Park, the Aquarium, Vancouver Lookout, a harbor cruise on the "MPV Constitution," and a walk on the Capilano Suspension Bridge.

As the fates would have it, there was a fireworks display at Vancouver harbor on our last night in Canada. You couldn't ask for a better send-off for such a memorial, truly special vacation trip.

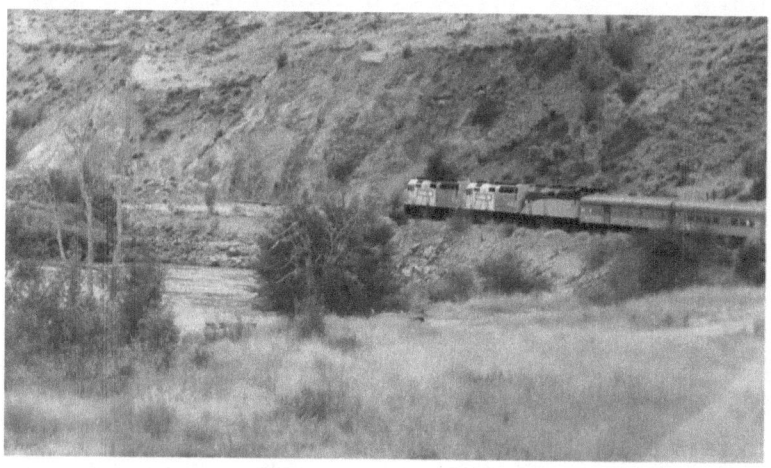

O Canada Via Railroad

75. Old Town Ocean City & the Wild Ponies of Assateague June 30, 2017

There is something special for me about the "Old Town" part of Ocean City, Maryland. This is the area that roughly runs from the beginning of the boardwalk at the Life-Saving Museum at South 2nd Street up to 27th Street, and from the ocean out and over to the Coastal Highway.

In the old days, they use to call the boardwalk - "Atlantic Avenue." I have plenty of fond memories of it to recall.

I've been going "down the Ocean," every summer for a visit of a week or less, even before the late Mayor Harry W. Kelley took office (1970-85). (The bridge on Rt. 50 going into town is named in his honor.) I've noticed some changes over the years to Old Town, but mostly for the good. It's cleaner-looking for sure, as is its beach. I like the fact that it has maintained its essential charming character from that bygone era.

The current Mayor of Ocean City is the popular Rick Meehan. He's a native of NYC, who grew up in Baltimore and graduated from my alma mater, the University of Baltimore. Meehan has been the Mayor since 2006, and by all accounts he's doing a very good job.

So, earlier this week, I enjoyed a three-night-and-four-day stay in Old Town. My motel bordered on the inlet that connects the Atlantic Ocean with the Ocean City Bay. So everything that I wanted to see, with the exception of Assateague Island and/or a movie, was within walking distance.

For travel in town, just take the "B" Line, the Beach Bus, that runs from its station in Old Town up to 144th St. on the Coastal Highway. It only cost $3 for an all-day ticket. Trust me, it beats driving in all of that automobile traffic.

The tourists were out in full. Old Town was packed with families, with their children in tow, enjoying all the amenities of the summer season. This included the arcades, "The Pier," the tons of amusement park rides, biking, the water and tram rides, and on and on. The kids particularly love strolling the boardwalk. It can be magical for them and also a great family bonding experience.

Naturally, I dove into the fast food the vendors were pushing on the boardwalk stores. My first strike was on a delicious crab cake. Some of the young workers at the sites were exchange students, here on a "Summer Work Travel" visa from sixty countries. Romania, Croatia, Slovenia, Turkey, Vietnam, Uzbekistan and Ireland were all in the mix. The students that I chatted with were all very happy for the experience to visit America.

I also soaked up the music coming from the solo violin and guitar players on the boardwalk. The guitar guy was blasting away with Johnny Denver's popular ballad - "Country Roads." Of course, I also bought myself an Ocean City T-shirt.

There was one dude on the boardwalk who was exceptional. He was dressed, rather painted, in gold! Really! At first, I thought it was a statue of some kind. Wrong! I waited for about 15 seconds or so. Then, he started gyrating. Amazing!

During the days, the beach, which for some reason looked larger than usual, had plenty of takers: swimmers; surf walkers; shower-takers; sun lovers; with soccer and volley ball games and kite flyers also getting in part of the action. The seagulls were in their glory. A sand sculpture artist showed off his skills with a respectful display of spotlighted "Jesus Crucified." The tattoo shops were busy, too, with customers.

One morning, I enjoyed a boat ride on Ocean City's bay, checking out all the fishing and sailing boats. Plenty of water sporting going on there, too, especially with the jet skis.

Another day, I drove over to the Assateague State Park to check out the wild ponies. That's just a short hop back over the Kelley Bridge, on Rt. 50, then take a left at Rt. 611 and you are there. The ponies always make my trip to the Eastern Shore extra special.

Ocean City, Maryland is a treasure. It's highly recommended.

With the 4th of July holiday coming up, you can expect thousands of travelers on Maryland roads. Some of them will be headed "down the ocean." To learn more about Old Town Ocean City, and environs, and all the family fun that it has to offer, go to: http://ococean.com/things-to-do/recreational/amusements/

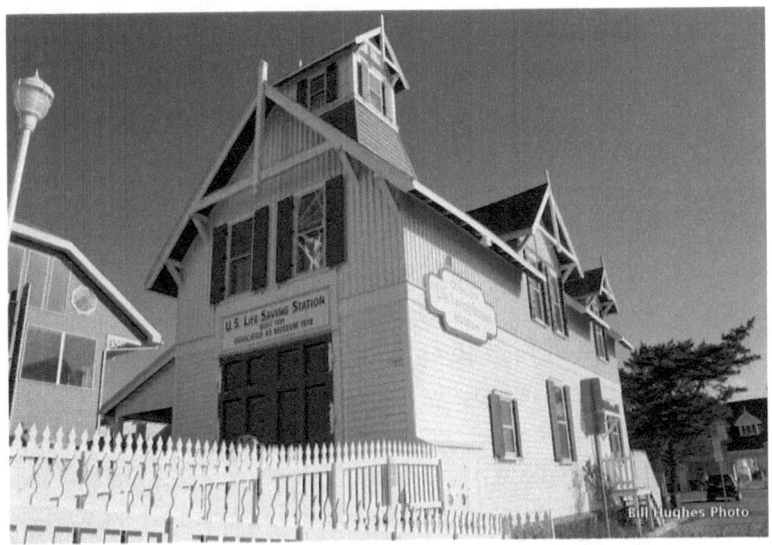

Old Town Ocean City, Maryland

76. Our Holiday Visit to "La La Land" LA Post-Examiner, January 4, 2017

Los Angeles, aka "La La Land," is one of my fave American cities. There is a lot to see and do in this colorful sprawling city by the Pacific and also in areas close to it. I've also always found the locals to be very friendly.

My wife, Ann, and I began our annual holiday trip on Christmas Day, December 25, 2016. We prefer to fly into the Burbank airport, named after the late comedian, Bob Hope, rather than LAX.

Burbank is smaller and easier to get in and out of. Besides, it's closer to where we were staying with relatives.

Our family members live on the fringe of Griffith Park. It is within spitting distance of the LA River, along which I enjoyed daily walks. It's also close to the fabulous LA Zoo and the Gene Autry's Museum of the American West.

Christmas night we got invited out to dinner at a home located over in the Studio City area of LA. They had a terrific spread of food laid out. There was also entertainment. Two of the young people played Christmas songs using the piano and the French horn. That made it a truly special occasion.

The next day we rested up, but not before taking in the movie "La La Land." It was playing at a theatre in Burbank, which was all lit up for the holidays. La La Land is a musical featuring two fine actors, Emma Stone and Ryan Gosling. It was just so delightfully over the top, that I had to give it "five stars."

The opening shot in that very entertaining film was of the intersection of Franklin and Argyle Avenue in Hollywood. It just so happened that our host family used to live there earlier in their marriage. We all almost fell out of our seats laughing.

That night in Burbank, we had dinner at the "Market City Cafe." I ordered steamed shrimp with rice and packed it all in. I thought I was home in Baltimore at Tio Pepe's restaurant.

The next morning, I did a solo jaunt to Hollywood. It was packed with tourists. The preachers were out, too, and in top form barking out prayers for "redemption." The tour buses were doing a brisk business, as I checked out the "stars" on the "Walk of Fame." For some inexplicable reason, there isn't any star for Baltimore's iconic filmmaker, John Waters! There was, however, one for the "Screen Actors Guild." Since I've been a proud member of that union for over 25 years, I am claiming it as my own.

Two nights and three days of our holiday were spent up in Big Bear Lake country, a popular recreation area about 100 miles northeast from LA. It rises to 6,800 feet, mostly snow-covered, with the temperature in winter going down to as low as 20 degrees and more at night. There was time here for some sledding in the snow and we also checked out the charming town of Big Bear Lake - population, 5019.

We stayed at the Best Western Big Bear Chateau, in comfortable rooms, and took a trolley tour of the town. Our charming conductor, "Mr. John," filled us in on its history. He mentioned how a dude from Tennessee, Benjamin David Wilson, came out West, married well and became a huge land owner in and around Southern California. I asked him if Mr. Wilson ever became a mayor of Los Angeles. He said he didn't know.

Well, I researched it when I got home. Mr. Wilson eventually became the second Mayor of Los Angeles (1851-52). He was also the grandfather of one of America's greatest son - General George S. Patton, Jr. - a WWII hero in the European campaign.

We followed up our trolley tour with a walk around the shopping area and finished our day in town with a very satisfying lunch at "The Old German" cafe and restaurant.

On our return to LA, we worked in a visit to the Famers Market. There's an old part and a newer, mall-like version, based in the Fairfax area of the city. We had a delicious counter-styled lunch in the old part at the "French Crepe" restaurant. It hit the spot. Then, we went shopping in the plaza-like mall. The weather was a little wet that day, but not enough to dampen our enthusiasm.

One night, the sky was clear for a change and I couldn't resist taking a photo of the crescent-shaped moon. I used my Nikon P900 that has a mega-zoom on it. I thought the shot turned out pretty well.

We liked going to LA's downtown area, too. City Hall is looking as great as ever. The downtown has had a spirited rebirth in the last few years. There's a lot happening there on an almost daily basis: festivals, music-making, dancing and theatrical shows of all kinds.

One night, we had dinner in the "Little Tokyo" area of the city, enjoyed some shopping. There was also a musical performance in its plaza by a talented entertainer - Arthur Nakane.

After going out just about every night, we spent New Year's Eve at our hosts' residence, enjoying a home-cooked meal and a celebratory apple cider toast to 2017. The next day, January 2nd, we watched the Sugar Bowl on cable. I was rooting for Penn State's Nittany Lions to win, but it wasn't to be. USC eked out a close win in a very exciting game by a score of 52 to 49.

Before going home to Baltimore, on January 3rd, I was hoping to get in some night shots at the Griffith Observatory. The city truly sparkles from there. It worked out that I could. The iconic observatory is a beacon to many visitors, myself included. It was a delightful way for me to finish a very enjoyable visit to the great city of Los Angeles and environs.

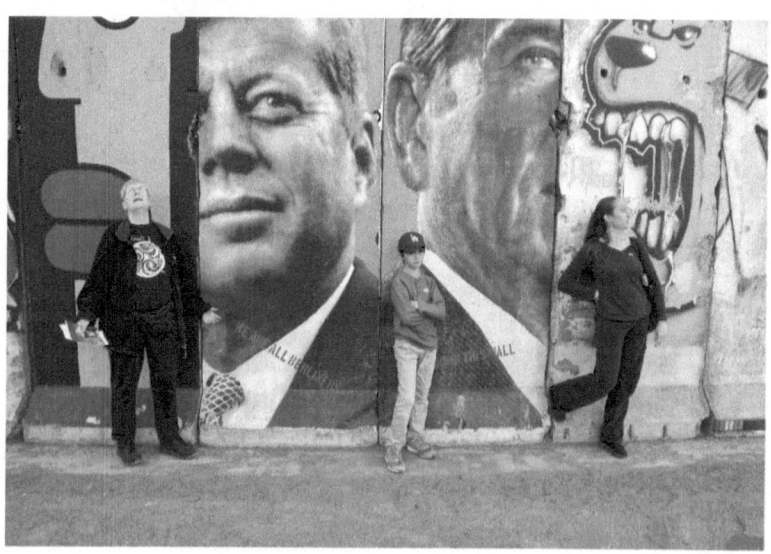

A Popular Tourist Site in Old Town, Los Angeles

77. Port Deposit, Conowingo Dam & the Susquehanna River
June 5, 2014

It's one of my favorite, small Maryland towns - Port Deposit. It sits on the upper bank of the Susquehanna River between the Conowingo Dam and I-95. It lies in Cecil County. Picturesque Route 222, with an abundance of green foliage, runs right through the town of about 700 citizens.

Another big plus for Port Deposit is that it's only a short one hour hop north of Baltimore City, via Route 1. Port Deposit is steeped in history going back to the days when it was a center of shad and herring fisheries.

Port Deposit is listed on the National Register of Historic Places. The Norfolk/Southern is one of the train lines that runs through it on a daily basis.

Port Deposit has a number of really nice restaurants, too. One of my favorites is "Lee's Landing." I highly recommend its cream of crab soup. The restaurant is located right in the middle of the town and on the water side.

If it's a nice evening, like it was on this Labor Day (09.04.17), consider sitting in the back of the restaurant. There, you can enjoy, not only your meal, but also a view of a beautiful sun set, along with the ambiance of the Susquehanna and its river traffic.

From the back of the restaurant, I could also check out two bridges that span the mighty river. The one that carries the busy I-95 traffic is name after the late Millard E. Tyding, a former U.S. Senator. (Sen. Tyding's son Joseph, 1965-71, was also a U.S. Senator from Maryland.)

The other bridge that moves traffic on U.S. 40 is called the "Thomas J. Hatem Memorial Bridge." Hatem was a popular Harford County politico who served in the General Assembly of Maryland with my former political mentor from South Baltimore, the late Harry J. "Soft Shoes" McGuirk.

Port Deposit also has a lot of heart and that's another reason I'm fond of it. From time to time, the Susquehanna overflows its banks, and the town takes a hard hit.

But, guess what? The town folks roll up their sleeves, make the necessary repairs and get back into action. You go, Port Deposit!

As we were leaving the town, the almost full harvest moon made its majestic appearance. You can't have a better way of saying adieu than that.

This leads me to another place I love to visit around this time of year - the Conowingo Dam. Earlier in the day, we made a stop at that site. It's right on Rt. 1 and only a few miles from Port Deposit. The bald eagle reigns here and it's a fave spot for fishing, and if the water is still warm - cool off in it.

The dam supplies electricity primarily to the Philadelphia area. The reservoir formed by the dam, however, provides some of Baltimore City's drinking water. The dam currently has 53 flood control gates.

The dam is situated about 10 miles from the mouth of the Chesapeake Bay and just five miles south of Maryland's border with Pennsylvania. It's at the town of Havre de Grace, down river, where the Susquehanna empties into the Bay.

When you ride across the top of the dam, on Rt. 1, you can't help but notice, there's always a lot of engineering/construction work going on.

The Conowingo Dam, built in 1928, is a work in progress. Its turbines are spinning 24/7 keeping up with the changing times and the growing demands of its customers. It plays an important part in the lives of so many.

It's easy to take the Conowingo Dam for granted, but, in this day and age, that would be a mistake.

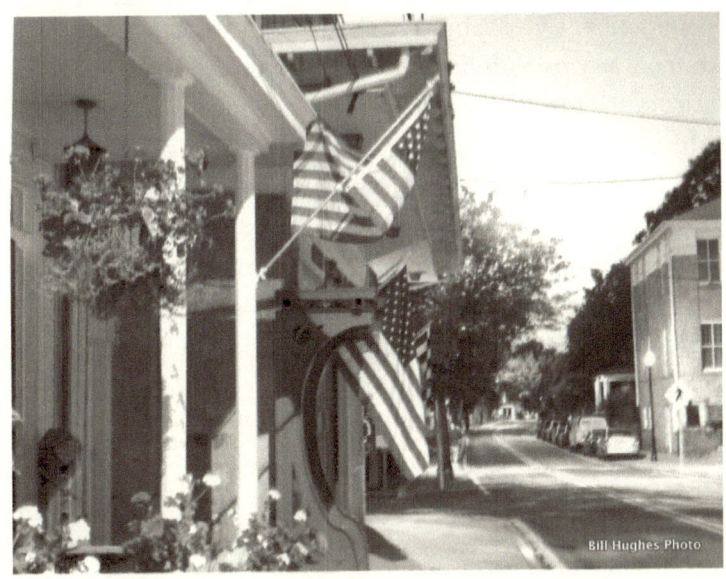

The Town of Port Deposit, Maryand

78. Touring Northern Spain & Portugal
November 19, 2016

The last time my wife Ann and I were in Spain was in 1987. On that occasion, she was an alto in the Tom Hall-led Choral Arts Society of Baltimore. The group was on a musical tour of Southern Spain. We took in Madrid, Costa del Sol, Seville, Toledo and Cadiz, among other cities. It was, indeed, an experience to remember.

On October 26, 2016, when we went back to Spain, we focused instead on the northern part of the country. To add interest, we put Northern Portugal on our 16-day Iberian agenda.

Our program was arranged by "Overseas Adventure Travel,"

aka OAT. We journeyed with them before to Ecuador and the Galapagos Islands. It's a first rate outfit in every respect. They take care of most of the meals, the accommodations and land transportation. Our tour guide, a native of Portugal, made the trip even more special with her scholarly insights about the history and culture of the towns, churches and institutions that we visited.

In the days of the Casesars, the people living in the area we covered in the North of Spain were known as Celtiberians, according to the author of the "Celtic World," Barry Cunliffe. (They were cousins to the Irish, among others). The provinces we visited were Galicia, Asturias, Navarra, Cantabria, and also the Basque province of Biscay. The climate was mild, the coast line on the Atlantic side was rugged and the mountains were very green. We were lucky and got little rain during our entire journey.

The Basque are known as a fiercely independent people, with their own culture and language.

Featured in the Biscay region was its capital city - Bilbao. At one time, (just like my home city of Baltimore), it was a hub of commerce; with shipbuilding, steel and manufacturing plants. In recent years, it has come back strong as a result of a boom in tourism. One of the gems it offers the public is its Guggenheim Museum. It's worth a visit to Bilbao to enjoy it. At night, the streets of Bilbao were filled with the locals enjoying a walk, a drink, some food. Many brought their youngsters with them - on foot, or in strollers. It was a pleasure to watch such Norman Rockwell-like scenes.

One evening, the singer-songwriter Huecco Lobbo was in Bilbao for an appearance. The paparazzi in me came rushing out. I chased across the street with my Sony mirrorless camera in hand, to get photos of him getting out of his black limo and being greeted by his adoring fans. That was great fun! (Bummer! I also dropped my glasses. When I went back later, I couldn't find them.)

On the Basque coast, we checked out the city of Guernica. Just prior to WWII, in 1937, the Nazis' air force bombed it in a three-hour terror raid. The artist, Picasso was commissioned by the dictator Francisco Franco to make a painting of the devastation, which forever etched the foul deed in the minds of humanity. The intrepid citizens of Guernica, however, bounced back. Although their city was badly damaged in the bombing, they have rebuilt it to its former glory. Viva Guernica!

Do you know the Spanish city famous for the running of the bulls? It's Pamplona. It was on our schedule, too. We were too late in the season to catch the actual event, but we enjoyed walking the same streets where the bulls are let loose to run every year. This event was an annual must-see as far as the late, great writer Ernest Hemingway was concerned.

Before we hit Pamplona, we enjoyed a brief visit to the seaside city of San Sebastian. We got a nice view of it and the hills surrounding it. We also surveyed the picturesque Lo Concha beach and the cloud-filled mountains that frame it.

Close to San Sebastian is the famous Camino de Santiago. It has been a pilgrimage route for centuries for the devout. The actress Shirley MacLaine wrote a book, "The Camino," about her spiritual experience on her journey along that well-tread path. We walked a total of about 3.5 mile walk on parts of the trail, through fields of green and a beautiful forest. We ended our walk at a canal. It was a unique experience.

The town of Burgos is steeped in history. We stopped there along the way to Leon. Burgos' Gothic Cathedral dates to the 14th Century. The locals believe it is the final resting place of the legendary El Cid. When the hero's name came up, I couldn't help thinking of the Hollywood actor Charleston Heston, who played him in the movie. I, wisely, kept that thought to myself.

After Leon, we stopped at the site of Las Medulas. This was where the Romans, for three centuries dug into the bowels of the earth to get to the rich gold deposits. The huge holes in the mountain sides reminded me of the harmful effects of strip coal mining in the state of West Virginia. We continued then onto Lugo. It has the distinction of being the only city left in the world "completely surrounded by a Roman Wall."

The city of Santiago and its beautiful Cathedral was up next. Like so many Spanish cities, it is filled with fine restaurants, cafes, an old town section, with winding streets and for its special feature - the Plaza de Espana.

Close by to Santiago is the lovely seaside town of Cambados. We talked with a woman there, who makes her living digging for shellfish. An entire industry is build around the digging for clams and cockles. The water was clear and sparkling blue at Cambados.

The next day we left Spain and traveled to Portugal's soil-rich Doure Valley. We had a delightful lunch in the town of Chaves with a local family. The grandmother of the House, as a warm welcoming gesture, sang some folks songs for us. Bless her heart!

Then, we hit the road to Pinhao, a grape-growing region that dates from the 3rd Century, A.D. The next morning there, after breakfast, we traveled to a winemaking complex, "Quinta de Pacheca." It is world famous for its Port Wine. We also had lunch at the facility and learn about its history of wine production that dates from - (would you believe?) - 1678!

We spend out last thee days of our fantastic journey in the beautiful city of Porto. It is one of the oldest cities in all of Europe and the second largest in Portugal. It is steeped in the charm and enchantment of Portugal. I particularly enjoyed the "Ribeira" area, which is located in the old town section, along the Douro River. One day, we took a boat ride in the morning on the river and we got an opportunity to see the city, and its spectacular bridges, from a different perspective. It was a photographer's dream come true. It was also "the trade route of the first wine sellers."

In the afternoon, we checked out a fabulous bookstore, in the town center, "LIvaria Lello & Irmao." It is Portugal's oldest and dates back to the 19th century. According to the celebrated author of "Harry Potter," J.K. Rowling, it was the inspiration for her "Hogwarts Library." Who knew?

I visited many churches and grand cathedrals on this trip, including in Porto, and lit many candles in them. It all reminded me of my days as an altar boy (Latin Mass), at Our Lady of Good

Counsel RC church in Baltimore, Maryland - near historic Fort McHenry. It brought back many fond memories for me.

On one of the last mornings of our tour, we enjoyed participating in a workshop drawing exercise, at an art house. I let the Piscasso in me come out! It was a great way reflecting back to say a fond "Adios" to Northern Spain and Portugal, which we finally did on November 17, 2016.

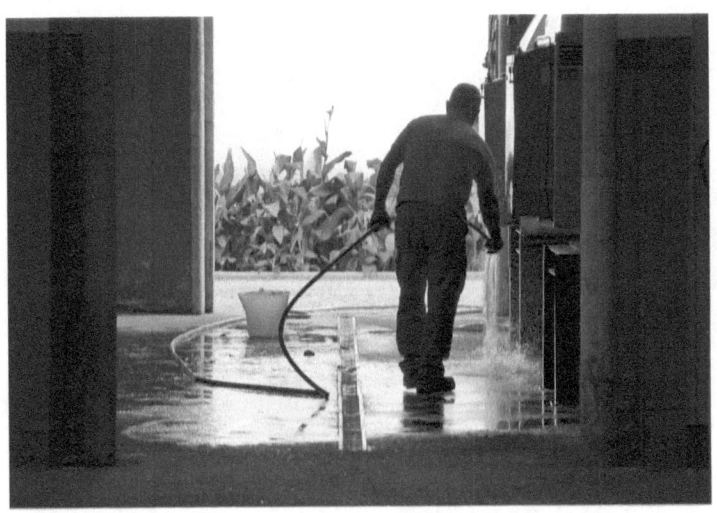

Cleaning the Winery

79. Visiting Historic New England in the Early Fall October 23, 2017

"By the rude bridge that arched the flood, their flag to April breeze unfurled. Here once the embattled farmers stood, and fired the shot heard round the world." - "The Concord Hymn," by Ralph Waldo Emerson

My journey to historic New England, via a bus excursion, starting on September 17th, 2017, in Boston, Massachusetts. It was met by the most agreeable weather: plenty of sun with temperate climate conditions. The meet up point was the Hilton Logan Hotel, which is right next to the airport, with a splendid waterfront view of the City of Boston.

We were blessed with a guide who was native son of the state with a deep knowledge of the areas we were going to visit. He also had a keen sense of humor, which always help on an eight day trip where you are sure to hit some bumps in the road, which we did. It comes with the territory.

Our first stop was downtown Boston and the Old North Church where Paul Revere began his legendary mission on April 18, 1775. As a result of Henry Wadsworth Longfellow's poem about that memorable event, he gained everlasting fame. You know that line, don't you? And doesn't it still stir you? "Listen my children and you shall hear of the midnight ride of Paul Revere."

We checked out the Old State House built in 1713. This is the site where five unarmed civilians were shot dead by British Redcoats. The lethal incident, March 5, 1770, became known as the "Boston Massacre." It helped to fuel the Revolutionary War fever (1775-83).

Patriots, like Sam Adams, used it to keep the heat on the Brits and to build wider support for independence. He was a master at propaganda, an intellectual and one of the country's founding fathers. Adams' monument stands near Faneuil Hall.

Unlike Karl Marx, who spent most of his time in a library in London, Adams was a hands-on fighter-for freedom. Social justice activists would do well to learn from his achievements.

However, Boston is a city with a checkered past. It once cultivated widespread anti-Irish Catholic sentiments. "No Irish need apply" signs were rampant. The Irish got even with them. They elected one of their own - John Francis "Honey Fitz" Fitzgerald Mayor from 1910 to 1913. Honey Fitz was JFK's grandfather.

Although the season was suppose to be changing, the trees weren't. The weather was still like late summer. We did see plenty of pumpkins, but missed the glorious Fall foliage. Maybe, next time!

We then moved on to first the Lexington Green where the heroic "Minutemen" engaged in the initial, but minor skirmish of the great conflict. Next, we traveled to Concord to view the North Bridge and the monument to the fabled Minute Men who fought and died there. This site is considered by some the spiritual center of the New England's resistance against the forces of the Crown.

Our tour moved on to Plymouth Rock. The Pilgrims landed there in 1620. A huge, 81 foot tall, national monument is found close by. It was completed in 1895, designed by Hammatt Billings, and is dedicated "to our forefathers."

A stop at Hyannis followed. This is where the family of our martyred President John F. Kennedy vacationed for many years. His promising service to the nation was cut short by cowardly assassins in Dallas TX, on Nov. 22, 1963.

The numbers are growing daily who believe JFK (1917-63) was a victim of a sinister plot orchestrated by "Deep State" terrorists and not killed by the "patsy" - Lee Harvey Oswald. JFK's death opened the way for the shadowy LBJ, and the Military Industrial Complex, to launch the Vietnam War debacle.

Our prime bump in the road came up fast. We couldn't do the planned trip on the ferry to Martha's Vineyard because the waters were just too rough. The remnants of those hurricanes that wrecked havoc in the Virgin Islands, Puerto Rico and Florida, just wouldn't allow it to happen. Bummer!

Our bus then headed south to Newport, Rhode Island. While there, we visited some of the huge mansions that line the waterfront. They date from the so-called "Gilded Age." The crown jewel of the homes is the 70-room, "The Breakers." It was the summer "cottage" of Commodore Cornelius Vanderbilt. Yes, I said, "cottage." Cheers to you, Commodore!

Newport, however, harbors a dark past. It was for a long time one of the slave-trading capitals of the country. Predatory merchants brought millions of black slaves to America in an evil business called, "The Triangle Trade." It lasted into the early 19th century.

Mystic Seaport, Connecticut, came up right after Newport. It featured a "living museum" of 19th century vessels, including the "Charles W. Morgan," the last survivor of a New England-based whaling fleet.

We turned north to visit the Norman Rockwell Museum in Massachusetts. He is America's most renowned painter and illustrator although dissed by nose-in-the-air purists. Rockwell's painting of a young black girl, Ruby Bridges, flanked by white federal marshals is one of his most famous. My favorite is his painting of Baltimore Orioles' Hall of Fame member, Brooks ("The Human Vacuum Cleaner") Robinson. Vermont was next on our agenda and the small home town, Plymouth Notch, of President Calvin Coolidge, in office from 1923-1929. He was known as "Silent Cal," an ultra-conservative. Coolidge broke the Boston "Police Strike of 1919." He also rejected the Wilsonian globalist line that America should police the world and go broke while doing it.

To its credit, Vermont prohibited slavery in its state constitution. It joined the Union in 1791.

On the way to Maine, via New Hampshire, and the pretty town of Woodstock, we stopped at one of its wooden covered bridges. Along the way, we also checked out the Green and White Mountains of the two states and enjoyed our stay in the resort town of New Conway.

On the seventh day of our trip we made it to Portland and Kennebunkport, Maine. The latter is where the George W. Bush clan hangout. I wonder if Dubya every sits out on his porch and ponders the disastrous mistake that his immoral Iraq War was? I doubt it. It was based on "fake evidence." We know Dick "Darth Vader" Cheney, his VP, doesn't give it a second thought.

Portland is a busy port city, which reminded me a lot of Baltimore and my days on its waterfront as a longshoremen. Picturesque lighthouses are one this state's main features.

It was privileged to witness a specular sunset on our last night in Maine before heading back to Boston the next day for my flight home. My trip was sponsored by Caravan tours. Our accommodations were all first-rate. I've traveled with them four other times to countries of Central America. I'm giving them my highest recommendation for this one.

You realize on this kind of journey into the past, that good coexisted with evil back then, just like it does today. Mercifully, in the past, the good prevailed and a new nation, a Republic, was born.

I suspect that there are many who might want to put this kind of experience, revisiting the noble struggle for independence, on their to-do list. I'm afraid some, however - probably those who need it the most - will take a knee on that one!

See more of my photos on my Facebook page, at: https://www.facebook.com/media/set/?set=a.10214458470798949 .1073742265.1334685315&type=1&l=94e16e8c1d

80. Northern Vancouver Island, Bluewater Adventures & the Mighty Orcas
August 18, 2018

This year after our Mount Hood, Oregon family related holiday, Ann and I took off for the wilds of Northern Vancouver Island, which included the blue, Inside-Passage waters of the Johnstone and Queen Charlotte Straits. The Pacific Ocean feeds its waters. It's the most western part of the country, and, despite what President Donald Trump insinuates, Canada is still our friendly neighbor to the North.

We started our journey on August 2nd with a jet-airplane flight from Portland, Oregon to Vancouver, Canada. Then, we got into a twin engine plane to get to Port Hardy - only about one hour and 290 miles away, on northeast Vancouver Island. We then hopped a shuttle taxi to Port McNeill. It was a 40 minute ride along a two-lane highway, full of green woods on both sides of the road. No stop signs or red lights to deal with on this part of our journey.

The driver, a long time resident, filled us in on what to expect in Port McNeill. "We are now in the heart of timber country," she said. We found out that McNeill was originally a base camp for loggers. The town also has a charming museum documenting its early days.

Our trip brochure revealed that this area is the largest one containing "a pristine old-growth coastal forest in North America." It is a full-time job, it continued for conservationists to "protect this remaining wilderness. Wales, bears and salmon require this wilderness to flourish. The forest industry, however, wants to log the old-growth areas." The battle to preserve these precious declining resources continues unabated.

We stayed overnight in Port McNeill in a motel close to the docks. The next morning, August 3rd, we embarked on our exciting one-week tour. We met the captain of our vessel, the "S/V Island Reporter" a 68' sailing/power/boat vessel, and the other ten passengers.

The captain, a young, very competent and charming individual, who was clearly a "safety-first" kind of seaman, introduced us to the three members of his crew; one of whom was the cook,(and a darn good one she turned out to be). Another one was an avid "naturalist," with a keen interest and deep knowledge of the Orcas (the killer whales), and the final crew member assisted the captain with just about everything else that needed to be done.

The naturalist, a soft-spoken, erudite fellow, also shared his knowledge about the grizzly bears, the salmon, the old growth forests, seabirds and eagles, and of the culture and traditions of the native peoples - the Kwakwakas. Every day with him was like being in a natural history class! Simply delightful!

It didn't take long for us to sight our first group of Orcas. They were located by our skipper swimming off our port bow about 200 feet away. The orcas are the oceans' greatest predator and they usually swim in a team. I found it a little hard to get a good photo of them. They are moving very fast, and so is our boat. But, I did, after many failed efforts, get off some decent shots of them.

As a local newspaper pointed out, the killer whales faced, up until the late 60s, an abundance of "human violence." In fact, in the areas where we were traveling, the local fishery department once hunted them down and killed them with a (double gasp) machine gun! Mercifully, people's perception of the Orcas has changed radically over the years for the better. To learn more about the Orca species, and the preservations efforts, go to: www.orcalab.org.

Besides the Orcas, who are forever foraging for salmon just about every day, we saw schools of humpback whales and Dall porpoises. The porpoises liked to swim, too, along side our boat as though they were racing us.

If you like sea kayaking, this is the trip for you. Everyday, the opportunity was presented to explore the protected waters of the Inside Passage. Even on some mornings where the fog was kind of dense, some of the passengers indulged in their favorite water sport.

The bird life on the waters and coast line was simply amazing. One morning, I spotted a huge flock of birds of every description: eagles, swans, ducks and mallards feeding off the salmon.

On board our vessel, I also got a view of some our winged friends, smaller sized, enjoying a respite from all of the frenzied sea action.

Along an inlet, known as "Knight Inlet," a brown grizzly bear, probably a cub, chose to make an appearance walking slowly along the coast. This is one of the best places for the bears to fish for salmon.

We did get a chance on this trip to visit an abandoned Native American village - Minquimlees. When we explored it, we found fallen totem poles and evidence of a once rich heritage. This village also was located in Knight Inlet.

Malcom Island, 14 miles long, was also on our itinerary and its main town of Sointula. The town is steeped in history. It was the base for a "group of Finnish immigrants who wanted to set up a utopian society" around the end of the 19th century. The idea couldn't be sustained. There is a museum in town which tells their amazing story.

A journey like the one we took wouldn't be complete without a visit to a Native American museum, such as the "U'Mista Cultural Centre." It housed a collection of marvelous potlatch masks. This facility was found in the modern Kwakwaka community of Alert Bay.

In closing, I can't tell you how many beautiful sunsets I encountered along the way.

On August 9th, we headed back to Port McNeill. Our seven day odyssey was complete. I'm giving "Bluewater Adventures," the sponsor of our fulfilling, captivating excursion, five stars and the highest recommendation.

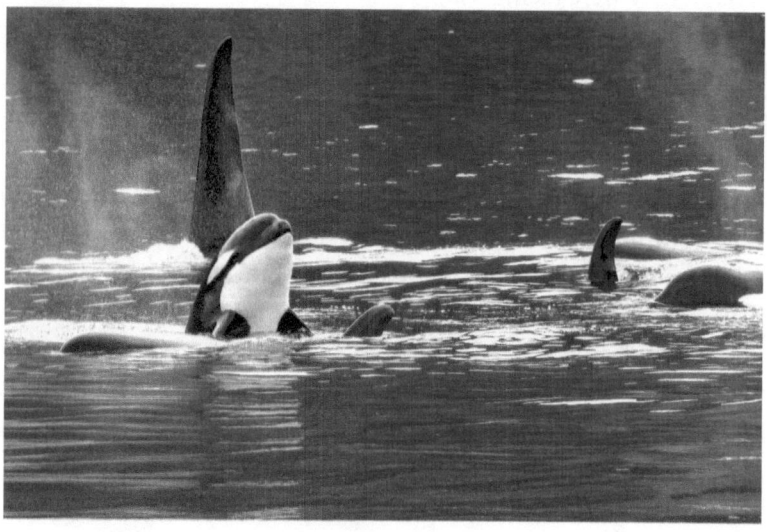

The Mighty Orcas

81. The Baltimore Colts of 1958
& "The Greatest Game"
February 13, 2013

My personal memory of "The Greatest Game," the Baltimore Colts versus the New York Giants, on Dec. 28, 1958, is now close to sixty years old. Both teams had won their respective divisions that year, and they were slated to play for the NFL championship. This was before there was a mega-event k/a "The Super Bowl."

Back then, I was working on the Baltimore docks as a longshoreman for the Alcoa Steamship Co., at Pier 9-A, Locust Point. It's located in Locust Point, just west of historic Fort McHenry. I was a member of the ILA Local 1429. My dad, Dick Hughes, a "ship runner" was a boss for Alcoa.

I was 21 years old, lived on Hull Street, across the street from ILA Local 829, and was close enough to the waterfront that I could walk to work. I had recently purchased from Fox Chevrolet, then located on Hanover St. & the Key Highway, a 1957 Bel Air Chevrolet, blue and white. I felt like I was at the top of my game.

Like many, I was excited about the upcoming Colts game against the Giants. After a very good 1957 season, where the Colts just missed winning their division, the team looked like the real thing in '58. Quarterback John Unitas, running back Lenny Moore and wide receiver, Ray Berry, all had had banner years, along with many of their talented teammates; such as Gino "The Giant" Marchetti, Alan "The Horse" Ameche, L.G. "Long Gone" Dupre, Art "Fatso" Donovan, Bill Pellington, Fred "Fuzzy" Thurston, Gene "Big Daddy" Lipscomb, Jim Mutscheller and "Big Jim" Parker.

In addition to a formidable team, the Colts had a terrific coach, Weeb Ewbank. He was a perfect match for his players. He knew his job and they respected him for it.

Another big plus was the owner of the Colts, Carroll Rosenbloom. He was a local who'd made a lot of money in the garment business.

Mr. Rosenbloom was also smart enough to get out of the way and let Ewbank do his thing.

Although Baltimore had recently gotten a new major league baseball franchise, thanks to the herculean efforts of its then Mayor, the Tommy "The Elder" D'Alesandro, (Rep. Nancy Pelosi's father), the city was in a little bit of a slump. In fact, it was mostly boring.

This was long before Jim Rouse built "Harborplace;" the reign of Mayor William "Do It Now" Schaefer; the founding of the Meyerhoff Symphony Hall; Center Stage's move to Calvert Street; and the rebirth of Fell's Point. The development of that $800 million subway system was still just a dream; and, entertainment icons; like John Waters, David Simon and Barry Levinson, via their celebrated movies, television and cable productions, weren't yet a reality.

Can you believe a ticket to that championship game, in 1958, cost $10? You can't buy a beer and park your car at Camden Yards, to see the Orioles play for that today!

I bought two tickets to the game at the now defunct Memorial Stadium on 33rd Street; one for myself and one for my then girlfriend, Carol, from Highlandtown. She was an original "Hon" from Patterson Park H.S. and later wife #1. We took a train to NYC on the morning of the game. It was awfully crowded and we were really lucky to get a seat.

After arriving at Penn Station, on 34th St., we caught the subway to the Bronx and to fabled Yankee Stadium. I had a rush of adrenaline when I came up from the underground and sighted the legendary arena, aka "The House That [Babe] Ruth Built," rising like a magnificent European Cathedral.

And, don't forget, that Ruth was one of Baltimore's greatest baseball sons. His dad had a popular tavern on South Eutaw Street, close to what is now, Camden Yards. Ruth was also baptized at the now-defunct St. Peter the Apostle RC Church in Pigtown.

When we got to our seats in the stadium, the usher politely wiped them off and then suddenly stuck out his hand. I thought to myself, "He wants to welcome me to New York City!" Wrong! I quickly found out by the look on his frowning face, that he wanted (double gasp) a tip! Under coercion, I gave him a quarter. In return, he gave me a really dirty look.

For morale purposes, I was please to see some other Southsiders sitting close by. I spotted John "Hopit" Haspert and Emmett Prenger. They both worked on the waterfront. Eli Burkum was there, too. Eli owned a fresh meat store on Fort Avenue in Locust Point,

Soon after the game started, however, I got another jolt. This time from the New York fans. When we would stand up to cheer for the Colts, the locals would invariably scream at us, in a loud, mocking voice: "Sit down you, farmers!" Huh?

I had never thought of myself as being "a farmer,' although my late mother, Nora Thornton, was raised on a farm in County Mayo, in the Wild West of Ireland. This quasi-hostile reaction to us put a modest damper on the festivities.

Nevertheless, we still continued to cheer for the Colts, when appropriate, but without standing up for fear of getting whacked on the head by a flying object tossed by one of the rabid fans of the Giants.

I'll leave the actual description of the legendary contest, rightly labeled as "The Greatest Game," to the sports writers. My recollections of the sudden death overtime win will forever center on the pinpoint passing of quarterback Unitas, (Yes, the man with the "golden arm"); the record breaking 12 catches by the left end, Berry; and the final touchdown run by the full back, Ameche, with a terrific block by half back Moore clearing his way.

As it turned out, the train ride south to Baltimore was a special happening unto itself. The cheering fans were at a "Mach-3" level of unbridled celebration. Some of them were carrying parts of the goal post with them through the train; others could barely walk to their seats from having one beer too many.

It was a party train like no other; with singing, yelling and laughing all the way back to Penn Station, in midtown Baltimore. There, the still mostly-delirious fans spilled out into the chilly night onto Charles Street to find their cars and, finally, to head back to their homes.

I felt then as I still feel today, that the thrilling victory by the Colts over the Giants by a score of 23-17, in the first NFL televised overtime championship game ever, placed Baltimore in the pantheon of pro sports towns. It also helped to give the city the national recognition it richly deserved as one of America's best.

Finally, the fact that it all happened at a venerable edifice, such as Yankee Stadium, which was so steeped in the history of professional sports, made it even more memorable.

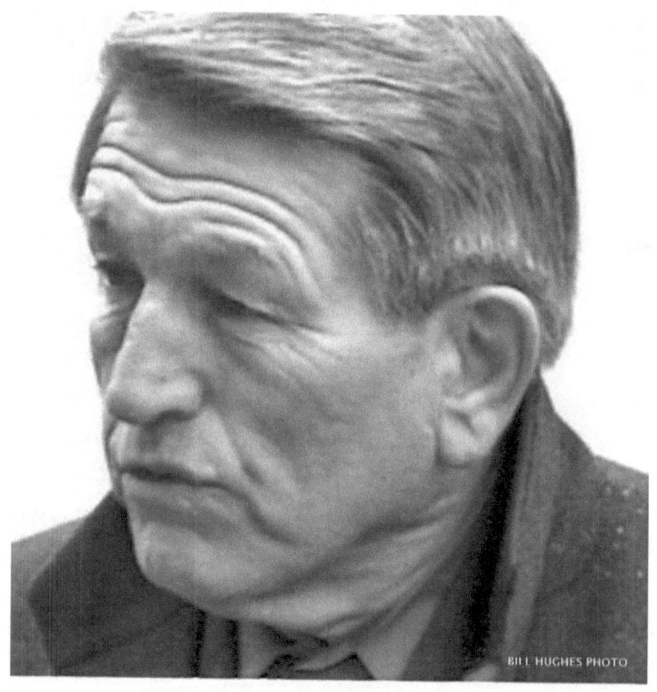

BILL HUGHES PHOTO

John Unitas at the Funeral Mass for "Baltimore Sun" Reporter, John Steadman